ORGANIZATION DEVELOPMENT

ORGANIZATION DEVELOPMENT

V.G. Kondalkar
Professor and HOD
VNS Institute of Management
Bhopal, Madhya Pradesh

PUBLISHING FOR ONE WORLD

NEW AGE INTERNATIONAL (P) LIMITED, PUBLISHERS
New Delhi • Bangalore • Chennai • Cochin • Guwahati • Hyderabad
Jalandhar • Kolkata • Lucknow • Mumbai • Ranchi
Visit us at **www.newagepublishers.com**

Published by New Age International (P) Ltd., Publishers
First Edition: 2009
Reprint: 2010

Branches:

- No. 37/10, 8th Cross (Near Hanuman Temple), Azad Nagar, Chamrajpet, **Bangalore**- 560 018. Tel.: (080) 26756823, Telefax: 26756820, E-mail: bangalore@newagepublishers.com
- 26, Damodaran Street, T. Nagar, **Chennai**- 600 017. Tel.: (044) 24353401, Telefax: 24351463, E-mail: chennai@newagepublishers.com
- CC-39/1016, Carrier Station Road, Ernakulam South, **Cochin**- 682 016. Tel.: (0484) 2377004, Telefax: 4051303 E-mail: cochin@newagepublishers.com
- Hemsen Complex, Mohd. Shah Road, Paltan Bazar, Near Starline Hotel, **Guwahati**- 781 008.Tel.: (0361) 2513881 Telefax: 2543669, E-mail: guwahati@newagepublishers.com
- No. 105, 1st Floor, Madhiray Kaveri Tower, 3-2-19, Azam Jahi Road, Nimboliadda, **Hyderabad**- 500 027. Tel.: (040) 24652456, Telefax: 24652457, E-mail:hyderabad@newagepublishers.com
- RDB Chambers (Formerly Lotus Cinema)106A, 1st Floor, S.N. Banerjee Road, **Kolkata**- 700 014. Tel.: (033) 22273773, Telefax: 22275247, E-mail:kolkata@newagepublishers.com
- 16-A, Jopling Road, **Lucknow**- 226 001. Tel.: (0522) 2209578, 4045297, Telefax: 2204098 E-mail: lucknow@newagepublishers.com
- 142C, Victor House, Ground Floor, N.M. Joshi Marg, Lower Parel, **Mumbai**- 400 013. Tel.: (022) 24927869 Telefax: 24915415, E-mail: mumbai@newagepublishers.com
- 22, Golden House, Daryaganj, **New Delhi**- 110 002. Tel.: (011) 23262370, 23262368, Telefax: 43551305 E-mail: sales@newagepublishers.com

ISBN : 978-81-224-2399-0

Rs. 200.00

C-10-06-4657

Printed in India at Glorious Printers, Delhi.
Typeset at In-house.

PUBLISHING FOR ONE WORLD
NEW AGE INTERNATIONAL (P) LIMITED, PUBLISHERS
4835/24, Ansari Road, Daryaganj, New Delhi-110002
Visit us at **www.newagepublishers.com**

Dedication

3 DOGRA Regiment was deployed in Poonch Sector in Jammu and Kashmir in 1965. The Infantry Battalion was assigned the task of capturing Rani Post (Chand Tekri) across the Cease Fire Line (CFL) during Indo-Pak Conflict of 1965. The Battalion mounted an attack on the night of 5/6 September, 1965 and captured the post at 05 a.m. Later Ring Contour and Kahuta Bridge were captured by A and D Company respectively during the day. This operation led to link up with the force advancing from Uri in the North, thus capturing the Hajipir Buldge. Rani Post was strategic. Major Girish Varma, Company Commander B Company and Captain Gurudeo Singh Bawa, Company Commander C Company, both leading company commanders laid their lives among many soldiers in this operation. The Battalion was awarded Battle Honour—"Jammu and Kashmir" by the President of India and Major Girish Varma VIR CHAKRA (posthomos) among galaxy of awards. ***The author was then 2/Lt (Intelligence Officer) and the part of this operation.***

"I experience great sense of pride and honour to dedicate this book in the memory of martyrs of 3 DOGRA"

Preface

Organizations in the past were operating in a stable environment where external pressures were relatively less and markets predictable. Changing market conditions marks the scenario in the 21st century. The organization structure is radically changing. Restructuring, flattening, downsizing, rightsizing, and a quest for global competitiveness are real. In the turbulent environment of the day, managers have to confront an accelerating change in an innovative and information technology era. Entrepreneur may be able to assemble resources and take ample risk, yet he may not be able to sustain the pressures of the environment.

I am extremely happy to bring forward a book on "Organization Development" (OD) that was my long desire. OD is a management discipline aimed at improving organization growth and effectiveness by increasing use of human resources. OD is an emerging behavioural science discipline that provides methodologies for systematically bringing about high performing organization. OD is about teaching people how to identify and solve problems, take advantage of opportunities, and learn how to do things better over time. The goals of OD are to make an organization more effective and to enhance the opportunity for the individuals and teams to develop their potential. It relates to human side of the organization.

It is essential for the organization to invent and discover a suitable organization culture. Employ people with required skills; introduce various processes and systems that are competitive; possess world class technologies; evolve suitable training and development programmes, and apply organization development strategies so that the organization is competitive in world and that the social obligations of the society are met. In the light of the above, the book offers a practical and realistic approach to the study of OD. Through the new paradigm, each of the OD stages is described from the standpoint of its relationship to an overall programme of change. The book is written basically for the students of MBA and OD practitioners in the corporate world. The concepts, theories explain in detail how it can be applied to the practical problems that face the organizations. The book is intended for those who are learning OD for the first time. Needless to say that it is written in simple language and supported by illustrations and diagrams.

There are a very few books on Organization Development. The book written by French and Bell (PHI) is the most comprehensive and a basic (foundation) book on the subject. The writers have chronologically docketed the growth of OD and very systematically enumerated various OD interventions from the standpoint of Western countries that is equally applicable to Indian scenario. I have taken help of this publication in formulating the style and contents. Keeping in mind the present environment, additional chapters have been included in the book. The book contains Foundation of Organizational Development, a chapter on Values, Assumptions and Beliefs; Diagnostic Strategies and OD Processes; and a chapter each on various intervention strategies. Organization Culture, Power and Politics, Training and Development have been discussed in greater details. It was considered necessary to include chapters on Emotional Intelligence and Employee Productivity, Empowerment, Learning Organization, Quality of Work Life and Future of OD. Each chapter begins with chapter plan that contains the outline of the chapter, followed by the text. At the end of each chapter, a detailed summary is given. Text questions, bibliography and a relevant case study are also appended to every chapter. Together, I hope it makes a very comprehensive book on the subject in Indian context.

V.G. Kondalkar

Acknowledgement

I have consulted various books, journals, periodicals, cases, and notes of various renowned Indian and foreign writers that I have referred in my book. I have acknowledged their contribution in the script wherever it appears. It is quite possible that I may have inadvertently forgotten to mention somebody; I whole-heartedly request to be pardoned. Without their contribution, the book would not have taken the present shape. It was also not possible for me to approach each of the case writers whose cases I have incorporated in my book, I request that they grant me their ex-post-facto permission. I very humbly acknowledge their contribution.

I would like to thank Mr. Sanjay Pandey, Chairman, VNS Group of Educational Institutes and President of All India Bruhan Maharashtra Samiti. It is because of his kindness that I have been able to write this book. I am grateful to Mr. Jay Kumar Singh, advisor VNS Group of Educational Institutes and Dr. D.K. Swami, Advisor for their encouragement and assistance rendered to me in performance of my duties in the Institute. I am grateful to Prof. P.K. Chopra, Director of VNS Institute of Management who has always been cooperative and has extended full support in this venture of mine. Dr. V.D. Garde, Advisor VNS Group of Educational Institutes has always been a source of inspiration to me in my endeavor. He has helped me in various ways for which I am grateful to him. I thank Mr. Jay Singh, Director of VNS Group of educational institutes, Dr. D.S. Swami, Dr. S.K.Yadav, Dr. Rajesh Tripathi, Dr. Kalpana Dixit, Prof. H.N. Dhabaliya and Dr. S.K. Srivastava for the support extended to me in performance of my duty and writing this book.

I thank Dr. P.K. Mishra, Dean Faculty of Management Studies for his kind support. I would also like to place on record the encouragement and advice received from Dr. D.P. Sharma, Ex.-VC Barkatullah University, Dr. Nageshwar Rao, Dean and Director, Department of Management, Vikram University, Ujjain, Dr. Upinder Dhar, Director, Nirma Institute of Management, Ahmedabad, Dr. Kailash Tyagi, Department of Defence and Strategic Studies, M.V.M., Bhopal. I express my deep appreciation and grateful to all my colleagues namely Prof. CA C. Rama Gopal, Dr. Sameer Sharma, Dr. Neeraj Singh, Prof. Archana Nema, Prof. Akhilesh Mittal, Prof. S.K. Mathur, Prof. Neha Patel, Prof. Shirish Verma, Prof. Amrish Saxena, Prof. R. Satyanarayan, Prof. Vineeta Manish, Prof.

Lakhnesh Pandey, Prof. Suruchi Saxena, Mr. M.P. Singh who have contributed in some form or the other. They have assisted me in formulation of the contents, the text and in editing and evaluating the appropriateness of the issues involved. I thank Mrs. Sarita, Shree Mishra, Mukesh, Akhilesh, Leeladhar, Devkant, and Yagya Narayan for they have always been ready to extend their helping hand. Mr. Vikas Varshney has done a great help to me in assisting in typewriting the script at odd hours.

My children Rahul, Sudeep, Avinash, Sapna, Anuradha, Ujwala, Rhitwik, and Udita have been very kind to me and always extended the desired support. The little ones kept me amused that gave me energy and freshness to start the work of writing again. I would like to express my grateful thanks to each one of them.

I convey my thanks to Mr. Saumya Gupta (Managing Director) and the team of New Age International (P) Limited, Publishers, New Delhi, for their involvement in the project right from the day the idea was conceived till its publication. They have brought out an admirably designed book. This is the second book published by them, first being "Organizational Behaviour", I hope they will continue to extend the same support in the future too.

I feel a great sense of pride and happiness in handing over this book to the readers. I am sure they would enjoy studying the book as I have enjoyed writing it. I request them to bring to my notice, the improvement they desire for which I shall remain ever grateful to them.

V.G. Kondalkar

Contents

Preface vii

Acknowledgement ix

CHAPTER 1 FOUNDATION OF ORGANIZATIONAL DEVELOPMENT **1–13**

- An Overview of Organizational Development 1
- Definitions 3
- Profile of Organization Culture 5
- History of Organizational Development 8
- Objectives of Organizational Development Programme 10
- Od Characteristics/Competencies 10

Summary 11

Text Questions 11

Bibliography 12

Case Study: Action Plan for CSR 13

CHAPTER 2 VALUES, ASSUMPTIONS AND BELIEFS IN ORGANIZATION DEVELOPMENT **15–23**

- Introduction 15
- Definition 16
- Historical Background of Values 16
- Early Statements of OD Values and Assumptions 18

Summary 21

Text Questions 21

Bibliography 21

Case Study: QWC—The Balancing Act 22

CHAPTER 3 DIAGNOSTICS STRATEGIES AND OD PROCESSES **25–35**

- Introduction 25
- Diagnosis 26
- The Six-Box Model 27
- Considerations and Action Components of OD Programme 27
- Nature of OD Interventions 28
- Phases of OD Programme Management 29
- Managing Change (Cummings and Worley's Model) 29
- Eight Steps for Successful Organization Transformation: Kotter's Model of Change 31

Summary 32
Text Questions 33
Bibliography 33
Case Study: Growing Pains of the Pennathur Tyre Company 33

CHAPTER 4 ORGANIZATION DEVELOPMENT INTERVENTION STRATEGIES **37–50**

- Introduction 37
- Concepts 38
- Organizational Strategies for Personal Concern 39
- Process Consultation 41
- Job Related Interventions 44
- Socio-Technical Interventions 45
- Structural Interventions 46
- Learning Organizations 47

Summary 48
Text Questions 48
Case Study: The Quality Conundrum 49
Bibliography 50

CHAPTER 5 ACTION RESEARCH AND ORGANIZATION DEVELOPMENT **51–55**

- Introduction 51
- Definition 52
- Understanding Action Research 52
- Action Research as Approach to Problem-Solving 54

Summary 55
Text Questions 55
Bibliography 55

CHAPTER 6 LEARNING ORGANIZATION 57–66

- Introduction 57
- Definitions 57
- Learning Organizations 60
- Skills Needed for Learning Organizations 61
- Phases of Learning 62
- Quality of Work-Life 63

Summary 63
Text Questions 64
Bibliography 64
OD in Practice 64
Case Study: A Success Story 65

CHAPTER 7 CONSULTANT-CLIENT RELATIONSHIP 67–81

- Introduction 67
- Entry and Contracting 68
- Defining the Client-Consultant System 69
- Diagnosis of the Problem and Implementation of Intervention Strategy 71
- Dependency and Terminating the Services of Consultant 72
- Ethical Standards 73
- Responsibilities of the Client System 74
- The Change Agents 75

Summary 77
Text Questions 79
Bibliography 79
Case Study: Impact India Foundation 80

CHAPTER 8 TEAM BUILDING INTERVENTIONS 83–99

- Introduction 83
- Understanding Teams 84
- Teams and Work Groups 84
- Types of Teams 85
- Characteristics of Effective Teams 86
- Team Building Interventions 88
- Process Consultation Interventions 92
- Techniques of Team Building 93

- Force Field Analysis 95
  - *Summary* 96
  - *Text Questions* 98
  - *Bibliography* 98

CHAPTER 9 COMPREHENSIVE OD INTERVENTIONS **101–103**

- Introduction 101
- Whole System in One Room 101
- Confrontation Meeting—Beckhard 102
  - *Text Questions* 103
  - *Bibliography* 103

CHAPTER 10 INTER GROUP AND THIRD PARTY INTERVENTIONS **105–125**

- Introduction 105
- Collaboration and Conflict 106
- Inter Group Operating Problems 106
- Transactional Analysis (TA) 109
- Strategies for Reducing Inter Group Conflict 114
- Stress Management 114
- Inter Group Team Building Interventions 119
- Third Party Peace Making Interventions 120
- Confrontation 121
- Organizational Mirroring 121
  - *Summary* 122
  - *Text Questions* 123
  - *Bibliography* 124
  - *Case Study* 125

CHAPTER 11 STRUCTURAL INTERVENTIONS **127–150**

- Introduction 127
- Job Redesign 128
- Quality of Work Life 131
- Quality Circles 131
- Management by Objective (MBO) 132
- Difficulties in Managing MBO Concept 136
- Six Sigma 138
- Total Quality in Human Resources Management 140

- Re-engineering 144
- Systems Approach to Management 145
- Benchmarking to Improve Competitive Performance 147

Summary 148

Bibliography 149

Case Study: Voltas Limited 149

CHAPTER 12 TRAINING AND DEVELOPMENT INTERVENTIONS 151–160

- Introduction 151
- T-Group Training 152
- Behaviour Modeling 153
- Coaching and Mentoring 153
- Instrumented Training 154
- Career Anchors 154

Summary 157

Text Questions 158

Case Study: (1) Training Skill Sets 158

(2) Succession Planning – Keeping the Seat Warm 159

CHAPTER 13 EMPOWERMENT 161–172

- Introduction 161
- Definitions 162
- Factors Favourable for Empowerment 162
- Why Empowerment? 163
- Process of Empowerment 164
- Factors Contributing to Empowerment 164
- Redesigning Organizational Structure 165
- Team Based Work Environment 167
- Types of Empowerment 167
- Model of Empowerment 168
- Benefits of Empowerment 168
- Barriers of Empowerment 168
- Career-Life Planning 169

Summary 170

Text Questions 170

Bibliography 171

Case Study: People Power at Jet Airways 172

CHAPTER 14 NORMATIVE RE-EDUCATIVE STRATEGY 173–177

- Introduction 173
- Examination of Various Strategies 174
- OD is an Applied Behavioural Science 175

Summary 176
Text Questions 176
Bibliography 176
Case Study: Managing the Mind 177

CHAPTER 15 MANAGEMENT OF ORGANIZATION CHANGE 179–197

- Introduction 179
- Understanding Change 180
- Organizational Growth as a Factor of Change 180
- Forces of Change 182
- Force Field Analysis 183
- Change Process 183
- Seven Stage Model 185
- Levels of Change 185
- Types of Change 188
- Steps in Managing Change 189
- Change Agents 190
- Resistance to Change 191
- Managing Resistance to Change 192

Summary 193
Text Questions 194
Bibliography 195
Case Study: Magic Kingdom 196

CHAPTER 16 POWER, POLITICS AND ETHICS IN ORGANIZATION DEVELOPMENT 199–212

- Introduction 199
- Definitions 200
- Bases/Sources of Power 201
- Organization Based Power 202
- Politics 204
- Techniques of Political Plays 206
- Machiavellianism (1469–1527) 206
- Strategies Used by Executives Ethics in OD 207
- Ethics in OD 209

Summary 211
Text Questions 212

CHAPTER 17 QUALITY OF WORK LIFE (QWL) **213–228**

- Introduction 213
- Definitions 214
- Features of Quality of Work Life 214
- Model of QWL 215
- Mental Health 219
- Burnout 220
- Quality Circle (QC) 222

Summary 223
Text Questions 224
Bibliography 225
Case Study: QWL in Bhilai Steel Plant 227

CHAPTER 18 EMOTIONAL INTELLIGENCE AND EMPLOYEE PRODUCTIVITY **229–235**

- Emotions 229
- Terminology 230
- Emotional Dimensions 230
- Emotional Intelligence at Work 231
- Framework of Emotional Competence 232
- Affective Events Theory 233

Summary 234
Text Questions 234
Bibliography 234
Case Study: Emotions 235

CHAPTER 19 ORGANIZATION CULTURE AND CLIMATE **237–248**

- Introduction 237
- Definitions 238
- Understanding Organization Culture 238
- Functions of Organization Culture 239
- Levels of Culture 240
- Organizational Climate 245

Summary 247
Text Questions 248
Bibliography 248

CHAPTER 20 FUTURE OF ORGANIZATION DEVELOPMENT **249–259**

- Introduction 249
- Strength of OD 250
- Challenges for the Organization 251

Summary 254

Text Questions 255

Bibliography 255

Case Study: (1) Esprit De Corporate 256

(2) Rebuilding Nalanda 258

INDEX **261–264**

CHAPTER 1

Foundation of Organizational Development

CHAPTER PLAN

- *An Overview of Organizational Development*
- *Definitions*
- *Profile of Organization Culture*
- *History of Organizational Development*
- *Objectives of Organizational Development Programme*
- *OD Characteristics/Competencies*
- *Summary*
- *Text Questions*
- *Bibliography*
- *Case Study:*
  1. *Action Plan for CSR*
  2. *Emerging Areas of Corporate Social Responsibility*

AN OVERVIEW OF ORGANIZATIONAL DEVELOPMENT

When an individual develops, organization develops automatically. OD refers to development of following elements of the organization:

1. Developments of individuals, teams and the organizations.
2. Development can only take place when an appropriate knowledge is achieved and passed on to subordinates. Hence it is necessary to study various fields of studies that contribute heavily to the field of OD. In this context, study of psychology, social and industrial psychology, economics, politics, commerce, medical, and sociology is important. These fields of study are already rich. OD envisages acquiring skills through already proved models and applying the same for improvement based on situations on hand.

3. As part from the above, OD is related to study of organization structures, organization designs, job analysis and management of change if required.
4. Organizations are dependent on each other for their very survival. It is therefore necessary to study other organizations with particular reference to their culture, perception, attitude and the climate they have established and enjoy. Quality of work life is an important factor in this respect.
5. As per Wendill L. French and Cicil H. Bell, Jr.[1] "Organization development offers a prescription for improving the 'fit' between the individuals and the organization, between the organization and the environment, and among the organizational components such as strategy, structure and process. The prescription is implemented through inventions and activities that address specific problematic conditions."
6. Organizational development can be achieved by carrying out research to identify problem areas and by applying various interventions to resolve the same. It is about bringing change in the organization. The areas of change may include anything under the sun. To name a few it may relate to implementing strategies to bring about positive change in employee morale, improvement in quality of product and productivity itself. It may include issues relating to personal behaviour of employees and may deal with management of work stress, conflict management between individuals and groups. Scant attention paid to environment protection and social issues that may have direct or indirect impact on the individual and group performance.
7. To achieve organization effectiveness and bring changes in human resource, various processes and systems.
8. Organizational development is a continuous process. The programmes are implemented on short-term as well as long-term basis.
9. The responsibility to implement programmes lies with leaders and OD practitioners. They are also called facilitators. They are consultants trained in theory and practice of OD. They may be members of the organization they are working or outsiders. The basic aim of OD is: (1) To improve functioning of individuals, teams and affect overall improvement in the organization. (2) To impart necessary skills and knowledge so that the organization efficiency is achieved. Consultants assist in incorporating required changes.
10. Leaders identify blocks, problems in the organization and seek its solution in consultation with OD practitioners. OD is a people's movement, central theme being, get as much people as possible to participate in a planned change. OD programmes are planned in details implemented and results evaluated for desired outcome. Modifications are carried out while programmes are in process of implementation with an aim of meeting changed environment.
11. Due to introduction of latest technology, computers, information technology and resultant social change, the importance of OD has increased many folds. Communication has made a total revolution in the organization. Individual expectations have increased. It has therefore become mandatory to handle situations in time so that problems are averted.

Latest Trends in OD

Organization Development (OD) is applied behavioural science. It is a strategy to develop people in the organization. It aims at improving the people side of the organization by planned change. It focuses on people, relationship, policies, procedures, processes, norms, organizational structure and improving the very culture of the organizations. It is a mission initiated by the top managers and practiced down the line in the organizational hierarchy. Total involvement makes OD efforts successful. It must be remembered that organizations are made up of human systems aimed at achieving individual and organizational goals, priority being given to the latter. In the present era of information technology and knowledge management, it has added a new dimension to the study of OD. Organization Transformation (OT) may be called as the second generation OD as suggested by Porras and Silvers. They suggest that the "planned change interventions can be divided into two parts. The first comprises the more traditional approach, Organizational Development (OD), which until recently synonymous with term planned change. The second generation as OT. Cummings an Worley describe OT as follows":

> "Organization transformation can occur in response to or in anticipation of major changes in the organization's environment or technology. In addition these changes are often associated with significant alterations in the firm's business strategy, which, in turn, may require modifying corporate culture as well as internal structures and processes to support the new direction. Such fundamental change entails new paradigm for organizing and managing organizations. It involves qualitatively different ways of perceiving, thinking, and behaving in the organizations"[2].

It involves culture change, strategic change and self-designing organizations. It also involves development of behavioural science theories, models, practices and interventions to facilitate organizational transformation.

DEFINITIONS

Several definitions of OD exist. We will examine a few of them.

Beckhard (1969), has defined organization development as an effort (1) planned, (2) organization wide, (3) managed from the top, (4) increase organization effectiveness and health through (5) planned interventions in the organization's "processes," using behavioural science knowledge.

Bennis (1969), OD is a response to change, a complex education strategy intended to change the beliefs, attitudes, values, and structure of organizations so that they can better adapt to new technologies, markets and challenges, and the dizzying rate of change itself.

Beer (1980), the aim of OD are (1) enhancing congruence between organizational structure, processes, strategy, people, and culture; (2) developing new and creative organizational solutions; and (3) developing the organization's self-renewing capacity.

Organizational development is a set of behavioural science based theories, values, strategies and techniques aimed at the planned change of the organizational work setting for the purpose of enhancing individual development and improving, organizational performance, through the alteration of organizational members' on the job behaviours (Porras and Robertson, 1992).

OD is a system wide application of behavioural science knowledge to the planned development and re-enforcement of organizational strategies, structures, and processes for improving an organization's effectiveness (Cummings and Worley, 1993).

OD is a planned process of change in an organization's culture through the utilization of behavioural science technologies, research and theory (Burke, 1994).

From the above definitions following points emerge:

(*a*) OD is a field of applied behaviour science technologies.
(*b*) It is related to planned change.
(*c*) The study of OD is concerned with the total organizational systems and processes.
(*d*) OD is related to achieving congruence among organizational components like structure, culture and processes.
(*e*) OD is a long-term strategy intended to change beliefs, attitudes, values and organizational structures. It is carried out to achieve organizational effectiveness and meet the challenges of changed environmental factors.
(*f*) The study of OD is aimed at developing overall organization with particular reference to development of organizations renewing capacity.
(*g*) It involves initiating actions so that organization's are transformed into Learning Organisations.

The author suggests the following definition of organizational development:

> "Organizational Development is a long-term behavioural philosophy initiated by the top management. It relates to use of latest technologies and organizational processes to affect planned change by establishing cultural framework based on vision, empowerment and employee well being leading to attainment of quality of work life and organizational effectiveness thus creating a learned organization."

Dynamics of OD

OD is a continuous process where problem areas are identified, alternative solutions are sought and evaluated and workable solution is identified for implementation. It is a long-term process because development takes time to be of some value. It relates to permanent change of individual and group behaviour. It is a continuous improvement phenomenon that is never ending. Organization sets goal for itself. Once the goal is achieved, a new and higher goal is set for achievement. OD is required to be initiated and led by top management. It is a hard and sustained effort. Whenever any programme fails, it is generally because of the lack of management commitment. Achieving change in various organizational processes is a serious affair and it should be treated so throughout. Vision is a process of visualising in advance as to how a product or service will look and what would go into make it happen. It is related to sustained efforts on the part of all members of the organization to put in the best foot forward. It is possible by empowerment process. All the members should have self-confidence and an ability to build a vision, develop a suitable strategy and implement the same so that the organization is transformed. OD takes place by evolving various processes. Individual must develop and so should the teams, with suitable modification to job design, organizational structure and appropriately analyzing the environment, a solution can be sought to resolve current problem. An organization should be a learning organization where development is unending. Culture plays a vital role in organizational development.

Organizational Culture

In OD, there is a reciprocal influence between culture, strategy, structure and processes; each is important and each influences the other. But culture is of primary importance. Edgar Schein [3] defines culture as "(*a*) a pattern of basic assumptions, (*b*) discovered or developed by a given group, (*c*) as it learns to cope with its problems of external adaptation and internal integration, (*d*) that has worked well enough to be considered valid and, therefore (*e*) is to be taught to new members as the (*f*) correct way to perceive, think, and feel in relation to those problems."

Basic assumptions relate to values, and norms of behaviour, which organizations can invent, discover or develop over a period of time. These values and norms are considered to be valid overtime and therefore practiced by the members of the organization. Teams are basic bricks of an organization over which an organization is built. Teams are assigned a specific work and they work under the guidance of superior—subordinate relationship, that is required to be built on the basic norms of the organization. Therefore, all OD programmes are generally directed towards team building. In some organizations teams may manage themselves. These may be self-directed and assume responsibility of planning and executing a work. In organizations members have to be trained in quality control, MIS, improvement of skills, management of time and have to undertake behaviour modification when required. These are generally implemented by carrying out organization development programmes. Before a programme is undertaken, need is identified, a suitable consultant is made responsible to implement change in a given area and OD programme is conducted. In the present scenario, it is necessary to scan the environment, bench mark the organization, and re-engineer various processes and systems. This is required to be undertaken on a continuous basis so that organization growth is achieved and maintained.

PROFILE OF ORGANIZATION CULTURE

Octapace is the first letter indicating eight values. Apart from an acronym for these values, OCTAPACE is a term indicating the eight (OCTA) steps (PACE) needed to create a functional ethos (Pareek, 2000). The eight important values relevant to any organisation are: (1) Openness, (2) Confrontation, (3) Trust, (4) Authenticity, (5) Proactivity, (6) Autonomy, (7) Collaboration, and (8) Experimentation. The above eight important values are discussed below briefly.

1. Openness

Openness can be defined as a spontaneous expression of feelings and thoughts and the sharing of these without defensiveness. It applies both receiving and giving directions without any resistance/hesitation. Individual should be open to criticism, aim being to correct oneself. Recent trend in organisations of sharing meals, accommodation in the offices irrespective of the rank and status is an example of openness.

2. Confrontation

Confrontation can be defined as facing rather than shying away from problems. It also implies a deeper analysis of interpersonal problems. It involves taking challenge to do the work. The outcome of the confrontation can be better role clarity, improved problem solving and willingness to work under adverse conditions.

3. Trust

Trust in the organisation is referred to maintaining confidentiality and mutual understanding. It is also reflected in a sense of assurance and that others will help when the need arises. Trust is accepting what other person is saying at the face value and not searching for the ulterior motives. The outcome of the trust is high empathy, support and simplification of office procedure. Trust is required for smooth functioning of the organization with reduced stress and negligible conflict environment.

4. Authenticity

Authenticity is the congruence between what one feels, says and does. It is reflected in owning up to one's mistakes and sharing of feelings without any reservations. It reduces dissonance between members of the orgnization.

5. Proactivity

Proactivity means taking initiative, preplanning, taking preventive actions and calculating payoffs of an alternative course of action. Proactivity gives a person initiative to start a new process or a set of modified behaviour. A person showing proactivity functions at the following three levels:

- *Feeling:* The person transcends logic and reasoning and reaches to the feeling of other person. In the process he crosses role boundary and ensure things happen leading to empathy.
- *Thinking:* A person may transcend his immediate feelings, emotions and reasoning. He may think of future plans and visualize the things to happen, he may even give suitable directions and evolve his own concepts/theory.
- *Action:* Looking at the problem, searching various alternatives and initiating a new process are the gist of action part of proactivity. Proactive individual does not fall in the trap but makes a move of his own in critical situation and puts opponent in the defensive situation. He shows a high level of maturity and displays adult-adult transactions.

6. Autonomy

Autonomy relates to wider degree of delegation. It refers to releasing power that the employees already possess. Individual enjoys freedom of action in his own area of responsibility. He sets for himself the way a particular works to be undertaken and lays down priority. Autonomy promotes initiative, greater degree of acceptance of responsibility and derives greater level of job satisfaction.

7. Collaboration

Collaboration refers to working together for mutual benefits. It develops team spirit. Collaboration promotes mutual trust, timely help in terms of sharing resources, experiences, leading to higher productivity and better interpersonal/group communication and behaviour in the organizations/groups.

8. Experimentation

Experimentation refers promoting creativity and innovation in the organizations. It uses feedback and reports to initiate corrective actions. It is a way of doing things differently away from the routine processes that springs added energy among the workers. In experimentation, the leader should promote mistakes of employees and should not snub them. He should initiate rewards liberally. He should promote organization learning.

Based on data, observation and discussion, following four organization profiles are discussed in Figure 1.1 below (Pareek, 2004).

Autocratic/Feudal Culture

An autocratic or feudal culture is primarily concerned with following proper protocol and is dominated by dependency ('de') a climate with affiliation ('af') as its secondary. People are recruited on the basis of relationship, and they are trusted. In 'deaf' (dependency-affiliation) climate, as already indicated, the top managers control the organization and employ their own ingroup members, who are extremely loyal to these leaders. The ethos of such a culture is closed, mistrustful, and self-seeking.

Profile of Organization Culture

Cultures	Focus	Climate	Ethos
Autocratic/Feudal	Proper protocol	Deaf (dependency-affiliation)	Rammassic (all opposite values of OCTAPACE)
Bureaucratic	Rules and regulations	Code (control-dependency)	Sick (playing safe, inertia, conflict, and closeness)
Entrepreneurial/ Democratic/Organic	Results and customers	Ace (achievement-extension)	OCTAPACE (all eight values)
Technocratic	Perfection	Expex (expert power-extension)	Pace (proactivity, autonomy collaboration and experimentation)

Figure 1.1 Profile of organization culture

(Source: Organization Behaviour by Udai Pareek, Oxford University Press, 2004)

Bureaucratic Culture

A bureaucratic culture is concerned with following proper rules and regulations. Its climate is dominated by control ('co'), backed up by dependency ('de'). Such a climate ('code') shows that bureaucracy and a rigid hierarchy dominate the organization. Because actions are generally referred to the higher levels for approval, decisions are usually delayed. It is more important to follow rules and regulations here than to achieve results. Senior employees protect those subordinates who do not make any procedural mistakes. The ethos of a bureaucratic organization is characterized by playing it safe, inertia, lack of collaboration, and being closed.

Entrepreneurial Culture

An entrepreneurial culture (also called organic or democratic) is primarily concerned with results and customers. Its climate ('ace') is generally that of achievement ('ac'), or concern for excellence, and extension ('e'), or concern for larger groups and issues. In such a climate, employees work on challenging tasks and devote equal attention to the social relevance of these tasks. The organization has a highly developed sense of social responsibility as well as a strong sense of its responsibility to fulfill employee needs. The ethos is positive and characterized by the eight values OCTAPACE.

Technocratic Culture

A technocratic culture generally has an 'expex' climate expert power (exp) being dominant, with a back up climate of extension ('ex'). Specialists play the major roles in the organization, working in a planned way on socially relevant matters. The organization pays attention to the employees' needs and welfare. The ethos is positive, featuring proactivity (initiative), autonomy, collaboration and experimentation.

HISTORY OF ORGANIZATIONAL DEVELOPMENT

Organizational development is a very young and recent field of study. OD is being carried out systematically. French (1996) has identified four "trunk stems" (as he calls it) under which the study of OD is carried out. The four trunk stems are as under:

(*a*) Innovations are carried out to solve complex organizational problems through laboratory training.

(*b*) Survey research and feedback methodology.

(*c*) Action research.

(*d*) Socio-technical and socio-clinical approach to organizational development.

Kurt Lewin had established a research center called Research Center for Group Dynamics (RCGDs) at MIT in 1945. Laboratory training methodology was practiced in the center to develop organization. Study of group dynamics, change process and action research was jointly carried out by distinguish people like Marian Radke, Leon Festinger, Ronald Lippitt and Dorwin Cartwright. A leader carried out sessions and "feedback" at the end of the day was practiced. That is how "T Group" emerged. Lewin who was pioneer in T Group died in 1947. Berne Bradford and Lippitt at National Training Laboratory undertook the work later. Organizational development included training into applied behaviour science, role-playing, concept in learning and change, transactional analysis and studies of environment. In 1940s intensive training was being carried out on performance of teams in organizations. It was largely a practical application of T Group laboratory experience. Later Chris Angyris was one of the first persons to carry out team building sessions at Yale University and subsequently at Harvard. Douglas McGregar was influenced by the work done by Kurt Lewin, Angryris and others. Two significant innovations were carried out during this period. (1) Managerial Grid and, (2) Team development, consultation and conflict resolution concepts by Blake and Mouton. "It was learning to reject T Group stranger type labs that permitted OD into focus" and it was inter group projects, in particular that "triggered real OD" states Robert Blake[4]. During World War II Blake served in the Psychological Research Unit of Army, Air Force where he interacted with large number of behavioral scientists. During this period Systems Theory and OD was evolved. The people involved in development of OD processes were Jane Mouton, Robert Blake, and McGregor. Richard Beckhard and Herbert Shepard during the period of 1940–50s, Beckhard quotes. We clearly did not want to call it management development because it was total organization wide, nor, was it human relations training although there was a component of that in it, we did not want to call it organization improvement because that is a static term, so we labeled the programme "Organization Development", meaning system wide change efforts[5].

Second generation OD efforts revolved around the following lines:

(*a*) Change is a continuous phenomenon: Organizations are required to study external and internal environmental factors, identification of drawbacks, obsolescence and carryout change. The change may take place in organizational structure, work design, processes and various operational systems. Change is required to be undertaken for organizational growth. There are two basic strategies of change namely (1) Fundamental change strategy and (2) Incremental change strategy.

(*b*) Organizational transformation: It refers to carrying out fundamental change in the organization. It is a commitment made by high-level managerial staff to carry out modification to existing systems. It is a systems approach. Organizational culture is required to be changed to adjust to the external environment.

(*c*) Learning organization: An all out effort is required on the part of managers to keep its employees educated on the latest technology, systems, knowhow and processes. It is a part and parcel of the OD requirement. More on learning organizations has been separately dwelt with in the separate chapter later in the book.

(*d*) Total quality management: Edward Deming and Crosby have done pioneering work on Total Quality Management (TQM). TQM involves employee involvement, teamwork, decision-making, problem-solving, high level involvement, adopting a work culture aimed at growth and quality of product and services. TQM requires total commitment, removing fear psychosis caused due to failure at lower levels, development of successful work culture and continuous improvement.

(*e*) Visioning: Visioning envisages as to what the organization would look like in the future. It is related to the shape in terms of HR facilities, the growth and the needs of people it is likely to fulfill. Based on the vision, database is required to be built, leading to interpretation of information, arriving at suitable decisions and setting a course of action leading to growth. Visioning refers to looking at the organization in "totality".

(*f*) **Virtual organizations**: Getting whole system in one room, evolving action plan and implementation.

Structural Changes

Structural changes are initiated to carry out organizational development. This includes research, use of change agent for implementation. The process involves identification of problem; courses open, selecting the best course of action and implementation. Services of OD consultant are central to implement change.

OBJECTIVES OF ORGANIZATIONAL DEVELOPMENT PROGRAMME

1. Individual and group development.
2. Development of organization culture and processes by constant interaction between members irrespective of levels of hierarchy.
3. Inculcating team spirit.
4. Empowerment of social side of employees.
5. Focus of value development.
6. Employee participation, problem-solving and decision-making at various levels.
7. Evaluate present systems and introduction of new systems thereby achieving total system change if required.
8. Transformation and achievement of competitive edge of the organization.
9. Achieve organization growth by total human inputs by way of research and development, innovations, creativity and exploiting human talent.
10. Behaviour modification and self managed team as the basic unit of an organization.

OD CHARACTERISTICS/COMPETENCIES

1. OD focuses on development of organizational culture.
2. OD focuses on overall development of organization and individuals with win-win strategy.
3. It relies heavily on action research.
4. It deals with improvement of on going processes.
5. OD focuses on total system change and views organization as complex social system.
6. Delegation of authority, empowerment, and quality of work life a sense of autonomy are the hallmark of OD programme.
7. OD practitioners are facilitators and collaborators. Their assistance in identification of problem areas, arriving at a solution, implementation and feedback is necessary. Their services are valuable.

8. OD is characterized by study and development of multiethnic culture that is supportive of work ethics. People with diverse value system, culture, and interests should be able to work effectively under one roof and achieve cordial relationship with fellow employees. It should be able to help achieve organizational effectiveness.
9. Organizational development is a joint responsibility of owners, employees, investors' society, government agencies and consumers. It must be understood that the organizations exist for all of them.

SUMMARY

Organization development offers a prescription for improving the ***"fit"*** between the individuals and the organization, between the organization and the environment, and among the organizational components such as strategy, structure and process. The prescription is implemented through inventions and activities that address specific problematic conditions. Organizational development is a continuous process. The programmes are implemented on short-term as well as long-term basis. Organization Transformation (OT) may be called as the second generation OD as suggested by Porras and Silvers. Organizational development is a set of behavioural science based theories, values, strategies and techniques aimed at the planned change of the organizational work setting for the purpose of enhancing individual development and improving organizational performance through the alteration of organizational members on the job behaviours.

In OD, there is a reciprocal influence between culture, strategy, structure and processes; each is important and each influences the other. When we study the profile of organization culture, it is identified as autocratic/feudal culture, bureaucratic, entrepreneurial, and technocratic.

Innovations are carried out to solve complex organizational problems through laboratory training, survey research and feedback methodology, action research and socio-technical and socio-clinical approach to organizational development.

Second generation OD efforts revolved around organizational transformation, learning organization, total quality management, visioning and virtual organizations. We should understand what are various objectives of organizational development programme before a beginning is made.

TEXT QUESTIONS

1. Define OD.
2. Explain in details the concept of organizational development.
3. What are the characteristics of an OD programme?
4. What objectives are being prompted by the OD programme?
5. Write a brief history of evolution of OD.
6. Define culture. What is its profile?

BIBLIOGRAPHY

1. French Wendil, L. and Bell Cicil, H., *"Organization Development"*, Fifth Edition, Prentice Hall India Pvt Limited, New Delhi.
2. T. G. Cummings and C. G. Worley, *"Organizational Development and Change"*, 6th Edition, West Publishing Co., 1993 p. 520.
3. Edgar, H. Schein, *"Organizational Culture"*, American Psychologist, 45 (Feb. 1990), p. 111.
4. Robert Blake and Jane Srygley Mouton, *"Why the OD movement is 'Stuck' and How to Break it Loose"*, Training and Development Journal, 33 (September 1979), pp. 12-20.
5. Beckhard correspondence.

CASE STUDY
ACTION PLAN FOR CSR*

There are several areas of action plan for undertaking corporate social responsibility. These are given in the succeeding paragraph.

1. Environments and Ecology

(*a*) Reduced consumption of energy, water and other natural resources and emission of hazardous substance, environment management systems have to be established.

(*b*) Recycled and recyclable products to be used.

(*c*) Durability of the products to be increased.

(*d*) Staff to be trained in environmental issues.

2. Health and Well-being

(*a*) Policies to ensure health and the safety of all employees.

(*b*) Involvement of employees in business decisions that affect men.

(*c*) Open-book policies of the corporate.

(*d*) Training for life management, retirement planning and dependents care.

3. Diversity and Human Rights

(*a*) Charitable job centers to redesign jobs to make them accessible to disadvantaged.

(*b*) Organization that promote fair trades and human rights compliance.

(*c*) Awareness among staff members about explicit policies against discrimination hiring, promotion, training, or termination of any employee on the basis of gender, race, age, ethnicity, disability and the like.

4. Community

(*a*) Surplus product and redundant equipment to be made available to local schools, charities and community organizations.

(*b*) Quality work experience for school children and students to be offered.

Emerging Areas of Corporate Social Responsibility

1. Social Responsibility

(*a*) Respecting human rights.

(*b*) Contributing to socio-economic development.

(*c*) Employee welfare: this includes right to organize, elimination of child labour, non-discrimination, living wages and social security, training, safety, health and empowerment of employees, etc.

2. Business Responsibility

(*a*) Compliance with tax laws and other regulations.

(*b*) Investing in developing in science and technology.

(*c*) Regulating suppliers and distributors CSR practices an transparent financial reporting.

3. Environmental Responsibility

(*a*) Respect for environment and environment friendly technologies.

(*b*) Conservation and discharge of energy material and water in eco-friendly manner. Adopting preventive and precautionary measure for environmental damage at source.

(*c*) Treating waste before disposing it.

(*d*) Preservation of biodiversity.

4. Stakeholders Involvement

Extension of principle and ethical values enshrined in organization to all the stakeholders such as authorities, customer groups, business partners and external influences. There are varying practices, and approaches on CSR in different economies due to the differences in social, cultural, and ethical systems in which different companies operate. In any developed country the issues of CSR relate to governance, business ethics, regulatory frameworks, cultural practices, public needs etc. However in a fast developing country like India, the issues primarily focus on the processes of nation building and socio-economic development in the areas like health, education, employment and rural development. Hence Indian corporate sector is fully aware and is striving to improve its public image. Undertaking social responsibility through upliftment and community development programme has become a common norm.

***Archana Nema and Hema Chura**

CHAPTER 2

Values, Assumptions and Beliefs in Organization Development

CHAPTER PLAN

- *Introduction*
- *Definition*
- *Historical Background of Values*
- *Early Statements of OD Values and Assumptions*
- *Summary*
- *Text Questions*
- *Bibliography*
- *Case Study: QWC The Balancing Act*

INTRODUCTION

1. Organization development relates to three major elements of society. These are, (1) the organization which desires to improve itself by way of applying OD intervention, (2) the change agent or an expert who has been working on projects to implement change in the organization by way of applying behaviour modification strategies and, (3) last but not the least the client system i.e., the team of people of the organization mentioned in Para 1 above, who in consultation with the change agent is to apply OD interventions to their sub-unit or the department or it may even be group of people.
2. For any efforts to be successful, it is necessary to understand and ensure that all the three elements mentioned above possess required values, beliefs and assumptions. No OD effort can ever be successful if they lack in this respect. Let us define value, beliefs, and assumptions.

DEFINITION

A belief is a proposition about how the world works that the individual accepts as true; it is a cognitive fact for the person. **Values** are about beliefs and are defined as: "belief about what is desirable or a 'good' (e.g., liberty of free expression) and what is an undesirable or 'bad' (e.g., disloyal)."[1] **Assumptions** are beliefs that are regarded as so valuable as obviously correct that they are taken for granted and rarely questioned or examined. Thus, values assumptions, and beliefs are all cognitive facts or propositions, with values being beliefs about good and bad, and assumptions being beliefs about good and bad, and assumptions being strongly held, relatively unexamined beliefs accepted as the truth.[2] It provides basic foundation for behaviour of the people around the world.

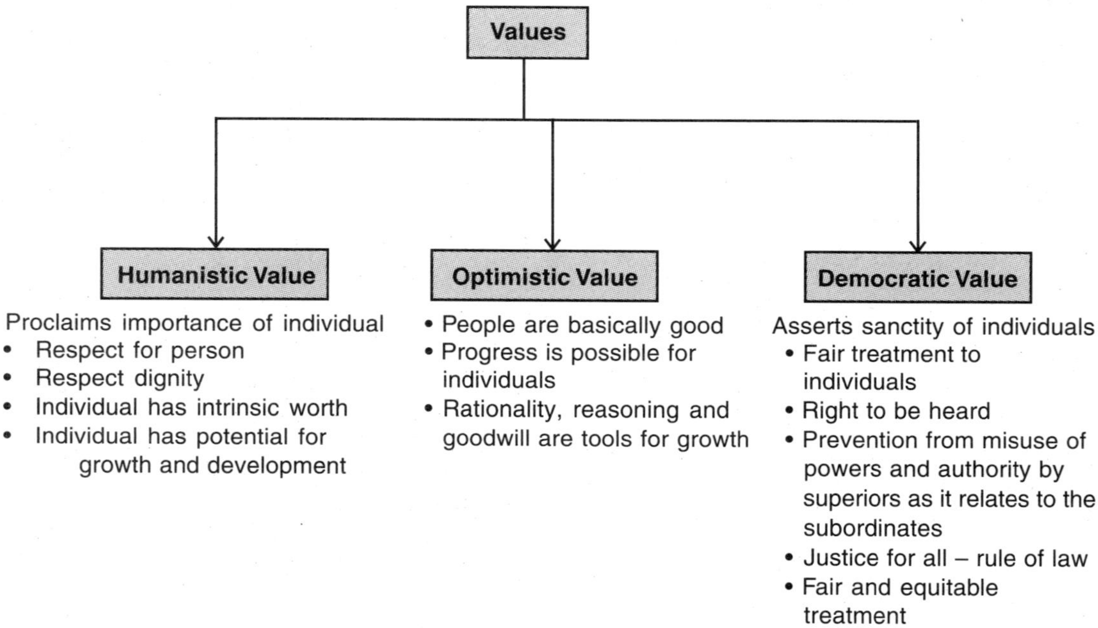

HISTORICAL BACKGROUND OF VALUES

Research, practices and experiments carried out in laboratories and industrial units by social scientists, psychologist and academicians have led to decide on various values, beliefs and assumptions. The details, in brief are given below:

(*a*) Principals of scientific management by Fredrick Winslow Taylor. He propagated time and motion studies, breaking of jobs into small jobs and thus developing expertise, piece rate of payment and separation of planning and doing a job. He thus brought revolution in organizations. His contribution to organization development is immense.

(*b*) 1992 the great German sociologist Max Weber introduced the concept of "bureaucracy" as the best, most efficient way to organize people. He believed and practiced a strong hierarch of authority, division of labour, impersonal rules, and strict procedures as the best way of running an organization.

(*c*) 1927–1932 Elton Mayo conducted the famous Hawthorne studies at the Hawthorne plant of Western Electric Company. The research demonstrated the *primacy of social factors* on productivity and morale. People came to work as a whole people; their feelings and attitude about the work, the work environment, and the supervisor determined their performance. *Group norms* had profound effect on productivity. People's *emotions* were to be honoured. The experiment gave a new twist to the studies of organizational behaviour. The new paradigm took birth, and bureaucratic, scientific way of operations was replaced by behavioural model of Mayo.[3]

(*d*) 1939 research by Lewin, Lippitt, and White demonstrated that democratic leadership was superior to authoritarian leadership and laissez-faire leadership in achieving group performance. They concluded that democratic leadership brings out best in the group and that the bureaucratic leadership promotes dependency, apathy, aggressiveness and poor performance.[4]

(*e*) Kurt Lewin and his students had launched the concepts of Group dynamics—the scientific study of groups using experimental research method in 1940s.[4]

(*f*) 1940s to 1960s the famous Hawthorne studies made its mark about Human relations era. It was full blown during this period. It advocated participative management, group phenomenon, full attention to human needs, training for supervisors in inter-personnel skills and developing work place and building social environment, that is conducive to higher productivity.

(*g*) 1946 and 1947 these years witnessed the beginning of the laboratory training, movement, a direct precursor of OD. Laboratory training taught the people how to improve inter-personal relationship, improve self-understanding and understand group dynamics. Humanistic and democratic values suffused the movement.[5]

(*h*) 1948 Ken Benne and Paul Sheats pioneered the laboratory training and proposed that a leadership function of a group is the joint responsibility of the leader and the group members.[6]

(*i*) 1948 Lester Coach and John R.P. French Advocated resistance to overcoming change. They proposed need for allowing the people affected by change to participate in planning of change.

(*j*) 1951 Eric Trist and Ken Bamforth introduced the concept of organization as socio-technical system, which postulates that the organizations are comprised of social system and technical system. Change in one system will have a corresponding effect in another system.

(*k*) 1954 Motivation and personality by Abraham Maslow presented a new view of human motivation. He classified human needs into five categories; physical needs being the most dominating lower-level need to self-actualization needs, a higher-level need. The theory postulates that when lower-level needs are satisfied, higher-level needs become dominant.[7]

(*l*) 1960 Douglas McGregor wrote the Human Side of Enterprise in which he described his famous Theory X and Theory Y assumptions. In addition the book popularized Maslow's motivation theory, and introduced practicing managers to the concepts of need hierarchy and self-actualization.

(*m*) 1961 Burns and Stalker described two different types of organizational structure, namely *mechanistic and organic*. Mechanistic structure, they say is suitable for slow moving organization where there is little or no change anticipated. While on the other hand organic structure is suitable for organizations that are fast changing.

(*n*) 1961 Rensis Likert's *new patterns of management* research work showing the superiority of democratic style of leadership over the autocratic style of leadership.

(*o*) 1966 Daniel Katz and Robert L. Kahn presented first comprehensive exposition of organization as the *open system.*[8]

(*p*) 1990s to date TQM, Business process reengineering, six sigma, Delegation, empowerment, Consumer relationship management, job redesigning, flatter organizational structure, collaboration, acquisitions mergers and takeovers are the new paradigm of organizational designs. Training and development and faster turnovers of employees have been notices especially in information technology industries. Knowledge management has become the corner stone of an organization that seeks growth. Group dynamics and transactional analysis is as important today as it was earlier. Emotional intelligence is important to measure employee performance and morale.

Based on the above research, organizational development practitioners have evolved a set of OD values, belief and assumptions about the people. These are humanistic, optimistic and democratic as is been explained in the succeeding paragraphs.

EARLY STATEMENTS OF OD VALUES AND ASSUMPTIONS

1. Values have been an integral part of any organization that has been successful in its endeavour. I shall append below the early statements that has had a tremendous impact on the success of the OD efforts.

Warren Bennis (1969)[9] proposed that OD practioners (Change Agent) share a set of *normative goals* based on their humanistic/democratic philosophy. These are as follows:

(*a*) Improvement in interpersonal competence.

(*b*) A shift in values so that human factors and feelings come to be considered to be legitimate.

(*c*) Development of increased between and within working groups in order to reduce tensions.

(*d*) Development of more effective "team management," that is, the capacity for functional groups to work more competently.

(*e*) Development of better methods of conflict resolution. Rather than the usual bureaucratic methods, which rely mainly on suppression, compromise, and unprincipled power, more rational and open methods of conflict resolution are sought.

(*f*) Development of organic rather than mechanical systems. This is a strong reaction against the idea of organizations as mechanisms which managers "work on." Like pushing buttons.

2. Richard Beckhard had immensely contributed to the field of OD. He gave certain assumptions about the nature and functioning of the organizations held by OD practitioners. The assumptions are listed below:
   (*a*) The basic building blocks of an organization are groups (teams). Therefore basic group of change are groups and not the individuals.
   (*b*) An always relevant change goal is the reduction of inappropriate competition between parts of the organization and the development of more collaborative conditions.
   (*c*) Decision-making in a healthy organization is located where the information sources are, rather than in a particular role or level of hierarchy.
   (*d*) Organizations, sub-units or organizations, and individuals continuously manage their affairs against their goals. Controls are interim measurements, not the basis of managerial strategy.
   (*e*) One goal of a healthy organization is to develop generally open communication, mutual trust, and confidence between and across levels.
   (*f*) "People support what they help create." People affected by a change must be allowed active participation and a sense of ownership in the planning and conduct of the change.[10]

Implications

1. **For Individuals**
   (*a*) Most individuals believe in their personal growth. Even today, training and development, promotion to the next higher position dominates the organization philosophy.
   (*b*) Majority of the people are desirous of making greater contributions to the organizations they are serving. Achievements of organizational goals are however, subject to limitations or environmental constraints. It is for the organizations to tap the skills that are available in abundance. This leads to adopt the following organization strategy for development:
   - Ask questions to resolve doubts.
   - Listen to superior's advice.
   - Support employees in their venture.
   - Accept challenge.
   - Leaders to encourage creativity and promote risk taking.
   - Give additional responsibility to subordinates.
   - Set high standards of quality.
   - Empower employees.
   - Initiate suitable reward system that should be compatible, if not more than the industry norms.

2. For Groups

(*a*) One of the most important factors in the organization is the *'work group'* around whom the organization functions. This includes the peer group and the leader (boss).

(*b*) More people prefer to be part of the group because the group accepts them.

(*c*) Most people are capable of making higher contributions to the group's effectiveness.

Following strategy is required to be adopted for group development based on the above assumptions:

(*a*) Invest in training and development of the group. Money and time spent on this is an investment for the organization. Leaders should also invest in development of skills and thus help create a position organizational climate.

(*b*) Let the team flourish. Teams are the best approach to get the work done. Apart from the above teams enjoy emotional and job satisfaction when they work in groups.

(*c*) Leaders should adopt team leadership style and not autocratic leadership style. To do this, jobs should be allotted to the team and not to the individual.

(*d*) It is not possible for one individual (leader) to perform both, the leadership and maintenance functions. It is therefore necessary for team members to assist leader in performance of his duties.

(*e*) Group should be trained in conflict management, stress management, group decision-making, collaboration, and effective interpersonal communication. This will improve organizational effectiveness. Empowerment is the corner stone of the successful organizations.

(*f*) Leaders should pay particular attention to the feelings of the employees. It should be understood that suppressed feeling and attitudes adversely affect problem-solving, personal growth and job satisfaction.

(*g*) Development of group cohesiveness.

3. For Organizations

(*a*) Create learning organization culture.

(*b*) Adopt win-win strategy for sustained growth.

(*c*) Create cooperative dynamics rather than competitive organizational dynamics in the organization.

(*d*) Needs and aspirations of the employees in the organization must be met. This leads to greater participation of the employees. Organizations should adopt developmental outlook and seek opportunities in which people can experience personal and professional growth. Such orientation creates a self-fulfilling prophecy.

(*e*) People must be treated with due respect and considered important. The credit of success must be given to the employees unconditioned.

(*f*) Promote organizational citizenship.

4. It is possible to create organizations that are humane, democratic and empowering on one hand and high performing in terms of productivity, quality of output, profitability, and growth on the other. It is the responsibility of every entrepreneur to ensure that the needs of the society are met.

SUMMARY

Organizational development relates to three major elements of society. These are, (1) the organization which desires to improve itself by way applying OD intervention, (2) the change agent or an expert who has been working on projects to implement change in the organization by way of applying behaviour modification strategies and, (3) last but not the least the client system. Values assumptions, and beliefs are all cognitive facts or propositions, with values being beliefs about good and bad, and assumptions being beliefs about good and bad, and assumptions being strongly held, relatively unexamined beliefs accepted as the truth. It provides basic foundation for behaviour of the people around the world. The OD values are humanistic value, optimistic value and democratic value. Research practices and experiments carried out in laboratories and industrial units by social scientists, psychologist and academicians have led to decide on various values, beliefs and assumptions. Richard Beckhard had immensely contributed to the field of OD. He gave certain assumptions about the nature and functioning of the organizations held by OD practitioners. The implications for individuals, for groups and for organizations are important and hence a subject matter for study and implementation by those who are closely associated with OD programmes.

TEXT QUESTIONS

1. Explain various values, belief and assumptions.
2. What are various values and assumptions Richard Beckhard has proposed?
3. Explain the strategies that should be adopted by various managers while implementing organisation development.
4. Define values, beliefs and assumptions.

BIBLIOGRAPHY

1. David Krech, Richard S. Crutchfield, and Egerton Ballachey, *"Individual and Society"* (New York: McGraw-Hill, p. 102).
2. Wendill, L. French, and Cecil H. Bell, Jr. "*Organization Development*", Seventh Edition, PHI, 2003.
3. Elton Mayo, *"The Human Problem of an Industrial Civilization"* (Cambridge, M.A. Harvard University, Graduate School of Business, Division of Research, 1933).

4. K. Lewin, R. Lippitt, and R. White, *"Patterns of Aggressive Behaviour in Experimentally Created Social Climate",* Journal of Social Psychology, 10 (1939), pp. 271–299.
5. D. Cartwright and A. Zander, *"Group Dynamics: Research and Theory"* (New York: Harper and Row, 1953).
6. K.D. Benne and P. Sheats, *"Functional Roles of Group Members",* Journal of Social Issues, 4, no. 2 (1948), pp. 41–49.
7. Abraham Maslow, *"Motivation and Personality",* (New York: Harper 1954).
8. Daniel Katz and Robert L. Kahn, *"The Social Psychology of Organisations"*, New, The Social Psychology of Organisations (New York: John Wiely & Sons, 1966).
9. Bennis, *"Organisation Development: Its Nature, Origins and Prospects"*, p. 15.
10. Beckhard, *"Organisation Development: Strategies and Models"*, pp. 26–27.

CASE STUDY
QWC—THE BALANCING ACT

Jim Bird, the President of wroklifebalance.com, a leader in work-life balance solutions, has a simple philosophy: "I just want to achieve something today and enjoy something too. And if I do both of these things everyday, for the rest of my life, I'm going to have a pretty good life," he says. A simple, yet profound concept, and is probably the best advice anyone can offer you for incorporating balance into your work-life. Balance is necessary, for it gives you a measure of control over your life. As work schedules become hectic and the customer expects 24 × 7 service from a company, the employee is under constant pressure to perform. "Today, most employees are reeling under long working hours and pressure," says Sanjay Salooja, Founder and CEO, Empower, a work-life value company. And if the pressure gets to you, then the balance could tip. The effect is, of course disastrous, with the employer and the employee suffering in the long run. A survey conducted on how personal problems could impact your work life, pointed out that 30 per cent of absenteeism is related to an employee's inability to cope with personal problems. And that nearly two out of every five employees are dissatisfied with the balance between their work and personal lives.

The symptoms of living in imbalance are quite obvious — mental duress and lack of concentration. "The employee is usually in a tearing hurry to shift from one task to the other and is unable to do justice to any," says Ajay Oberoi, Senior Vice President, Aptech, Limited. As a result, he feels tired constantly and eventually burnout sets in. "One can quote the example of Amitabh Bachchan who used to pump 17 hours into his workday. And this is, no doubt, one plausible reason for his illness," says Dr. R.L. Bhatia, CEO, Fun and Joy At Work.

So how does one go about achieving a work-life balance? There are five stages that one must go through to achieve this, the first one being the phase where you struggle, to understand what is wrong and what you are missing in life. Says Bhatia, "You just feel out of control." In the second stage, you juggle various responsibilities and develop tricks and techniques that allow you to create a sense of control. "This is a precarious stage and the skills that allow you to juggle two balls may fail as soon as a third ball is added to juggle," he says. Now comes the third stage – work-life balance – where you actually begin to fulfill your multiple responsibilities and enjoy a sense of equilibrium. The trick is to focus on all your energies and get through the day. The fourth is work-life integration where you are not only able to fulfill all your work responsibilities but also have enough energy to put towards career planning, career development and personal growth. You have a personal growth. You have a sense of where you are going, says Bhatia. In the final stage of work-life harmony, you are completely in control of all aspects of your work-life.

Even organizations have started realizing the importance of work-life balance and are taking some concrete steps to help employees snap out of the imbroglio. A company, for instance, has come up with a Wednesday Blackout policy, which essentially means that lights are switched off at 6 pm every Wednesday – a signal for employees to wrap up and push off. Then there are companies that have formulated flexi-hour policies for their employees. This allows people to adjust their workday while maintaining full-time hours-an ideal arrangement for someone who might want to start work early and leave early. "I know of a manager in a company who worked flexi-hours from December to May to meet with a family responsibility," says Bhatia.

A compressed workweek is another option. "Companies even allow employees to work the entire week and club the holidays together to meet family," says an Editor of publishing house.

For that to happen, you'll obviously have to look for an opportunity to talk to your employer. "It's better to be prepared in advance and not spring it onto a manager on a Friday afternoon in a fit of tears after an exhausting week," says Salooja. Let them know exactly what you are looking for and explain why. Do this not from the perspective of "I need to spend more time with my kids" but in terms of "In order for me to be the most effective employee possible, this is the work arrangement that I need in order to fulfill my commitment".

And if you are wondering whether flexi-arrangements would hamper your career, then let me tell you a flexible schedule does not always limit your career. "It can slow down your career path slightly because it may take you longer to get the necessary experience for promotion, but it shouldn't limit growth in the long run," says Bhatia. After all, it's good o remember that the more out of balance or out of control your life is, the more you pay in terms of physical and emotional health. "You probably won't eat properly or consume more caffeine, more alcohol, more sugar, and you are less likely to exercise on a regular basis. Your relationships, too, could become unstable – quite a heavy price to pay for an unbalance life," says Salooja. A stressed employee may spell trouble for companies too.

Hindustan Times
Dated 30 May 2006

Author: ***Sonali Majumdar***

CHAPTER 3

Diagnostics Strategies and OD Processes

CHAPTER PLAN

- *Introduction*
- *Diagnosis*
- *The Six-box Model*
- *Considerations and Action Components of OD Programme*
- *Nature of OD Interventions*
- *Phases of OD Programme Management*
- *Managing Change (Cummings and Worley's Model)*
- *Eight Steps for Successful Organization Transformation: Kotter's Model of Change*
- *Summary*
- *Text Questions*
- *Bibliography*
- *Case Study: Growing Pains of the Pennathur Tyre Company*

INTRODUCTION

In this chapter we will examine what leaders, organization members and OD practitioners do as they implement and manage OD programme. Organizational development programmes are required to be implemented by all the organizations irrespective their size, structure, location, and culture they follow. For organizational development to be successful, it is necessary to study the following basic component of any OD programme:

- Diagnosis component
- Action component
- Programme management

DIAGNOSIS

This is the first model of diagnosis being explained here. The diagnosis is carried out in the following four steps:

Step 1: The diagnostic component represents a continuous collection of data about the organization, system, or the process. The focus of the total exercise is to diagnose the state of the system. It aims at identifying its strengths, problem areas and unrealized opportunities. Vision statements are evaluated in depth in this stage and the discrepancies between the vision, the desired future and the current situation are identified.

Step 2: Step 2 relates to correcting problems that have been identified in step 1, seize opportunities and encash on the strengths of the organization. These are called organizational development interventions. OD interventions specifically tailored to address issues that are at the individual, group, inter-group and organizational levels. These interventions are also applied to various organizational processes or the systems so that optimum benefits are derived from them.

Step 3: Step 3 consists of fact finding. Once the OD interventions are applied to individual, group, or the department, it aims at its effectiveness. Has the problem solved? Have the opportunities resulted in desired output. If the answer is 'yes', then the expert moves on to apply interventions to the other problem. If the answer is 'no' the modified interventions are applied again and the problem is resolved or the opportunities have been realized.

Step 4: As explained in step 3, once the problem is solved the diagnosis stage is over. But if the problem remains, or if the opportunities have not been properly utilized to achieve the desired results, or the strength of the organization is not fully exploited, then stage 4 continues. There may be situations when various OD interventions may not bring the desired results, then the intervention will have to be changed and the whole process will have to be repeated. In such situations step 4, 5 and even 6 may have to be implemented. The diagnosis stage appears to be simple phenomenon, but it is not so. It is very complicated exercise especially when behaviour modification is aimed at.

Analysis

The objective of the diagnosis programme is to study the whole system, identify various strengths of the organization and also the weak points/areas. It is the responsibility of the change agent or the expert who has been assigned the duty of implementing the change by way of application of OD interventions so that weak areas are improved in a phased manner. OD interventions are applied in a graduated manner taking one issue at a time and dealing with it threadbare. Improvement strategy calls for concentrating on different organizational targets in a planned sequence. For example, the programme may start at an important sub-system, move to another sub-system, and then extend to the entire organization. It may even take a reverse approach namely to take on the entire organization first and then move on to the selected sub-systems in a graduated manner.

THE SIX-BOX MODEL

Marvin Weisbord has proposed 'six-box model', a diagnostic framework that is widely used by the OD practitioners. This model tells practitioners where to look and what to look for diagnosing organizational problems. He suggested six critical areas—purposes, structure, rewards, helpful mechanism, relationships and leadership. The model is explained in the diagram below:

Explanation: It is the responsibility of the OD practitioners to examine each of the box in detail. There are two ways of looking at the issue. One, the formal way and the other the informal way—the things actually happen. For example, the formal reporting relationship and organization of tasks and people prescribed in the structure box may not reflect the real structural arrangements found in formal system. The practitioner needs answer to two questions: First, are the arrangements and the process called for by the formal system correct for each box? Second, are the arrangements and the processes developed by the informal system correct for each box? On examination it will be noticed, that though the correct systems and processes may have been formed by the formal system, but the employees may not strictly follow these. On the contrary, there may be informal systems and processes that may be followed by the employees, which might not have been formalized. These are the indicators that the OD practitioners are supposed to look for, for the organizational development. The formal/informal distinction, that is, what's supposed to happen versus what is really happening, is a powerful OD diagnostic tool.

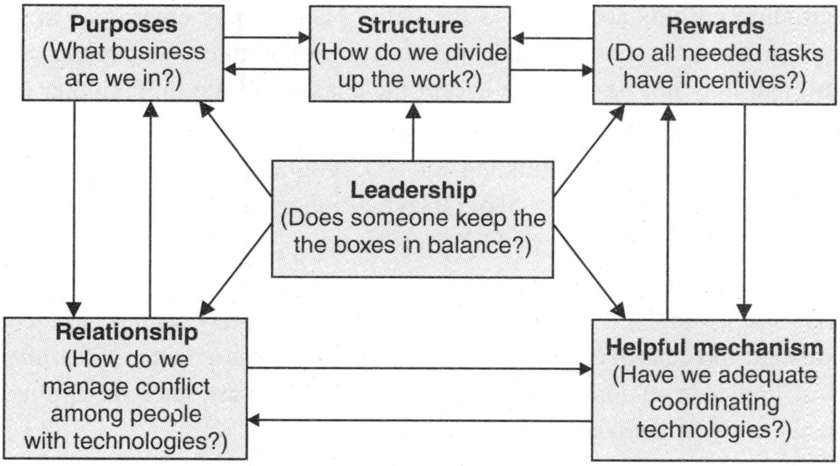

Figure 3.1 The six-box model of diagnosis

CONSIDERATIONS AND ACTION COMPONENTS OF OD PROGRAMME

OD interventions are set of structured activities in which selected organizational units engage in a sequence of tasks that will lead to organizational improvement. Interventions are planned set of actions to change situations; the organization members want to change. The following four conditions are required to be examined for action component of OD interventions. These are as under:

1. The organization has a problem. Therefore interventions are required to fix the problem.
2. The organization feels an unrealized opportunity; something it wants to achieve beyond. These are called enabling actions that the organization wants to achieve. Therefore interventions is developed to seize the opportunity.
3. Features of the organizations are working at cross-purposes. Alignment activities interventions are developed to bring back the organization in the synchronization stage, so that all departments, systems and processes work in tune with over all organizational objectives.
4. Environment is changing very fast. The vision that was fixed may not be in line with the changed environment. New action to build the necessary structures, processes, and culture to support the new vision-interventions are developed to make the new vision a reality.

NATURE OF OD INTERVENTIONS

1. Intervening in the client system refers to interposing activities so that intervention activities are done in addition to or are done instead of the normal activities. For example, carrying out brainstorming session before a meeting to find a solution to the existing problem. This is generally not done as matter of routine.
2. OD programme unfolds according to the game plan or may emerge as the event moves on. OD programme may be applied to production department as per the game plan, but the department may not be ready to accept the change. While on the other hand, research and development department may welcome the change (emerge).
   - Planning, executing and evaluating an OD programme is integral to organizational development. It is a powerful tool of OD practitioners hence detailed planning and action taken are powerful features of OD programme.
   - Most of the OD interventions have two goals. One 'to learn' and the second 'action aspects'. For example, top managers may evolve a two-day seminar to identify problem of command and control mechanism in the organization as a matter of learning or updating skills at higher-level managerial levels. The model may later be applied to the real problems in the organization as a action plan.
   - OD interventions focus on the real problems faced by the organization.
   - The group as a smallest entity generally applies the interventions.
   - Organizational development programmes depend heavily on various learning models like classical learning or social learning, etc.
   - Action programmes in OD are closely linked with explicit goals and objectives of the organization. It is therefore necessary, to pay attention to translating goals into observable, explicit, and measurable actions.

Organization development is about diagnosis, action taking, goal setting, collection of data, planning and taking actions and evaluating results are important steps of OD programme. Each step in itself is an independent OD programme.

PHASES OF OD PROGRAMME MANAGEMENT

Warner Burke described the following phases of OD programme:

1. *Entry*: Entry represents the initial contact between consultant and client. It also examines the reasons that led to client selection. It further determines smooth amalgam of the client, the problem— the consultant is hired to resolve, the extent opportunities have been aimed to be enchased and the smooth working relationship that should prevail.
2. *Contracting*: Establishing mutual expectations; reaching agreements on expenditure of time, money, resources, and energy; and generally clarifying mutual expectations.
3. *Diagnosis*: Identification of slot where the problem arises by way of carrying out data collection and interpreting the same. It may be related to department, system processes, and culture modification.
4. *Feedback*: Represents returning the analyzed information to the client system; exploration of information for understanding in relation to the problem; its application; trust between the client and the specialist, extent the problem is being resolved and opportunities realized.
5. *Planning change*: Client deciding what actions to be taken; alternatives available; critical analysis of the possibilities available; action plan devised/selected from among the available alternatives and implemented.
6. *Intervention:* Implementation of sets of actions designed to correct the problem or seizing the opportunities.
7. *Evaluation:* Assessing the results of the OD programme; its success, changes in the organization structure, processes, systems, job design, and analyzing the total difference made to the organization. It also relates to the effective of the OD programme.

MANAGING CHANGE (CUMMINGS AND WORLEY'S MODEL)[2]

Cummings and Worley have suggested the following five areas where change is required:

1. Motivating change
2. Creating a vision
3. Developing political support
4. Managing the transition
5. Sustaining momentum.

1. Motivating Change

It is important that the leader of the organization must create readiness to change. The motivation is achieved by adopting following guidelines:

- Sensitise people about the pressure of change.
- Show deficiency between the present situation and the future.
- Highlight advantage of change.
- Create pains in the minds of the people in the organization that things are not working as desired by them.
- Involve members right from the beginning of change efforts planning and implementing change.

2. Creating a Vision

Creating vision is visualizing how the future will look. Vision must have the following ingredients:

- It must be realistic.
- It should be beneficial to the majority of people in the organization.
- It should be attainable.
- Suitable mission statement backed up by organization values and making available the inputs required for achieving change is the essence of achieving the desired vision.

3. Developing Political Support

Cumming and Worley suggest that the practitioner assess his own power. He should identify the key players whose support is required for success of implementing change. He must persuade those key players to explain to the employees that it is for their benefit. Individuals who wedge power in the organization should be associated with the change efforts.

4. Managing the Transition

This stage is most important as we are leaving behind the old ways of doing things/processes or the systems and evolving a new set. It relates to maintaining momentum of various activities till the end is achieved. Unfreezing of the present state, the transition to the new future, attainment of desired goals and refreezing the outcome. "Activity Planning" achieves this. It involves preparation of checklist of various activities, sequence of events and people responsible for various activities. The total plan must serve as a road map for the change to be implemented. "Commitment Planning" is also important. It involves getting the support and commitment of the key players in the organization whose leadership, resources, and energy is so crucial to the success of transition.

5. Sustaining Momentum

Following actions are recommended for sustaining momentum:

- Regular meetings to review progress of the work done.
- Problem-solving.
- Ensuring that the resources are made available.
- Close interaction with the specialist/change agent/practitioner.

- Instituting reward system in the organization.
- Highlighting the gains.
- Reminding the employees that the change is for them and management is only an instrument to implement it.
- It must always be group/team effort.

It is felt that, this is a simple and practical model of implementing change. It is shown in Figure 3.2 below:

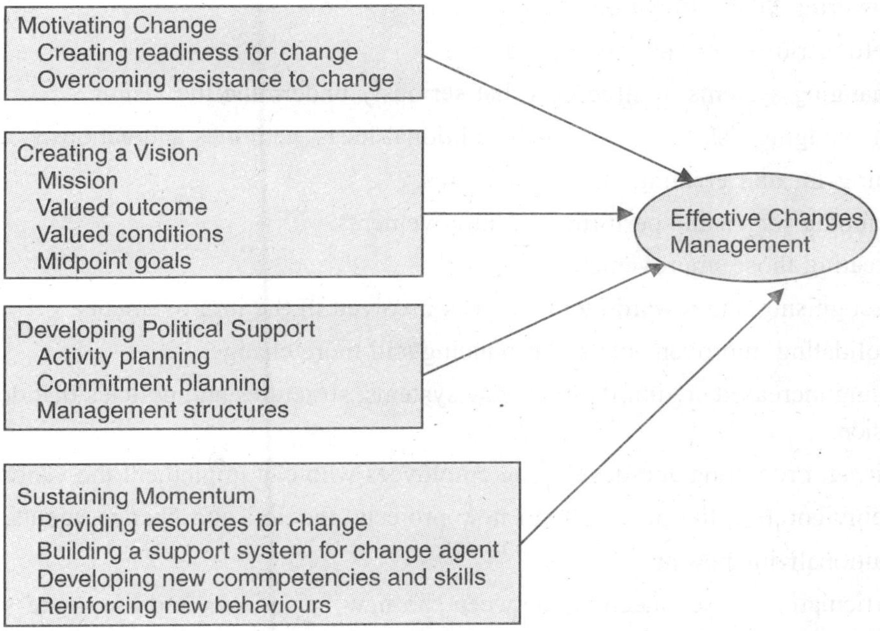

Figure 3.2 Activities contributing to effective change management

(Source: Organisational Development and Change, 5/e. T.G.Cummings and C.G. Worley)

EIGHT STEPS FOR SUCCESSFUL ORGANIZATION TRANSFORMATION: KOTTER'S MODEL OF CHANGE [3]

According to Kotter, change processes unfold in series of phases. To ensure successful change, Kotter has suggested the following steps:

1. Establish a sense of urgency.
   - Examining market and competitive realities.
   - Identifying and discussing crisis, potential crisis, or major opportunities.
2. Forming a powerful guiding coalition.
   - Assembling a group with enough power to lead the change efforts.
   - Encouraging the group to work together as a team.

3. Creating a vision.
   - Create a vision to help direct the change efforts.
   - Developing strategies for achieving the vision.
4. Communicating the vision.
   - Using every vehicle possible to communicate the new vision and strategies.
   - Teaching new behaviours by the example of the guiding coalition.
5. Empowering others to act on the vision.
   - Getting rid of obstacle to change.
   - Changing systems or structures that seriously undermine the vision.
   - Encouraging risk taking and non-traditional ideas, activities and actions.
6. Planning for and creating short-terms wins.
   - Planning for visible performance improvements.
   - Creating those improvements.
   - Recognising and rewarding employees involved in the improvements.
7. Consolidating improvements and producing still more change.
   - Using increased credibility to change systems, structures and policies that do not fit the vision.
   - Hiring, prompting and developing employees who can implement the vision.
   - Reinvigorating the process with new projects, themes, and change agents.
8. Institutionalizing new approaches.
   - Articulating the connections between the new behaviours and corporate success.
   - Developing the means to ensure leadership development and succession.

SUMMARY

Organizational development is a complex blend of skill of identification of problem; selection of suitable intervention strategy; its implementation and feedback throughout. It is the skill of the client, consultant, the implementation team and the organization as whole that make the OD programme success or a failure. Diagnosis, interventions, and programme management are critical to all the organizations that venture to OD programmes. The more people learn about these three components, the more effective they will become in organizational development efforts. Cummings and Worley have suggested the following five areas where change is required:

1. Motivating change
2. Creating a vision
3. Developing political support

4. Managing the transition
5. Sustaining momentum.

Kotter has suggested various steps to implement change. It is a very practical model that can be applied by any organisation with modification.

TEXT QUESTIONS

1. Explain various diagnostic components.
2. Explain six-box model.
3. What are various consideration and action components of OD programme?
4. Explain nature of OD interventions.
5. What are the various phases of OD programme?
6. Explain Cummings and Worley's model of change. Do you feel this is practical and a simple model of change?
7. Explain Kotter's model of change.

Exercise

After studying the diagnostic six-box model of OD programme, implement the same in your organization. After implementation examine whether the problem identified by you is worth the efforts for OD implementation strategies.

BIBLIOGRAPHY

1. Wendell, L. French, Cecil H. Bell, Jr. Veena Vohra; *"Organisation Development"*, Pearson, Sixth Edition, 2006.
2. T.G. Cummings and C.G. Worley, *"Organisational Development and Change"*, (St Paul, MN: West Publishing Company, 1993).
3. John P. Kotter, "*Leading Change: Why Transformation Fails*", Harvard Business Review March-April 1995, p. 61.

CASE STUDY
GROWING PAINS OF THE PENNATHUR TYRE COMPANY

The Pennathur Tyre Company (PTC) was incorporated, as a partnership firm in 1986 to fill what one of its partners, Mr. Mani, called a void that existed in South India. According to Mr. Mani, who had worked for a foreign tyre company for nearly 15 years, there was no company that really had for its major aim the production of tyres at the minimum cost and their sale to customers at an affordable price. "Four wheel vehicle owners pay through their nose for tyres, petrol and repairs.

Anybody who owns a car owns a care spends at least 35 to 40 per cent of his salary on its maintenance and that is not how it should be", Mani was often heard to say. Mr. Mani started the PTC in partnership with two close friends of his who had also extensive experience in the tyre business, working for other companies. Mr. Mani was very actively involved in the business and was at work everyday at the crack of dawn and never left the place before 8.00 pm. Sometimes when work was heavy, Mani would stay as late as 10.00 pm at the shop. One of the other two partners owned another business as well and was, for all practical purposes, a sleeping partner in this firm, and the third partner was much less involved in the day-to-day operations of the company than Mr. Mani.

PTC, though a small partnership firm, had enormous backing from the business community because of their appreciation of the goals of the company and the extreme dedication of Mr. Mani. Thus, PTC was off to a good start. Being very cost conscious, PTC set up a small Cost Analysis department. As business began to expand, more customer services were added and the company attained an excellent reputation for its wheel balancing service. As a result, the company was given sole dealership for helmets as well. In 1988, just two years after its incorporation, the company had to expand its premises, operations and personnel. With the expansion came the growing pains and Mr. Mani and the two partners has to encounter many small hurdles. Even as they were trying to solve one problem, several others seemed to crop up. Mr. Mani highlighted some of the more serious ones described them to me as follows. "Dr. Sekaran, sometimes I wish we had never expanded our business. When we were merely selling tyres we could comfortably handled the operations and the workmen, and we the partners were all happy. At first, it was exciting to expand the business and services to our customers. The smile on the customer's faces as they drive their cars away is still very gratifying. But because of our increased staff size, we are beginning to lose control. Often, the customers are not served as effectively as they could be. The personal touch that we had established with our customers seems to be slowly slipping away. I have been telling the employees that they should be more customer oriented, but they seem to be more concerned about their own inter-departmental problems and fights. For instance, last week, while a customer was waiting patiently, the mechanic who was to have changed the oil and filter in his car, was arguing for more than half an hour with the purchase clerk about some trivial matter. I almost lost my patience, and was about to give the mechanic a bit of my mind, when my partner took the mechanic aside and talked to him. The fact that customers are not serviced without delays bothers me. I wonder if it bothers my partners as well. I have not discussed these kinds of issues with them since I don't want them to think that I am getting unduly worried about small matters.

"Another potential problem lies in the way some of the employees come across to the others in the company. For instance, we have a rather brash young engineer. He is thoroughly knowledgeable about his work and is extremely productive, but he always wears a serious look on his face and talks in a very abrupt, and sometimes, abrasive manner. Some of his mechanics have told me that they are scared of him. I have a set of capable workmen and don't want to lose any of them. I am at a loss to knowhow to handle this particular situation. I guess if I happened to work for this engineer, I would also be scared of him; but he is really a nice person, you know. The only problem is that he is too intense and comes across to others as a grouch. We have a few others who are just the opposite, laughing and joking all the time, and I sometimes wonder if their workers take them seriously at all!

"Something else is also engaging my thoughts. Ultimately, I would like to see each of the service departments as individual profit centers and share the additional profits with the workers. That, of course, is down the road; perhaps three to five years from now. I am thinking that if the employees have a stake in the profits they will work harder and I shall not have to put in so much time supervising them. But then, they should all learn to work well together so that there is more collaboration and joint problem solving rather than competition and dysfunctional conflicts. I would like them all to see themselves as one big family where everybody works together harmoniously to reap the full benefits. If, somehow, we can develop that spirit of friendliness and cooperation, it would be great! Maybe, I am rambling too much, but these and similar issues keep engaging my thoughts and I was wondering if you have any advice for me on how I should handle some of these issues."

Assuming that diagnostic survey does indeed confirm Mr. Mani's statements, you are required to:

(*a*) Clearly identify the problem in the case;

(*b*) Recommend appropriate OD intervention strategies to resolve each of the issues;

(*c*) Explain in detail why you make the particular recommendation and how it would resolve the problem.

(Source:Organisational Behaviour by Uma Sekaran, The McGraw-Hill, NewDelhi, Second Edition 2006)

CHAPTER 4

Organization Development Intervention Strategies

CHAPTER PLAN

- *Introduction*
- *Concepts*
- *Organizational Strategies for Personal Concern*
- *Process Consultation*
- *Job Related Interventions*
- *Socio-technical Interventions*
- *Structural Interventions*
- *Learning Organizations*
- *Summary*
- *Text Questions*
- *Bibliography*
- *Case Study: The Quality Conundrum*

INTRODUCTION

In this unit we will discuss OD interventions and describe the important ones. OD interventions address a wide range of specific problems and opportunities. Work gets done in organization when organization leaders and members systematically address problems and opportunities, usually guided by an OD practitioner. Practitioners have over a period of time developed number of OD interventions to solve organizational problems. Interventions such as team building, survey feedback, role-playing, and inter group conflict resolutions were developed during early years of organizational development. Interventions such as Quality of Work Life (QWL) work design using socio-technical systems theory, learning organizations were developed in the later times. In addition to the above interventions, we have interventions aimed at developing self-directed teams, flexible work hours, and hosts of them.

OD interventions are set of *Structured activities* in which selected organizational units (target groups or individuals) engage in a sequence of tasks with goal of organizational improvement and individual development. Interventions constitute the action thrust of organizational development. The OD practitioner, a professional versed in the theory and practice of OD, brings four sets of attributes to the organizational setting; *the interventions*

1. a set of assumptions about people, organizations, and interpersonal relationship.
2. a set of goals for practitioner and the organization and its members.
3. a set of structured activities that are the means for achieving the values, assumptions and goals.
4. a set of values.

CONCEPTS

Organization development intervention strategies: Study of organizational development can be carried out on four different fronts as under:

(*a*) People side or organization, which includes personal counseling and career planning at intra personal level.

(*b*) Problem-solving, interpersonal communication and interpersonal relationship at dyadic level.

(*c*) Group goal achievement and aspects related to group dynamics at group level.

(*d*) Societal level, organizational development intervention may include assisting people to resolve their personal problems like housing, education, induction programmers and social acceptance especially for those who are new to the organization. Organizational development strategies can be broadly classified as under:

Classification of OD Strategies

OD Strategies for personal concern	Job related OD interventions
Sensitively training	Work flow
Transactional analysis	Job evaluation
Process consultations	Job redesigning
Team building interventions	
Third party interventions	
Individual counseling	
Life and career planning	
Role playing	

Socio-technical intervention	Structural interventions
System analysis	Change in physical setting
Flexible work hours	Formalization
Job sharing facilities	Organizational mirroring
Job evaluation and role analysis techniques	

Figure 4.1 Diagram showing intervention strategies

ORGANIZATIONAL STRATEGIES FOR PERSONAL CONCERN

1. Sensitivity Training

Kurt Lewin first introduced sensitivity training in 1945. Sensitivity training is also known as T-groups or Lab training. The method is used to train teams with an ultimate objective of organizational development. Sensitivity training envisages formation of unstructured small groups. Members of the group interact with each other and learn from various situations. Kurt Lewin was a theorist, researcher and practitioner of interpersonal and inter-group dynamics and a strong propagator of community relationship as an approach to overall organizational development. T-group developed various models of role-playing, learning, change and transactional nature of human beings. Team building dynamics was the major contribution of T-group. Sensitivity training involved organizational topic like deadlines, study pertaining to duties and responsibilities, policy, procedures and inter organizational group relationship.

Lewin carried out sensitivity training by field theory, group dynamics, evolving change processes and action research that was of profound importance to people involved in development. The method helped individual to change attitude, understand human nature, and modify behaviour to suit a particular situation and be a useful member of the team.

2. Team Building Interventions

Teams

Team is a small number of people with complimentary skills who are committed to a common purpose, set of performance goals, and an approach for which they hold, themselves mutually accountable. (Katzenbach and Douglas Smith) Teams have emerged as the most important group phenomenon in various organizations. Joseph Juran first tried to adopt "team approach to problem-solving". Today teams are becoming increasingly popular as a result of advanced information technology and concern for total quality management and organizational learning processes. Organizational development has shifted from a reliance on individual managers and workers to inter-functional management teams and work teams that focus on complex problems and tasks. Teams can be formed for any purpose. They can go beyond traditional formal work group by having a collective synergistic effect. Production teams, teams for rendering advice in the form of board and review panels are generally formed. Teams can also be formed for completion of the specific task like research and development, engineering work, etc. Action teams for sports, entertainment, expedition, surgery and negotiation are also formed. The objective of such teams is to plan, implement and receive feedback of the job done. However, Quality Circles and Self-Managed Teams are very common in most of the organizations.

Teams and Work-groups

"Team" is frequently used for any group, especially to get them to work together and to motivate them. Jon and Douglas differentiated team and work-group. A work-group's performance is a function of what its members do as individuals. A team's performance includes both individual results and what we call "Collective work products". A collective work product is what two or more members must work together. It reflects the joint, real contribution of team members.

Quality Circles and Self-managed Teams

Quality circles are made up of volunteers from the lower levels of operations in manufacturing and offer advice to management on improving quality and productivity. On the contrary, self-managed teams, sometimes called autonomous work teams, are formally designated by management and can be made up of employees from all levels. Self-managed teams may make decisions and do the real work of the organization. These teams have no appointed manager. They do their own managerial functions.

Development of Self-managed Teams

Self-managed teams can be developed to a great extent. These teams should be made up of dedicated people who enjoy working together, who maintains high standards and demonstrate high productivity. These teams should be monitored on a regular basis and evaluated in the following areas:

(*a*) Team mission
(*b*) Goal achievement
(*c*) Empowerment
(*d*) Open and honest communication
(*e*) Positive role and norms.

By controlling such key functions, self-managed teams can be effective and contribute to the performance goals of the organization Effectiveness of the team can be achieved by considering following points:

(*a*) A proper training and development schedule should be planned well in advance.
(*b*) A facilitator (trainer) must be coopted with the team right from the beginning. Team members and facilitator should develop rapport. Facilitator should create an environment where individual member can clear his doubts without hesitation.
(*c*) Group goals should be set up in advance and required resources made available to the team. Processes should be well established.
(*d*) Decision-making, delegation of authority and extent of empowerment be clearly spelt out by the organization. Members should experience autonomy in the work environment.
(*e*) The group should be trained in various methods of group decision-making, intra-group relations and have an adequate knowledge of various group functions.
(*f*) Intra-group procedures involving setting up of meeting format, involving taking down of minutes of conference and progressing each point should be known to each of the members of the group.
(*g*) Team members should be so trained that they are self-managed.

Transactional Analysis

Eric Berne first introduced TA in 1964. He stated that every individual has three ego states in varying degree. Person acts and reacts depending upon situation and the ego state displayed by the person with whom one is interacting.

(*a*) Parent ego state represents feelings of superiority, authority, being judgmental and so on.

(*b*) Adult ego state represents maturity, objectivity, logic and rationality in communication.

(*c*) Child ego state indicates dependant, impulsive and rebellious nature of behaviour.

Most of us have one dominant ego state. Any communication between two people is called transaction. The transaction can be analyzed in terms of ego state from which each of the transactions can be complimentary, crossed and ulterior. Complimentary transaction is those transactions where two people communicate verbally from a compatible ego state. For example adult-to-adult communication. Crossed transaction occurs when a message from one ego state is responded in an incompatible ego state. An adult to child communication falls in this category. Such type of communications is not good and it produces anger, resentment and frustration between the two individuals involved in the communication. Ulterior transactions take place when two parties involve themselves in communication where main issue is circumvented.

(*d*) TA is a useful technique to understand people, their attitude and behaviour. Communication should preferably be from adult-adult ego state. This will lead to better understanding and logical approach to the problem. Crossed and ulterior communication should be avoided while interacting with each other. TA helps to quickly identify and untangle crossed transactions. By understanding the extent to which ulterior transactions occur in organizations, efforts can be made, if necessary to minimize them since avoiding authentic encounters adversely affects the organizational effectiveness. It is therefore necessary for the employees to identify individual ego state, situations under which one is working, organizational stress and its effect on individual behaviour and transact accordingly. By practice, interpersonal problems can be reduced to a great extent and organizational growth is achieved.

PROCESS CONSULTATION

Process consultation requires combination of skills in establishing helping relationship, knowing what kinds of processes to look for in organizations and intervening in ways to improve organizational processes (Schein, 1969). The essence of process consultation is that a skilled consultant (facilitator) works with managers, groups and individuals with the object of developing their process skills. It involves diagnosing, understanding and solving process related problems. There are various processes in the organizations like enrolment process, administrative process having various sub-processes within it. A manager who has evolved a particular process should see to it that all the employees implement it. For example, communication process. In this process manager must ensure free flow of vertical, horizontal and diagonal information flow and that no work should suffer for want of required information in required format. Should there be any problem an outsider consultant is employed to examine the process, identify problem areas, suggest solutions, implement and obtain feedback. It involves ascertaining solutions to various issues in the organization. Major processes that are generally evaluated are as under:

(*a*) Organizational structure and organizational design modification.
(*b*) Dynamics of interpersonal relationship.
(*c*) Nature and scope of communication.
(*d*) Issues relating to leadership styles that are followed by various leaders.
(*e*) Group problem-solving on organizational, social and domestic issues.
(*f*) Decision-making process.
(*g*) Welfare measures.
(*h*) Training and development.
(*i*) Issues of production, quality control leading to product modification and thereby achieving organizational effectiveness.

The process consultation sensitizes the individuals who are directly or indirectly involved in above processes. Phenomenon is observed in the organizational systems where individual display their voluntary commitment to develop organizational processes and assist each other to resolve issues irrespective of their departmental boundary.

Third Party Peace-making Interventions

A facilitator to resolve conflict in the organization uses third party interventions. Walton (1969) suggest that a fundamental aspect of third party peace-making is for the consultant to make two disagreeing parties to confront and agree that the conflict does exist which is leading to situation where organizational development is hampering. The problem generally relates to emotional disagreement by conflicting parties. The facilitator resolves the issue by creating congenial atmosphere by way of selecting a place, mode and appropriate agenda for the meeting. During the conduct of the meeting, he evolves such techniques that both parties do agree that there exists a conflict between them. The facilitator identifies the problem and suggests remedial methods. If the problem is of structural nature like sharing scares resources, then the problem solving strategies are implemented. If the problem is of emotional nature like anger, distrust, fear the consultant has to adopt strategies for behaviour modification. This will take a reasonably longer time and efforts to resolve the problem.

Individual Counseling

Counseling refers to the process of advising an employee or preferably in most cases, listening to the statement of his problem and enabling him to form his own thinking and taking a solution for it.[5] Counseling relates to understanding and helping people. As counseling involves discussion, it forms a process of communication. Effective counseling is a function of communication skills by which an individual tends to share his emotions with another individual. Counseling deals with resolving emotional difficulties of individuals, which excludes mental illness. Although the emotional problems may not appear to be very significant or complex to others, they are important to the individual who has them and thus whose productive efficiency or performance they affect. The problems may relate to stagnation in promotion, job insecurity, feeling, inappropriate handling by superiors, job stress and the like. Apart from emotional imbalance, need for counseling may arise from varied on-and-off the job conditions such as dissatisfaction, resistance to change, alienation, frustration, stress and conflict Counseling provides to solve employee problems so that they develop self-confidence, self-worth, understanding and ability to work effectively. Various functions therefore of counseling are to advice, reassurance, communication, release of emotional tension, clarified thinking and reorientation. While performing the above functions, counseling may have several accomplishments. Maier indicates seven such accomplishments of counseling. These are

(*a*) Identification of attitudes and values.
(*b*) Reduction of frustration.
(*c*) Location and acceptance of true problems.
(*d*) Stimulation of problem-solving.
(*e*) Development of responsibility.
(*f*) Conformity of solution with value system.
(*g*) Availability of expert knowledge.

Types of Counseling

(*a*) **Directive counseling:** Directive counseling is process of listening to employee's emotional problems and advising him. Advice is not preferred as compared to listening. Facilitator may develop mutual understanding with the individual so that the later may be free to release his tension and thus modify self-behaviour. The advice and assurance provided by the counselor during the counseling process may be worthwhile if the employee has faith in the counselor. It is more of matter of trust and belief between the two.

(*b*) **Non-directive counseling:** Roger's, the founder of non-directive counseling states as, "within the client reside constructive forces whose strength and uniformity have been either entirely unrecognized or grossly underestimated. In most of us, if not all, there exits growth forces, tendencies towards self-actualization. The individual has the capacity and the strength to devise, quite unguided, the steps which will lead him to a more mature and more comfortable relationship to his reality. All of his capacities are realized in the individual if a suitable psychological environment is provided. This non-directive counseling is instrumental in the release of dynamic forces within the individual and resolving emotional problems.

Life and Career Planning

Life has become very fast because of automation, social change, and technological leap. Expectation of individual has therefore grown out of proportion. In a family both husband and wife are earning members and they desire growth and social recognition. It is the responsibility of the organization to plan growth of each of the officer/managerial cadre. This will enhance organization culture, growth and develop sense of belonging. This will also facilitate succession in the family run organizations. At supervisor and workers level, training and development is essential. It is the responsibility of the line managers to organize periodic cadres, refresher courses, and promotion cadres and ensure that the work force is kept updated. Career Manning Cell should be established in large organization, whose sole responsibility should be to plan, organize and conduct career planning courses in consultation with HR department, training institutes, government agencies and NGOs. One of the drawbacks of career planning is constant turnover of employees for various reasons. If career planning is effective, the employee turnover will reduce drastically. Career planning is one the important functions of the organization which should be taken seriously.

Roleplaying

Roleplaying is a spontaneous acting of a realistic situation. Real life situations are used to teach the trainees. When few individuals play role, the others observe and criticize at the end of the session. Roleplaying is a substitute for experience. It emphasizes techniques of observation, participation, copy and discussion. Trainees try to enrich by trying different approaches of roleplaying. Roleplaying as a tool of organizational development is an important instrument. It should be carried out under an expert so as to derive maximum advantage.

JOB RELATED INTERVENTIONS

1. Workflow

In highly technological environment, every job has to be reviewed periodically to ensure the job has the following attributes:

(*a*) **Task identity:** As far as possible a job must be identifiable in "Whole" from right from its inception to its completion. It is necessary because a worker identifies himself with the job and derives a greater satisfaction.

(*b*) **Meaningfulness:** While designing a job due care should be taken that every job should involve skill variety. The job should encompass use of abilities of individuals. The job should not be of routine nature.

(*c*) **Task significance:** Employees will derive maximum satisfaction if the job they are doing is of a great significance. For example, manufacturing of a firing mechanism in a petrol vehicle is of great significance.

(*d*) **Autonomy:** Employees should enjoy autonomy while they are performing. Freedom of action, decision-making and discretion in scheduling a job adds to the organizational development efforts. Autonomy envisages the content, structure and organization of the job is such that individuals or groups performing those jobs can plan, regulate and control their own work. Autonomy implies use of individual skills effectively, so that the contribution to accomplishment of the job is meaningful and should regulates the individual activities on the job. *Autonomy is self-governance.*

Job Evaluation

Wendell French defines job evaluation as "a process of determining the relative worth of the various jobs within the organization, so that differential wages may be paid to jobs of different worth." Relative worth of a job means relative value produced. The variables that are assumed to be related to value produced are such factors as responsibility, skill, efforts and working conditions. It is important to note that job evaluation is ranking of job, not the jobholder. Jobholders are rated through performance appraisal. Job evaluation provides basis for developing job hierarchy and fixing structure. It must be remembered that job evaluation is about relationship, and not absolute. That is why job evaluation cannot be sole determining factor for deciding pay structure. Various external factors like technological changes, labour market, collective bargaining capacity of the workers political and economic factors. It is important to note that regular review of various jobs should be done by the organization and suitable modification to pay structure made. Employees have a positive impact on personal development. It is at the work place that the individuals derive satisfaction and further organizational development in a long run.

Job Redesign Strategies

Job design refers to the study of jobs, tasks and constellations of tasks. It includes job enrichment, job enlargement, job characteristics models and social information processing perspectives. The traditional approach involved fitting people to job is not valid now. A more recent approach to designing jobs incorporates both objectively gathered descriptions of the jobs and the perceived requirements and relationships of jobholders. Since Hertzberg work on job enrichment, a great deal of interest has been aroused in job redesigning, apart from collecting data pertaining to the job and work, a great deal of emphasis on human values have also been added. Davis proposed the concept of job design as "the organization (structuring) of a job to satisfy the technical—organizational requirements of the work to be accomplished and the human requirements of the person performing the work". Job designs change as jobholder needs and work requirement change. Job redesign strategies seek to address these changes. Job redesign approaches aimed at enhancing productivity and employee motivation include job enlargement. Scope of the job, variety of activities, number of processes and required skills to accomplish work. Job extension, doing more of the same work, is a form of job enlargement.

SOCIO-TECHNICAL INTERVENTIONS

1. Systems Analysis

An organization should study both external and internal environment, analyze the socio-economic factors like prevailing standard of living, social demands on employees, aspirations of children and the ability of the individual to fulfill the same. Demographic factors also play a dominant role in the organizational development paradigm. Based on the above factors an organization should design its reward system so that the employee is able to live in a desired level and meet its social obligation. This is important because the systems so evolved would be able to generate enthusiasm and desire to excel in the job that will bring growth to the organization. Contingency approach should be adopted by the managers in this respect and aspirations of the employees be met. Off late the individual has started comparing his status vis-vis the status of the workers world over. Certain amount of parity is required to be adopted by the organizations. In the light of the above discussion following system needs attention:

(*a*) Recruitment system
(*b*) Reward system
(*c*) Appraisal system
(*d*) Training and development
(*e*) Organizational mission with particular reference to growth potential
(*f*) Technical upgradation
(*g*) Social recognition
(*h*) Ability and will of the organization to plan for the growth of children of the employees to enable them to be competitive in the present social scenario.

2. Flexible Work Hours

Organization should plan working based on brick pattern. The responsibility to produce is assigned to teams and work-groups. The work should be assigned to them based on timings. All the resources are made available and no interference be made by the senior members thereby providing them the total autonomy. Flexible work hours are necessary for dual career families. For instance, dual career members, who are now trying to combine their family and work lives, face problems managing their work family interface. Workshop conducted for both spouses on time management, childcare, stress management, and management of the overlaps among the work and family boundaries will be immensely helpful for the members.

3. Job Sharing Facilities

Organizations should create job-sharing facilities within the organization and may also have tie-ups with other organization for sharing the job. This is particularly required for research and development branch of any organization. Job sharing creates additional facility without any monetary burden on the organization and optimum utilization of resources is achieved. If the facilities are available for performing the work, employees can meet the dead line of their tasks.

4. Job Evaluation and Role Analysis Techniques

An individual should be trained in handling more than one job so that, should there be need, he could be gainfully employed in a different role (job). Job evaluation and job analysis techniques have already been studied by you earlier. Individual has to play different roles in the organization. He should be made self-sufficient so that he can fulfill his obligation. It is important that an individual should be satisfied on the job he is performing. Job redesign, job rotation, job simplification, job automation are some of the methods where organizational development takes place.

STRUCTURAL INTERVENTIONS

1. Change in Physical Setting

Physical setting and its importance on productivity is a subject on which lot work has been done.

The objective of ideal physical setting of machinery is to reduce physical fatigue to the worker and afford him maximum physical convenience in doing the job. This involves layout of the machinery, position of the operator, availability of tools and raw material. This also involves the supervision that is required to be carried out by the superiors. For example, you would see the layout in the banks or in a bottling plant. There are standard tailor made layouts available and the organization can adopt them with suitable modification. The objective is to improve productivity. Taylor has done the pioneering work on the subject in early twentieth century when management concepts were in the evolution stage.

2. Formalization

Formalization refers to the extent to which policies, procedures, rules, regulation exists in the organization. Policies are basic guideline and principles based on which the organizational objectives are to be fulfilled. Policies are laid down with great thought and deliberation and are indicative of the culture the organization wants to follow. Policies are mandatory requirements of any system. Policies are general in nature and give basic guidelines to the manager how to operate. For example, recruitment policy or training and development for managers. While rules and regulations are strict in nature and individuals have to obey those. There is no scope for deviation. These are prescribed codes of conduct that needs to be strictly followed. Procedures are method which are practical in nature to carryout any work and the steps involved in it. These are generally stated in the standing orders for an organization. These are necessary to relieve managers of any necessity of directing so that he can concentrate on the job exclusively. There are certain situations that are not covered in the policy of the organization. Under this situation manager has to interpret the event/situation and give his decision. This phenomenon is called "management by exception". Thus formalization of rules regulations, policies and procedures help managers to focus on the primary managerial functions. Too much of formalization is not advisable as it reduces the personal contact between employees and managers. It also gives the feeling of too much of bureaucracy and lack of operational freedom. For creativity and innovation less of formalization is recommended. For organizational development, it is therefore necessary to ensure mix of both formalization and work autonomy to the employees.

LEARNING ORGANIZATIONS

Major work towards learning organization was made by Frederick W. Taylor by introduction of scientific management; however, beginning of use of term learning organization is usually attributed to seminal work of Chris Argyris and his colleagues, who made the distinction first order or "single-loop" and second order or "double-loop" learning.

1. Single-loop Learning

Single-loop learning involves improving the organization's capacity to achieve known objectives. It is associated with routine and behavioural learning. Under single-loop, the organization is learning without significant change in basic assumptions.

2. Double-loop Learning

Double-loop learning re-evaluates the nature of the organizational objectives and the values and beliefs surrounding them. This type of learning involves changing of the organization's culture. Double-loop learning consists of the organization's "learning how to learn". From single-loop and double-loop learning organizations have made a drastic change in the present times. Adoptive learning is another concept of achieving double-loop learning. It is based on implementing change in basic assumptions of the organization like culture, value and structure. Generative learning on the other hand, involves creativity and innovations. Generative process leads to a total reframing of an organization's experiences and learning from that process. Senge propagated generative learning. This learning creates tension that stems from the gap between the organization's vision and reality and suggests to the learning organizations, and continually questioning and challenging the status quo. The systems thinking refer to the ability of learning organization to recognize the shared vision of employees throughout the whole organization and the openness to the new ideas and the external environment. The third major characteristic is the organization culture. It must place a high value to learning and setting up of a mechanism for introduction of suggestions, empowerment and empathy for the operating teams. The factor of empathy reflects for the genuine concern for, and interest in, employee suggestions and innovations that can be backup by reward system. The congruence of these three systems can be called, as truly a learning organization.

SUMMARY

We have in this chapter studied in details the OD interventions that pertain to development of individual, teams of various types. We have also studied intervention pertaining to the job, and structural interventions. Application of OD intervention is not a simple job, it requires energy, time, money, and right person as a specialist to implement and achieve modification that is desired. All the people in the organization must also be psychologically ready for the change. Last but not the least, the management commitment should be total for such a mission is to be possible.

TEXT QUESTIONS

1. Explain the concept of team building. Does this concept exist in your organization.
2. What are various strategies relating to personal concern that is carried out by organizations for its development?
3. Explain job evaluations and how can the job be re-designed. Explain the concept after visiting an organization in close vicinity of your work place.
4. Evaluate the present environment of the organization and apply socio-technical intervention.
5. Change in physical setting improves the organization. Explain.
6. Write detailed notes on the following topics:
   (*a*) Systems analysis
   (*b*) Organizational culture
   (*c*) Formalization
   (*d*) Learning organizations.

CASE STUDY
THE QUALITY CONUNDRUM

How Indian Industry is Managing Quality

By Surinder Kapur
Chairman,
CII Mission for Manufacturing Innovation,
and Chairman and Managing Director,
Sona Koyo Steering Systems

Innovating for the Bottom of the Pyramid

A major objective of the Confederation of Indian Industry (CII) Mission for innovation in manufacturing is to sensitize the business community to look at the bottom of the pyramid, where innovations are really required. For the upper and middle sections of the society innovations products will always be available from the West. However, these products cannot be and will not be used by the bottom of the pyramid. To ensure the participation of this section in economic activities and the growth of the country, Indians must themselves innovate. Today's column focusses on one such innovation.

Cosmos Ignite Innovations is one of the most innovative Indian companies I have come across. The company has not only brought out an innovative product but has also established a highly innovative business model. Mightily Light is disruptive product targeted to meet a social need; at the same time, the company is modeled to function not as a charity, but like any other business organization —with an eye on the bottom line.

Amit Chugh and his team at Cosmos Ignite have worked relentlessly to develop an innovation product that will help solve the electricity problems of millions of people—not only Indians living below the poverty line in the remotest corners of the county but also the poor of developing countries facing the problem of inaccessibility of power. Mighty Light uses the latest LED technology combined with solar energy and is designed to be a waterproof, shockproof and multiple-function lamp that can be used as a room light, reading lamp or flashlight.

It uses a best-in-class 1-watt super-bright white LED bulb to illuminate and is capable of holding an eight-hour charge and designed to last an extraordinary 100,000 hours (up to 30 years on use of eight hours daily). It is cost-effective as it uses solar power to recharge and provides light enough to illuminate any room, especially helping the poor forced to use dangerous, polluting and expensive kerosene oil lamps. While solar energy has been around for a long time, what is innovative is its use in combination with the revolutionary LED technology in Might Light, suddenly opening up a whole new market to more than 1.6 billion people without regular lighting around the world. Moreover, this is being done in a "green" manner, contributing to climate change control.

Further, the company consciously chose to be a profit-oriented venture to make the project sustainable in its aim to effect social change. This philosophy is based on the belief that capitalism, not charity, leads to sustainable growth.

Never before has a start-up organization tried to make social impact its business. Companies undertake social projects as a part of their corporate social responsibility, but they don't usually make it the nucleus of their business. Cosmos Ignite likes to call this business model Social Entrepreneurship and works "for profit", but "profit maximization". In arriving at this business model, Chugh faced numerous challenges such as those related to new technology and market, entrepreneurial organization and running an international operation with cross-cultural team—the design from the US, manufacturing in India, and marketing around the world. But he never gave up and continued to provide full support to his team.

The light is also energy efficient and environment friendly and could provide the foundations for the developing world to "leap frog" development to the next generation of lighting, even more efficient than both incandescent as well as CFL bulbs, while avoiding the pitfalls of dangerous mercury vapour in these bulbs.

Following a "design-based approach", the company studied consumer behaviour as well as the consumer need and tried to come up with a product that would fit these consumer needs. Chugh understood the need gap and that this need gap could be met only be a disruptive change.

Thus, the company developed a product that was not technology-or-state-dictated, but was driven by customer needs. Mighty Light provides "off-the-grid" electricity using a source that is distributed (solar power) and is close to the customer. The team listened to the "voice of the customer" and developed a product to meet the need.

Today, Mighty Light is in use in India, Afghanistan, Pakistan, Cambodia, Nigeria, Kenya, Rwanda, Panama, Guyana, Colombia and has become integrated into numerous international projects by NGOs, the UN, World Bank, with commercial distribution now underway.

I would like to conclude by high-lighting some principles of visionary leadership that drive innovation:

- A visionary leader must be noble-minded.
- The leader must never give up.
- He should be emotionally attached to the idea.
- Listening to the voice of the customer is the key to success.
- Innovation opportunities are all around us. We need to prepare ourselves to identify ad capture these when they present themselves— "chance favours the prepared mind".

BIBLIOGRAPHY

Dr. Surinder Kapur writes "*The Quality Conundrum*" from Business Standard, 14 August, 2007.

CHAPTER 5

Action Research and Organization Development

CHAPTER PLAN

- *Introduction*
- *Definition*
- *Understanding Action Research*
- *Action Research as Approach to Problem-Solving*
- *Summary*
- *Text Questions*
- *Bibliography*

INTRODUCTION

Action research is the bedrock of organizational development. It is related to theory and practice in the field of OD. It relates to identification of problem, collecting data, applying the data to the problem and evaluating results. In case the results do not arrive at expected solutions, additional data collection and application is resorted to. The process is carried on till the problem is solved. Action research is a very common phenomenon in various fields of life. It relates to identifying problems (diagnosis), collect data relating to the problem, apply the data (solutions), and thus solve the problems. Research should follow action mode of thinking. Action research projects may be directed towards diverse goals, which give rise to several variations to the model. Lewin suggested two broad categories of action research—the investigation of general laws and the diagnosis of the specific situation. Lewin believed that research and action programmes, especially social change programmes, was imperative if progress were to be made in solving social problems. Action research, would address several needs simultaneously: the pressing need for greater knowledge about the causes and dynamics of social ills—the need to understand the laws of social change; the need for greater collaboration and joint inquiry between scientists and practitioners; the need for "richer" data about real world problems; the need to discover workable practical solutions to problems; and the need to discover general laws explaining complex social phenomenon.[1] Action research is a comprehensive tool to solve problems and has very wide application to identify problem areas and seek solution through collecting data and interpreting against a standard laid down.

DEFINITION

"Action research is the application of the scientific method of fact-finding and experimentation to practical problems requiring action solutions and involving the collaboration and cooperation of scientists, practitioners and layperson". (French and Bell)

Types of Research

1. **Basic research or pure research:** It is carried out to generate the body of knowledge about some phenomenon of interest to the researcher. For example, to carry out investigations in various organizations to identify motivational or the leadership qualities of various successful managers.
2. **Applied research or the action research:** To find out the solution to a specific problem confronting to an organization. Like falling sales, increased absenteeism of employees in an organisation or steps to be taken to improve organizational effectiveness. It is called action research or the applied research because the recommendations of the research are to be acted upon to solve the problem. Most of the consultants are generally engaged in applied research. The job is tough as it involves interaction with the body of people; it could be an individual, team or the department. It may relate to systems modification or the change of process or the behaviour.

UNDERSTANDING ACTION RESEARCH

Action research as process comprising of various activities: Action research is the process of systematically collecting research data about an ongoing system relative to some objective, goals, or the need of the system; feeding these data back into the system; taking action by altering selected variables within the system based on the data and on hypothesis; and evaluating the results of actions by collecting more data.[2] The definition considers action research as activity comprising the process. Activities in the process involved are, (*a*) the existing situation of the organisation under research, (*b*) setting the goal—what is expected to be achieved, (*c*) collecting data, (*d*) applying data to various parts of the organization or to the subjects, (*e*) manipulating variables that are under control (Because all the variables cannot be manipulated easily. For example, changing of organizational culture overnight.) and, (*f*) finally the expected outcome of the total research programme. The definition further suggests collection of additional data and its application till results or the objectives are achieved.

Action research as a process: The study by Whyte and Hamilton is an example of action research as a process. They describe their work as follows:

"What was the project? It was an action research programme for management. We developed a process for applying human relations research findings to the changing of organization behaviour. The word *process* is important, for this was not a one-shot affair. The project involved a continuous gathering and analysis of human relations research data and the feeding of the findings into the organization in such a way as to change behaviour."[3]

Action Research as a Generic Process in Organizational Development Programme

French has explained how action research can be used as a generic process in organization development. The process is iterative and cyclical. He explains:

> " The key aspects of the model are diagnosis, data gathering, feedback to the client group, data discussion and work by the client group, action planning, and action. The sequence tends to be cyclical, with the focus on new or advanced problems as the client group learns to work more effectively together."[4]

Example: Client system desires to improve the effectiveness of their organization. They decide in consultation with the consultant to apply various OD interventions to improve organizational effectiveness. To start with, *group decision-making* is resorted to, and following sequence of processes takes place:

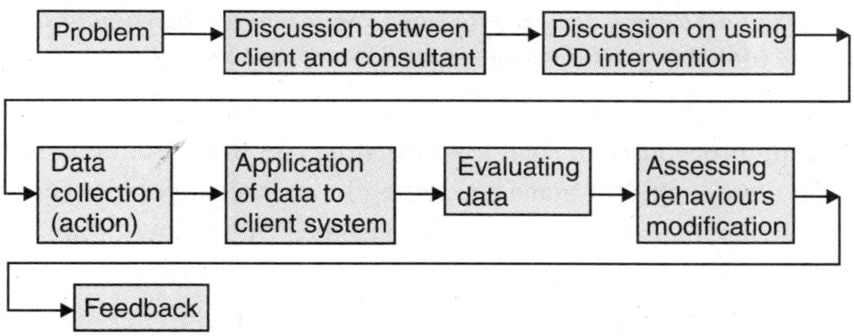

In case the desired results are not achieved, a second cycle (with new OD intervention) is put into action and the next process of various activities take place. In this example, we take team building as the next step to improve organizational effectiveness. The sequence of various processes will take the following steps:

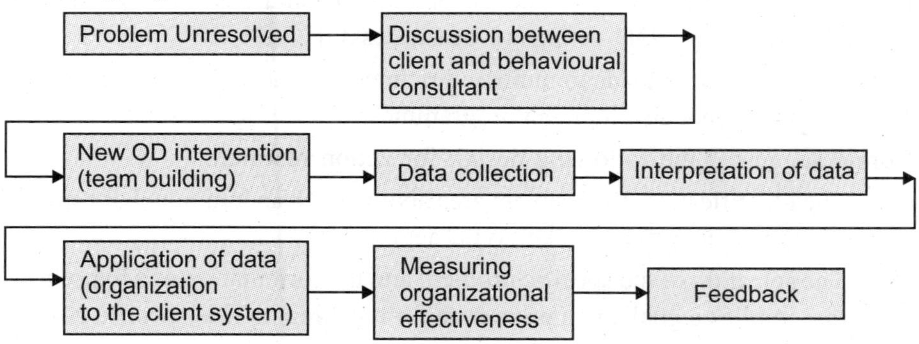

ACTION RESEARCH AS APPROACH TO PROBLEM-SOLVING

1. Action research involves sequence of events and concurrent activities of the client system (organization) and evaluating the effects of OD programme continuously. Action is the application of the scientific methods of fact-finding and experimentation to practical problems requiring action solutions and involving the collaboration and cooperation of scientists, practitioners and the client system. Action research suggests solutions to the burning problems of the organization and adds scientific knowledge to theory. Shepard's concept of action research model as a problem-solving approach is given below:

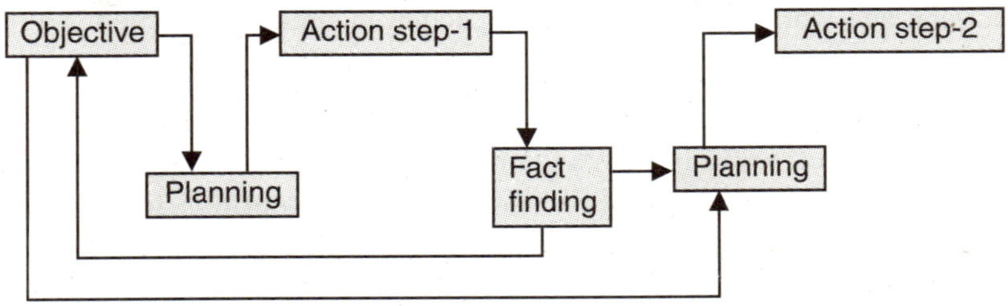

***Source:* Herbert A. Shepard, An Action Research Programme for Organisation Improvement (Ann Arbor, MI: Foundation for Research on Human Behaviour, (1960).**

2. In an action research approach. The role is to help manager plan his actions and design his fact-finding procedures in such a way that he can learn from them, to serve such ends as becoming a more skillful manager, setting more realistic objectives, discovering better ways of organizing. In this sense, the staffs concerned with follow-up are research consultants. Their task is to help managers formulate management problems as experiments.[5]
3. Features of action research as an approach to problem-solving are as under:
   (*a*) Centrality of objective, normative nature of the model and close interaction with consultant and the client system is basic feature of the action research method of OD.
   (*b*) Action research envisages scientific method of investigation of the problem.
   (*c*) Collaboration between scientist, practitioner and the client system is of paramount importance for OD efforts to be successful.
   (*d*) Action research leads to increased richness of knowledge that can be used for further organizational development programmes.
4. Corey[6] suggested the following design for action research:
   (*a*) The identification of a problem area about which an individual or a group is sufficiently concerned to want to take some action.
   (*b*) The selection of the specific problem and the formulation of a hypothesis or prediction that implies a goal and a procedure for reaching it. This specific goal must be viewed in relation to the total situation.

(*c*) The careful recording of actions taken and the accumulation of evidence to determine the degree to which the goal has been achieved.

(*d*) The interface from this evidence of generalizations regarding the relation between the actions and the desired goals.

(*e*) The continuous retesting of these generalizations in action situation.

SUMMARY

Research is of two types, **basic research** or **pure research**. It is carried out to generate the body of knowledge about some phenomenon of interest to the researcher. Second is **applied research** or the **action research**. It is intended to find out the solution to a specific problem confronting to an organization. Action research is a process comprising of various activities action research as a generic process in organizational development programme is as under.

It starts with identification of problem. Client and consultant sit down together and identifies as to which of the OD interventions are to be applied to solve the problem. They take a deliberate decision in this regard. A hypothesis is then formulated and data about various elements is obtained. The data is then applied to the client organization and its effects are later evaluated. It is examined in the light of the desired behaviour modification is achieved. If the feedback is not positive, a new set of OD interventions is later applied. The process continuous till the problem is resolved.

TEXT QUESTIONS

1. Explain the concept of action research.
2. Explain with the help of a diagram, action research as approach to problem-solving.

BIBLIOGRAPHY

1. Lewin, *"Action Research and Minority Problems"*, pp. 34–46.
2. French Wendell, H. Bell Jr. Cecil H., *"Organisational Development"*, PHI of India, 2003.
3. William, F. Whyte and Edith L. Hamilton, *"Action Research for Management"* (Homewood, IL; Irwin-Dorsey, 1964), pp. 1–2.
4. French Wendell, H. Bell Jr. Cecil H., "*Organisational Development*", PHI of India, 2003.
5. *Abid.*
6. Corey, "*Action Research to Improve School Practice*" (New York: Bureau of Publications, Teachers College, Columbia University, 1953), pp. 40–41.

CHAPTER 6

Learning Organization

CHAPTER PLAN

- *Introduction*
- *Definitions*
- *Learning Organizations*
- *Skills Needed for Learning Organizations*
- *Phases of Learning*
- *Quality of Work-life*
- *Summary*
- *Text Questions*
- *Bibliography*
- *OD in Practice*
- *Case Study: A Success Story*

INTRODUCTION

Information technology has taken a big leap forward. The need of total quality management, consumer satisfaction and provision of services have made it necessary for organizations to achieve competitive advantage. For survival, it has become necessary for organizations to be the leader and to remain so. The concept of learning organization is a natural extension of organizational learning.

DEFINITIONS

1. Gravin (1993),[1] p. 80, ***defines the learning organization as "An organization skilled at creating, acquiring, and transferring knowledge, and modifying its behaviour to reflect new knowledge and insights."***

2. McGill *et al.* (1992),[2] ***Suggested that the learning organization is one that "can respond to new information by altering the very 'programming' by which information is processed and evaluated through internal reframing of process and managerial practices that put these ideas into action."*** McGill *et al.,* has suggested the following attributes of learning organizations:

   (*a*) Openness
   - Commitment to cultural–functional diversity in HRD practices.
   - Use of multifunctional and cross-functional work groups.
   - Absence of Jargon and 'expert' domain.
   - Conflict-surfacing and conflict-resolving skills.

   (*b*) Systems Thinking
   - Sharing of accurate organizational histories for continuity.
   - Recognizing the importance of relationship based on exchange.
   - Removing the artificial distinction between line workers and white-collar staff.
   - Attention to relationship between actions in organization and external forces.

   (*c*) Creativity
   - Long-term policies.
   - Mobility across divisions and functions.
   - Growth-oriented.
   - Supportive culture.

   (*d*) Personal Efficacy
   - Clean vision.
   - Celebrating what people do that makes a difference.
   - Linking learning to change and innovation.

   (*e*) Impartiality
   - Strong sense of ethics in dealing with employees and customers.
   - Active corporate citizenship.
   - Recognition and encouragement of employees' contribution outside the organization.
   - Willingness to take responsibility for relationship.

3. Senge (1990),[3] who popularized the term *'learning organization'*, has stated that the following five 'learning disciplines' have their foci within individuals and their loci within an organization's culture.

   (*a*) **Develop personal mastery:** The discipline of continually clarifying and deepening our personal vision, of focusing our energies, of developing patience, and of seeing reality objectively.

(*b*) **Use mental models:** Analyzing one's mental models and envisioning alternative ways of thinking about the world working with mental models means exposing our own ways of thinking as well as making that thinking more open to the influence of others.

(*c*) **Build a shared vision:** Unearthing shared pictures of the future that foster genuine commitment and enrolment rather than compliance.

(*d*) **Understand the power of team learning:** Learning as team, which starts with dialogue, and the skill of overcoming defensiveness and other patterns of interaction that keep members form learning, individually and as a team.

(*e*) **Use systems thinking:** 'Thinking' systematically, seeing patterns and the invisible fabrics of interrelated actions, which often take years to fully play out their effects on each other.

4. Chris Argyris[4] evolved the following two concepts of learning:

(*a*) **Single-loop learning:** It involves organizations capacity to achieve known objectives. Under this concept, the organization learns without significant change in basic assumptions. It is related to behavioural learning.

(*b*) **Double-loop learning:** Under this concept, organization revaluates organizational objectives, values and beliefs. It involves changing organization culture based on the need of the time.

5. Peter Senge coined following two terms:

(*a*) **Adaptive learning:** It is a first stage of learning organizations. It involves adapting to environmental changes and does not entail a change. Adaptive learning is associated with employees' results in short run solutions.

(*b*) **Generative learning:** It involves creativity and innovation. The generative process leads to a total reframing of organizations experiences and learning from that process. Generative learning emphasizes on experimentation and feedback. Employees in generative organizations are taught how to examine the effect of their decisions and to carryout behaviour modification. It may be mentioned that his book. "The fifth discipline" emphasises 'systems thinking' as a major factor for learning organization. Senge identified difference between traditional organizations and learning organizations. The difference is shown in Table 6.1.

Table 6.1 Difference between Traditional and Learning Organizations

Functions	Traditional organization	Learning organization
1. Determination of overall direction	Vision is provided by management	There is a shared vision. Top management is morally responsible to nurture it.
2. Formulation of implementation of ideas	Top management decides what is to be done, rest of the organization members act on the idea.	Formulation and implementation of ideas take place at all levels of the organization.
3. Nature of organizational thinking	Each person is responsible for his/her job responsibilities. The focus is on the individual competence.	Individual understands his own job and that of the others. Interrelationship of influence is considered important.
4. Conflict resolution	Conflicts are resolved through the use of power.	Conflicts are resolved through the use of collaborative learning
5. Leadership and motivation	The role of the leader is to establish organizations vision, provide reward and punishments as appropriate and maintain overall employee activities.	The role of the leader is to build a shared vision, empower the personnel, inspire commitment, and encourage effective decision-making.

LEARNING ORGANIZATIONS

Fred Luthans carried out a comprehensive review to identify the major characteristics of learning organizations; the same is explained below:

1. **Presence of Tension**
   (*a*) Gap between vision and reality
   (*b*) Questioning/inquiry
   (*c*) Challenging status Quo
   (*d*) Critical reflection.
2. **System Thinking**
   (*a*) Shared vision
   (*b*) Holistic thinking
   (*c*) Openness.
3. **Organization Culture Facilitating Learning**
   (*a*) Suggestions
   (*b*) Teamwork
   (*c*) Empowerment
   (*d*) Empathy.

1. **Presence of tension** (Creative Tension) that stems from the gap between what is existing (reality) and the vision. Employees in the organization should always challenge the organization's status Quo. Creative tension always serves as catalyst.
2. **Systems thinking** imply that the organization recognizes the shared vision of employees of the organization. A culture of openness to new ideas should prevail in the organization based on holistic approach.
3. **Organization culture** should be on high value on the process of learning. Organization should have appropriate mechanisms in place for suggestion, teams, empowerment and empathy. An organization should reflect itself by the genuine concern for the employees that should be appropriately rewarded.

SKILLS NEEDED FOR LEARNING ORGANIZATIONS

Learning organizations need to be skilled at five main activities (Gravin, 1993):

1. **Systematic problem-solving:** For this, among other things, employees need to be provided with tools in four areas:
   (*a*) Generating ideas and collecting information (brainstorming, interviewing and surveying).
   (*b*) Reaching consensus (list reduction, rating forms and weighted voting).
   (*c*) Analyzing and displaying data (cause and effect diagrams, force field analysis).
   (*d*) Planning actions (Flow charts and Gantt charts).
   (These tools need to be applied to real problems by business unit teams.)
2. **Experimentation with new approaches:** This activity essentially involves the systematic searching for and testing of new knowledge through the use of the scientific method. It is usually motivated by opportunity and expanding horizons, not by current difficulties or problem-solving. It may involve stages of knowledge from superficial to deeper understanding, from knowing ***how*** (standards of practice and setting of equipment) to knowing ***why*** in terms of underlying cause and effect relationships; and interpreting operating knowledge, for example can be depicted in a hierarchy moving from limited understanding and the ability to make few distinctions to more complete understanding in which most or all contingencies are anticipated and controlled. Experimentation and problem-solving foster learning by upgrading knowledge from lower to higher stages.
3. **Learning from experience and past history:** This implies that companies review their successes and failures, assess them systematically, and record the lessons in a form that employees find open and accessible. It requires a mind-set that enables companies to recognize the value of productive failure in contrast to productive success.
4. **Learning from the experiences and best practices of others:** This involves "benchmarking", among the other things. Benchmarking refers to investigating and learning from the best industry practices after careful study of one's own practices and performance. It involves uncovering, analyzing, adopting and implementing such practices.

5. **Transferring knowledge quickly and efficiently throughout the organization:** Knowledge and ideas have the most impact when they are shared broadly. Transferring knowledge is best done through teaching the behaviour needed and creating opportunities for activity experimentally. Knowledge is more likely to be transferred when the right incentives see new ideas as being in their own best interest, their innovation to accept and adopt them will be high.

PHASES OF LEARNING

Organizational learning can usually be traced through, the following phases (Gravin, 1993)[5]: The phases are overlapping in nature. See Figure 6.1 given below:

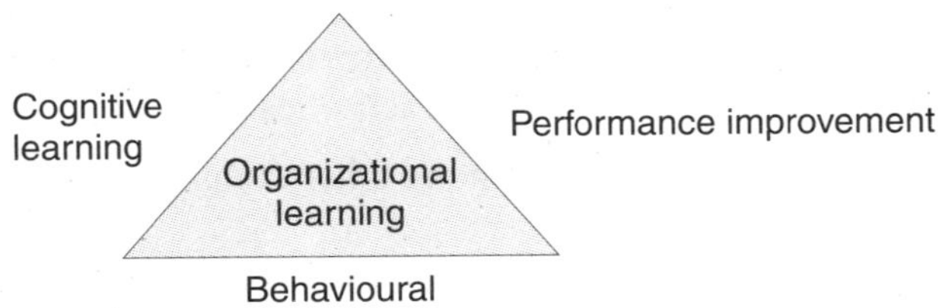

Figure 6.1 Phases of organizational learning

1. **Cognitive:** The first phase is **cognitive**, wherein members of the organization are exposed to new ideas, concepts, and insights, expand their knowledge, and begin to think and look at things differently.
2. **Behavioural:** The second phase is **behavioural**. In this, employees begin to internalize new insights and alter their behaviour.
3. **Performance improvement:** The third phase relates to **performance improvement** with changes in behaviour. The changes lead to measurable improvements in results with tangible gains.

Organizational effectiveness is expressed by:

- Production
- Quality
- Efficiency
- Flexibility
- Satisfaction
- Competitiveness
- Development
- Survival.

QUALITY OF WORK-LIFE

QWL is the overall quality of human experience in the work place. Today many concepts and theories discussed and adopted for organizational development reflect QWL and theory Y themes. The hallmark of excellence in management of organizations includes the following:

(*a*) **Empowerment:** Involving people from all levels of responsibility in decision-making.

(*b*) **Trust:** Redesigning jobs, systems, and structures to give people more personal discretion in their work.

(*c*) **Rewards:** Building reward systems that are fair, relevant, and consistent, while contingent on work performance.

(*d*) **Responsiveness:** Making the work setting more pleasant and supportive of individual needs and family responsibilities.

(*e*) **Work-life balance:** Organizations should ensure that the demands of the job are a reasonable fit with one's personal life and non-work responsibilities.

SUMMARY

1. The concept of learning organization is an extension of organizational learning. Learning organizations are skilled at creating, acquiring and transforming knowledge leading to behaviour modification, new knowledge generation and thus evolving growth and competitiveness. It involves managerial practices of high order that put ideas into practice. This involves openness, systems, and impartiality. Learning involves behaviour modification based upon organizations existing capacity. Organization is further required to re-evaluate its objectives, values and beliefs and implement change in organizational culture that may be required due to environmental changes. Senge has suggested adaptive learning and generative learning. Former is associated with employee reactions to environmental changes that is of routine nature and leads to standard responses. While generative learning leads to creativity and innovation. It emphasizes on experimentation and feedback. Major characteristics of learning organizations are, (1) presence of tension, (2) systems thinking, and (3) enriched organizational culture that facilitates learning. It is important that organizations should adopt a new approach to organizational effectiveness. It includes aspects like transformational leadership, empowerment, delegation of authority and bringing cultural change.
2. Following skills are required for learning organizations:

   (*a*) Systematic problem-solving skills.

   (*b*) Experimentation with new approaches.

   (*c*) Learning from past experience and past history.

   (*d*) Learning from best practices of other organizations.

   (*e*) Transfer of knowledge quickly and effectively throughout the organization.

Learning is generally carried out in three phases (Gravin's model). These are, (1) cognitive learning, (2) performance improvement, and (3) behaviour alteration.

TEXT QUESTIONS

1. Define learning organizations.
2. What are the attributes of learning organizations?
3. Senge who popularised the term "learning organization" has suggested the five learning disciplines. Discuss.
4. What are various characteristics of learning organizations? Explain with the help of a diagram.
5. Carryout comparison of traditional organizations vis-a-vis learning organizations.
6. What are various skills that are necessary for learning organizations?
7. Explain Gravin's model of organizational learning.

BIBLIOGRAPHY

1. Gravin, D.A. (1993), *"Building a Learning Organisation",* Harvard Business Review, 4, pp. 78–91.
2. McGill, M.E., "Management Practices in Learning Organisations", *Organisational Dynamics,* 21 (1), pp. 5–17.
3. Senge, P.M. (1990), "*The Fifth Discipline: The Art and Practice of Learning Organisation",* New York: Double Day.
4. Chris Argyris, *"Double Loop Learning in Organisations",* Harvard Business Review.
5. Gravin, D.A. (1993), *"Building a Learning Organisation",* Harvard Business Review, 4, pp. 78–91.

OD IN PRACTICE

Learning Through Creativity and Innovation

Given strong consumer resistance to price hike, organizations go to great lengths to find alternative approaches that will allow them to avoid increasing prices when they otherwise would have done so. Following are some of the examples of organization learning through creativity and innovations.

(*a*) Shrinking the amount of product instead of rising price. (Hersey foods).
(*b*) Substituting less expensive materials or ingredients.
(*c*) Reducing or removing product features.
(*d*) Removing or reducing product services.
(*e*) Using less expensive packaging materials.
(*f*) Creating new economy brands.

CASE STUDY
A SUCCESS STORY

Lawrence Bossidy became CEO of Alliedsignal, Inc. in 1991. A company forecast right at the start of his tenure predicted negative cash flow for 1991 and 1992. Bebt was 42 per cent of capital, and survey showed that executive morale was lower than the company's bottom line.

Clearly, change was needed. And it was clear that leadership was required to create a vision and to direct the change. Bossidy, who had left a job as Jack Welch's right-hand man at GE to take an Alliedsignals, was hailed in 1993 by Fortune magazine as one of the few "master of corporate revolution."

"We went into 1992 with three objectives, Bossidy says. To make our numbers; to make total quality, not just a slogan; and to make Alliedsignal a unified company."

Bossidy's use of phrase of Total Quality is a shrewd stroke of leadership. What he did was engage Business Process Reengineering with a zeal few other corporate leaders have? But, since Alliedsignal was already involve with a TQ efforts Albeit with mixed results to that point Bossidy retained the nomenclature in an efforts to enhance morale around subsequent results and to try head off the resistance that often occurs when employees feel that executives are engaging in the "change programme of the month". Maintaining this focus, not fitting from one change fad to another, helps employees to understand that there really is commitment from the top to set a course and stick with it.

Bossidy used the report he received on the first day as Alliedsignal CEO as the key example of the compelling need to change. Along with this, he set as the desired future state a set of aggressive goals for performance on a variety of measures:

(*a*) 6 per cent annual gains in productivity.

(*b*) Increasing operating profits from 4.7 per cent in 1991 to 9 per cent in 1994.

(*c*) Increasing working capital turnover from 4.2 times per year to 5.2 times per year.

(*d*) Raising return on equity from 10.5 per cent to 18 per cent by 1994.

Bossidy also worked with Alliedsignal's top 12 executives to develop the country's "to-be" vision, which commits the company to "strive to be the best in the world". The vision specifies a customer focus, teamwork, innovation, and speed as key means to the end. The vision also specifies that Alliedsignal will become a "total quality company by continuously improving all our work process to satisfy our internal and external customers."

Alliedsignal's definition on a total quality company includes:

(*a*) Producing satisfied customers.

(*b*) Focussing on continuous improvement.

(*c*) Having highly motivated and well-trained employees.

It also includes taking high quality steps to achieve excellent business results, such as managing by facts, taking a process orientation, and using a business process that has quality goals, steps to achieve them, and the means to measure them.

Questions

1. Read the case and carryout SWOT analysis.
2. What are the business process objectives set by the CEO for Alliedsignal?

The case has been adapted from the script of "Best practices in reengineering", by David K. Karr and Henry J. Johnson, McGraw-Hills Inc., New York.

CHAPTER 7

Consultant-Client Relationship

CHAPTER PLAN

- *Introduction*
- *Entry and Contracting*
- *Defining the Client-Consultant System*
- *Diagnosis of the Problem and Implementation of Intervention Strategy*
- *Dependency and Terminating the Services of Consultant*
- *Ethical Standards*
- *Responsibilities of the Client System*
- *The Change Agents*
- *Summary*
- *Text Questions*
- *Bibliography*
- *Case Study: Impact India Foundation*

INTRODUCTION

Organization development is a continuous process. The quality of change that is intended to be implemented will largely depend upon the diagnosis of the problem areas where change is required, selection of interventions and its implementation by the consultant. The process of OD implementation of strategies is long and takes a long time to be of any value. Consultant-client relationship is discussed in following stages:

(*a*) Entry and contracting.
(*b*) Defining the client-consultant system.
(*c*) Diagnosis of the problem and implementation of intervention strategy.
(*d*) Dependency and terminating the services of consultant.
(*e*) Ethical standards.

ENTRY AND CONTRACTING

1. A person within the organization generally carries out OD interventions. The ideal person for this purpose would be HR manager or any manager who has the complete knowledge of the organization's policies, approach, and knowledge of employees. Person from within the organization may be biased towards a particular department or the group of people and therefore may not be able to do full justice to the job of implementing OD interventions. On the contrary a person who has an expertise about OD intervention implementation and is known for that skills can be hired and entrusted with the job of identifying the problem areas, diagnosis of the problem, selecting an appropriate OD intervention, applying the same to the group of people who are involved in the operation of the job and finally to see that desired changes have taken place, thus leading to resolution of problem. The consultant being a person from outside may not have complete knowledge of the organization and therefore would need assistance from the client side. To that extent the consultant is at a disadvantage as compared to the person implementing the OD intervention from within the organization. Both systems have their strong and weak points.

2. **Invitation and assigning of contract:** An introduction of a consultant to a client may be through some friend or the business fraternity may know the consultant. After a brief description of some of the problems and the discussion of the extent to which the consultant's expertise is a reasonable fit for the situation, an agreement is made to pursue the matter over business meals or through an appointment at the executive's office. During the face-to-face meeting, the consultant explores with the potential client some of the deeper aspects of the presenting problem. If "communication between managers aren't as thorough and as cordial as they ought to be," the consultant asks for example to get a better fix on the nature of the problem and its dynamics. In this event he may like to get in touch with various departments or the teams. This will depend upon the nature of the issue involved and the depth of initial discussion. Following points merit attention in the initial meeting, as the success of OD intervention will to a large extent depend upon the mutual trust achieved.

(*a*) Introduction with the organizational set up.
(*b*) Detailed briefing with manager with whose group the OD interventions are to be applied.
(*c*) Scope of the OD interventions.
(*d*) Discussion with the top management and assurance of their total commitment for the OD project.
(*e*) In house discussions with various team leaders/members to identify themes.
(*f*) Conduct of workshop to identify the problem areas.
(*g*) Consultant should come to a conclusion at this stage as to who is to be included in the OD intervention and who is not to be included. This is a very sensitive aspect as no one is to be hurt in any way. The consultant must therefore be very clear in his mind on the issue.

3. All kinds of nuances can arise in this discussion. In addition to problems of who can and who should attend a workshop other matters concern when and where it could be held, whether the management group can be away from their offices for the desired period, whether person is to be briefed about interviews themes prior to the workshop, the extent of confidentiality of the interviews, and so on. An overriding dimension in this preliminary discussion is the extent of mutual confidence and trust that begins to develop between consultant and client. If both parties agree, these conditions become part of overall psychological contract between consultant and the client. To be more formal, a contract should be signed and handed to the consultant. The fees may be based on an hourly basis, daily basis, or it even could be on a turnkey basis. Thereafter, a bill might be sent for time spent, or a bill might be submitted for the total agreed upon price for the particular project.

4. Contracting, is both a psychological and financial sense, occurs over and over in OD consulting. Drawing on Weisbord[1] and focussing on psychological contract:

Contracting, like the seasons, is repetitive and continually renewable. If I have a long-term, contract (*e.g.,* four days a month for a year) I also have a separate contract for each meeting, which I present on a flip sheet and discuss at the outset. If I have contract with a boss to help him build his team, I need to extend it to the team before we go to work. In short, I'm never finished contracting. Each client meeting requires that reexamine the contract. Does it cover everybody I am working with? Is it clear what we're doing now? And why?[2]

DEFINING THE CLIENT-CONSULTANT SYSTEM

In the initial stage single manager is a client and a single consultant is working as a consultant. But as the trust develops it is the whole organization as client and the team of consultant as consultant. Client-consultant functions with mutual trust, concern for each other's job, and desire to the core to develop the organization. The whole department is then the client.

1. The trust issue: The important point in the OD is the relationship between the client and the consultant. The client (CEO/Manager) of an organization may be fearful that things will go out of hands with an outsider intervening in the **system.** The employees will also feel that someone else has come to give them the lessons they are so used to, when the things go wrong. In the same fashion, the junior manager would generally feel that the system might be changed against them with little attention paid to them. These kinds of concern mean that the consultant will need to earn trust in these and other areas that high trust will not be immediate.

2. The consultant may start his trust on a neutral note: He would be trying to understand the minds of the people who matter in implementation of the OD programme. He may assess the validity and practicability of any OD intervention. He understands that no one should be hurt in the process of implementation of a particular programme. On the positive note, the client may see OD as a means of increasing both the client's and the subordinate's effectiveness, and that the successful OD efforts may bring recognition from their superiors. Such positive behaviour will enhance the trust between the consultants and the client leading to a very successful OD intervention implementation and lasting ties between both the organizations. Confidentiality must be maintained if the trust is to be maintained. Even unintentional error can be disastrous to the consultant-client relationship.

3. Expertise: Client is generally not aware of the outcome of the OD interventions. Client therefore tries to put the consultant in the role of an expert on substantive content like personal policy or the business strategy. It should be remembered that a consultant is a common person like anyone of us; he has been in the advisory capacity for a long time with various organizations tackling different issues. He therefore is considered the consultant. His skills should not be stretched far too much. In fact, it is the duty of the consultant to clarify the results that a particular OD programme can achieve so that the picture is clear right from the beginning.

4. OD consultant should avoid being called the expert or he should avoid the expert role for the following reasons:

(*a*) Major objective of OD effort is to help the client system to develop its own sources. The expert role in this context creates a kind of dependency that typically does not lead to internal skill development.

(*b*) Expert role almost inevitably requires the consultant to defend his recommendations. With reference to an initial exploratory meeting, Schein mentions the danger of being "seduced into a selling role" and states that under such conditions "We are no more exploring the problem."[3] In short, finding oneself in the expert role and defending one's advice tend to negate a collaborative, developmental approach to improving organizational processes.

(*c*) There are situations when consultant may have to submit a confidential reports or advice to the management. Application of such an intervention should not be inimical to members of the client group. For example, reduction in the number of managers from 10 to 6 for better efficiency or cost cutting is likely to be met with widespread alarm and distrust in the consultant. The very concept of improving the system or the organization by application of OD interventions will be questionable.

(*d*) The last reason is related to the expectations. If the consultant goes very far in directing, he is bound to loose the touch of improving the processes in the organization, which is his basic job of being consultant. The client in the process will expect more and more from the consultant, and consultant will drift away from improving the processes. That will defeat the very purpose of OD interventions.

Following points may be remembered in this regard:

- Advice of a facilitator should usually be facilitating like advising on the structure of the organization or assist client in preparation of questionnaire.
- Advice should be perspective enlarging and not prescriptive in nature.
- We believe that more extensive OD consultant's knowledge on management and organization, more effective the consultant can be. Consultant's basic job is facilitator-educator and not the adviser-giver. The difference should be noted carefully and the facilitator should not be dragged in discussion among clients system.

DIAGNOSIS OF THE PROBLEM AND IMPLEMENTATION OF INTERVENTION STRATEGY

1. It is the general tendency of the consultant to use a familiar OD intervention in which he had the success on number of occasions. Selection of intervention will largely depend upon the organization, its culture, and number of options available to the facilitator. It will depend largely on skills and expertise of the facilitator, interaction with client system and the trust he believes he enjoys.
2. Harrison [4] states that a major aspect of selecting appropriate interventions is a matter of *depth of intervention*. The depth of interventions can be assessed using the concepts of *accessibility and individuality*. Wendill French *et al.*,[5] in their book Organisation Development beautifully explains the concepts of Harrison. "By *accessibility* Harrison means the degree to which the data are more or less public versus being hidden or private and the ease with which the interventions of self-skills can be learned. *Individuality* means the closeness to the person's perceptions of self and the degree to which the effects of an intervention are in the individual in contrast to the organization. We assume that the closer one moves on the continuum to the sense of self, the more the inherent processes have to do with emotions, values, and hidden matters and, consequently, the more potent they are to do wither good or harm. It requires a careful diagnosis to determine whether these interventions are appropriate and relevant. If they are inappropriate, they may be destructive or, at a minimum, unacceptable to the client or the client system.
3. To minimize these risks, Harrison suggests two criteria for determining the appropriate depth of interventions:

   First to determine at a level no deeper than that required to produce enduring solutions to the problems at hand; and; to intervene at a level no deeper than that at which the energy and resources of the client can be committed to problem-solving and to change.
4. These criteria require that the consultant proceed no faster or deeper than the legitimation obtained from the client system culture and that he or she at the level of consciously felt needs. We believe these are sound guidelines. Harrison does recognize, however, that the change agent is continuously confronted by the dilemma of whether to *'lead and push'* or to *'collaborate and follow'*. Harrison's orientation is to the latter. Consultant should handle the sensitive issue of personal data of individuals in a imaginative way. He should proceed in such situations progressively: and ask the answers to the following questions:

   - "How well are we performing?
   - How well are we doing as a large unit?
   - How well are we doing as a team?
   - How well are you and I working together?
   - How well am I doing?"

5. Consultant needs the following skills:
   (*a*) Extensive repertoire of conceptual models.
   (*b*) Full knowledge of intervention techniques.
   (*c*) Sensitivity to be helpful to the client at various levels.
   (*d*) Self-awareness of own capabilities and weaknesses.
   (*e*) Ability to see each situation independently and not to take decisions on the past history.
   (*f*) He should possess collaborative and follow up approach and should not lead and push.
6. Consultant-client team as a microcosm:

   Consultant-client team can be viewed as microcosm of the organization they are trying to create. They should
   (*a*) set an example of their team for enhancement of credibility.
   (*b*) improve team effectiveness by continuous growth and renewal of their skills.
   (*c*) the quality interrelationships within the consulting team carries over directly into the quality of their diagnosis, their intervention designs, and the implementation of interventions.

DEPENDENCY AND TERMINATING THE SERVICES OF CONSULTANT

As studied earlier, that consultant can be internal or the external person. When internal expert takes on the duties of the facilitator, he identifies the problem, selects appropriate OD interventions and implements it. He also carries out the analysis of the desired improvement and at the later stage reverses back to his assigned job. The problem of continuity or reversion does not arise if the consultant is insider. Following points should be considered for analyzing dependency factor while utilizing services of the facilitator/consultant.

(*a*) The consultant is in the business to improve the client system to identify problems and evolve problem-solving capabilities rather than to create a dependency relationship.

(*b*) The consultant should be clear in his mind about the notion of being expert or the facilitator as discussed earlier in this chapter. He should believe that it is a shared technology and that growth of the client system is the prime objective of the OD strategy. This will automatically lead to less facilitator dependency.

(*c*) Argyris suggests that if the consultant intervention is to be helpful in an on-going sense, it is imperative for the client to have "free, informed choice". And to have this free choice, the client requires a cognitive map of the overall process. Thus the consultant will have to be quite open about such matters as the objectives of the various interventions that are made and about the sequence of planned events. The OD consultant should continuously be part educator as he or she interveners in the system [6]. Once he feels that the objective of his employment has been achieved, he should honorably cease to function. His withdrawal should be gradual and not abrupt.

(*d*) Consultant should not seek personal importance. He should not work for improving his personal resourcefulness, longer utility and feel needed in the organization. Gradual reduction in external consultant use as OD efforts reaches maturity. His skills can best be utilized at highest possible levels like universities or professional organizations and to set the renewed higher standards of skills, value system and innovations for other organizations to emulate at a later stage.

(*e*) There may be a situation when consultant feels that his utility is declining and the progress of the OD effort are not encouraging; in such situations, the consultant should raise the issue with client and ask for more details about the dynamics of the OD efforts, and not shy away even if consultants approach appears to be self-serving. He must maintain the momentum of OD efforts by involving client system.

(*f*) Every organization has power centers. Consultant may not have foreseen it. The powerful person may wish to maintain status quo and that the OD efforts may not take off as desired. The threat may be the practitioner or the OD efforts or the threat may be wholly unrelated to the OD process. But if the people in the organization get caught up in the political power maneuvering, the OD efforts may not take off, or even if it has taken off it may not lead to desired conclusion. The money, time, and efforts will be wasted.

(*g*) At times, people in key positions are deeply involved in handling the external environmental factors and are not available for OD efforts. In such situations, the strategy may be one of reducing more formalized OD interventions and letting people carry on with their enhanced skill and then returning to the more formalized aspects at a later date. The services of the OD practitioner need not be suspended but deferred for certain period to time.

ETHICAL STANDARDS

1. Louis White and Kevin Wooten[7] see five categories of ethical dilemmas in organization development practice stemming out of actions of either the consultant or the client or both. These are as under:

   (*a*) Misrepresentation and collusion: Consultant is basically a free-lancer and generally in search of an assignment. It is quite possible that he may inflate his credentials for want of a job and thus behave in an unethical way. He must understand that to be a consultant is in itself a big responsibility. While carrying out OD programmes, he is dealing with modification to the human behaviour, which is very delicate issue.

   (*b*) Misuse of data: OD involves gathering of data in respect organizational members. It involves data pertaining to attitude, behaviour, and decision-making abilities, inter-personal behaviours and hosts other factors depending upon the requirement of the OD intervention being applied. It is the responsibility of the OD practitioner to keep the same confidential. Leakage of information may lead to conflict between the managerial staff and disastrous for the organization.

(*c*) **Manipulation coercion:** It is not ethical to force a member of a client team to give information about another person or the organization, which he desires to keep to himself. It is better to go and implement OD strategy without any information than to have information that is undesired.

(*d*) **Value and goal conflicts:** Client and consultant should maintain a high degree of openness, ethics, and visible commitment to improve the organizational standards. Their personal goals should not conflict with that of the organizational goals. They must maintain very high value standards. They must dedicate themselves to development of people. This can only be achieved if the practitioner possesses honesty, integrity, voluntarism, confidentiality, professional skills, and last but not the least self-awareness.

(*e*) **Technical ineptness:** Consultant should have full knowledge about the OD interventions being implemented. He should not carry out trials on the people and try to be wise about it. A person not having team building skills need not carry out that intervention in the organization. It is unethical. Professional incompetency cannot survive in this profession. If OD interventions perceived as methods of getting anyone or getting anything done, the OD process is doomed to failure.

RESPONSIBILITIES OF THE CLIENT SYSTEM

1. **Top management team is the key players:** Top management team consists of CEO/ GM and departmental heads. They must play a pivotal role in implementing OD intervention. They should not be silent spectators, but the key players. They should lead the OD efforts. Their contributions is observed by the subordinates that has a long lasting impact on their personality that propelles the organization in correct direction.
2. **Develop collaborative management style:** Development of collaborative style of management is an essence of OD efforts. Areas of conflicts should be identified and the situations are brought under control so as to lead them to collaboration. Teams should be formed and assigned the job to them. Inter group, inter department relations be improved and cooperation should be the theme of work culture. Difference between competition and collaboration must be understood.
3. **Capitalise on informal systems:** There are formal and informal groups in any organization. Grapevine is also prominent phenomenon. Informal and formal system should work in collaboration to each other and be congruent to each other. Emotions of the employees should be respected and canalized to higher productivity. Management should praise their employees for good work done and institute reward system effectively.
4. **Knowledge management:** Tacit knowledge (knowledge possessed by the employees by virtue of their skills) should be valued with great care and retention of the employees should be ensured. If an employee leaves the organization he carries with him the knowledge he possesses. This is a great loss to the organization. Knowledge base of the organization should

be increased, training and development activities carried out regularly and the status of the employees improved.

5. **Have latest processes and systems:** Organizations having traditional processes may not be able to compete with fast growing organizations. Management must ensure that the organizations are technologically advanced, having latest processes. Periodic revisions in organizational structures, job designs and adopting latest technology are some of the important factors that the management is required to pay attention to.
6. **Be seen:** Times have gone that the managers could sit in their chambers and control the organization. There is no difference between workers and managers. We believe, that the leaders should lead the organization by being visible, by setting personal example and by working (physically and mentally) more. A platoon can only be more effective if the officer (captain) is physically fit, professionally sound, mentally tough and alert, has a high skill in handling weapon systems and a lover of his men. He can influence them by being physically present with his command. The same is applicable to the corporate world today.

THE CHANGE AGENTS

1. The management can bring about changes in strategy, structures and processes. The workers generally accept these. Bringing about change in human behaviour is a complex phenomenon and it may require a number of strategies to implement desired changes in human behaviour. Theses are called change agents these either initiators of change or act as catalysts in bringing about the desired changes in the human behaviour in the organization. Tichy *et al.*,[8] has suggested the following factors as change agents:
   - (*a*) **Outside pressures:** These are pressures from external environment. These may be in the form of government orders and instruction that are necessary for organizations to follow. These may be in the form of maintaining the quality control. Adhering to various standards in the factory for the safety and welfare of the employees. Provisions of Factories Act fall under this category.
   - (*b*) **Internal organizational developments:** These are various measures the organization adopts over a period of time. This may be work redesign, team development or adopting various measures for total quality management. These are initiated with the consent of various employees and leads to behaviour modification.
   - (*c*) **Individual change:** This change is the modification of behaviour within the individual where his personal goals would be better served. Reprimanding an individual may lead to changed behaviour and that may lead to personal development. Soldiers are generally given physical punishment for improvement of personal behaviour. That leads to over all discipline in the regiment.

(*d*) **Changes from central management:** Top management may import better technology, systems and suitably modify organizational structure. Virtual organizations are typical example of such organizational changes. These are external factors that act as the major source of change or push the change for betterment. This act as catalysts.

2. The change agent may also be in the form of a person who helps the client system to solve organizational problems and bring change. It could be in the form of trainer who trains the client to achieve higher skills that could be used to achieve higher organizational effectiveness. This has been discussed at greater length in this chapter. The way the change agent manages the process of change is indicated by certain factors and characteristics that have been identified by Havelock and Shaskin. The first letter of these factors together spell "HELP SCORES". These are given below:

(*a*) **Homophily:** It is the degree of closeness and similarity between the change agent and the client. The closer the relationship, the easier and more successful the change.

(*b*) **Empathy:** It involves understanding of feelings and emotions, and thoughts. The similarity between the client and the change agent leads to successful implementation of change strategies.

(*c*) **Linkage:** It refers to the degree of collaboration between the change agent and the client. The tighter the linkage, the more likely is the success.

(*d*) **Proximity:** The change agent and the client should have easy access to each other. The closer the proximity, better the relationship and easier to develop collaborative efforts.

(*e*) **Structuring:** Client and the change agent should plan implementation of interventions by mutual consultations and structure various strategies step by step.

(*f*) **Capacity:** This factor refers to capacity of the organization to make available resources required for implementation of the change strategies. Higher the capacity easier to implement change.

(*g*) **Openness:** Openness refers to the conceptual environment that is favourable for both the parties. Client must have respect for the ideas, feelings and needs of the change agent. Who has made his services available for the improvement of the clients' organization. This is in any case a mutual respect for each other.

(*h*) **Reward:** Change brings potential benefits to the organization. Strategies should be so planned that the short-term rewards are visible to the participants in the change programme. Once this is achieved, the employees will display higher degree of enthusiasm and keenness in implementing long-term strategies for change programme.

(*i*) **Energy:** Energy refers to the amount of efforts spent in implementing the change programme. Client may be able to spend physical and psychological energy for his employees who are directly or indirectly involved in the change process, the same may not indeed be possible for the change agent. For that matter the efforts will be scattered and the outcome though well intended may not be visible and subsequent effort may not bear the desired results.

(j) **Synergy:** Synergy simply means that the whole is more than the parts we have discussed. The total of individual efforts brought together should be higher, and then only synergy is deemed to have been achieved.

3. These ten factors describe the skills that are required by the change agent. The role of client is also important for the success of the orgnizational development programme. Mutual support, covering fire for each others ideas and thinking and sincerity in implementation of programmes can bring sustained development in the organization.

SUMMARY

A person within the organization generally carries out OD interventions. The ideal person for this purpose would be HR manager or any manager who has the complete knowledge of the organization's policies, approach, and knowledge of employees. On the contrary, a person who has an expertise about OD intervention implementation and is known for that skills, can be hired and entrusted with the job of identifying the problem areas, diagnosis of the problem, selecting an appropriate OD intervention, applying the same to the group of people who are involved in the operation of the job and finally to see that desired changes have taken place, thus leading to resolution of problem. Introduction with the organization, detailed briefing with manager with whose group the OD interventions are to be applied. This should include:

- Scope of the OD interventions.
- Discussion with the top management and assurance of their total commitment for the OD project.
- In house discussions with various team leaders/members to identify themes.
- Conduct of workshop to identify the problem areas.
- Consultant should come to a conclusion at this stage as to who is to be included in the OD intervention and who is not to be included. This is a very sensitive aspect as no one is to be hurt in any way. The consultant must therefore be very clear in his mind on the issue. In the initial stage single manager is a client and a single consultant is working as a consultant. But as the trust develops it is the whole organization as client and the team of consultant as consultant. Client-consultant functions with mutual trust, concern for each other's job, and desire to the core to develop the organization. The whole department is then the client.
    - The important point in the OD is the relationship between the client and the consultant is trust and expertise. Following points may be remembered in this regard.
    - Advice of a facilitator should usually be facilitating like advising on the structure of the organization or assist client in preparation of questionnaire.
    - Advice should be perspective enlarging and not prescriptive in nature.

We believe that more extensive OD consultant's knowledge on management and organization, more effective the consultant can be. Consultant's basic job is facilitator, educator and not the adviser-giver.

Diagnosis of the problem and implementation of intervention strategy is important step in implementing the OD programme. Selection of intervention will largely depend upon the organization, its culture, and number of options available to the facilitator. It will also depend largely on skills and expertise of the facilitator, interaction with client system and the trust he believes he enjoys. Harrison states that a major aspect of selecting appropriate interventions is a matter of depth of intervention. First to determine at a level no deeper than that required to produce enduring solutions to the problems at hand and second, to intervene at a level no deeper than that at which the energy and resources of the client can be committed to problem-solving and to change. An agent is continuously confronted by the dilemma of whether to 'lead and push' or to 'collaborate and follow'. Consultant needs the following skills:

Extensive repertoire of conceptual models

(*a*) Full knowledge of intervention techniques.

(*b*) Sensitivity to be helpful to the client at various levels.

(*c*) Self-awareness of own capabilities and weaknesses.

(*d*) Ability to see each situation independently and not to take decisions on the past history.

(*e*) He should possess collaborative and follow up approach and should not lead and push.

Dependency and terminating the services of consultants is an important factor. The consultant identifies the problem, selects appropriate OD interventions and implements it. He also carries out the analysis of the desired improvement and at the later stage reverses back to his assigned job. The consultant should be clear in his mind about the notion of being expert or the facilitator. Once he feels that the objective of his employment has been achieved, he should honorably cease to function. He must maintain the momentum of OD efforts by involving client system.

Every organization has power centers, if the people in the organization get caught up in the political power maneuvering, the OD efforts may not take off, or even if it has taken off it may not lead to desired conclusion. The money, time, and efforts will be wasted. At times, people in key positions are deeply involved in handling the external environmental factors and are not available for OD efforts. In such situations, the strategy may be one of reducing more formalized OD interventions and letting people carry on with their enhanced skill and then returning to the more formalized aspects at a later date

> Louis White and Kevin Wooten see five categories of ethical dilemmas in organization development practice stemming out of actions of either of the consultant or the client or both. These are misrepresentation and collusion, misuse of data, manipulation, coercion, value, goal conflicts and technical ineptness. Client system has great responsibility. It should be understood that the top management team is generally the key players. They should

develop collaborative management style, capitalise on informal systems, knowledge management and introduce latest processes and systems. They must also be seen at the place of work.

Tichy *et al.*, has suggested the following factors as change agents. These are outside pressures, internal organizational developments, individual change, changes from central management. The change agent may also be in the form of a person who helps the client system to solve organizational problems and bring change. It could be in the form of trainer who trains the client to achieve higher skills that could be used to achieve higher organizational effectiveness. These are homophily, empathy, linkage, proximity, structuring, capacity, openness, reward, energy and synergy.

TEXT QUESTIONS

1. Explain the concept of diagnosis of the problem and implementation of intervention strategies.
2. Explain the concept of dependency and terminating the services of consultant.
3. What is the ethical responsibility of OD programme implementer?
4. What is the responsibility of the client system?
5. What are various change agents? Explain.

BIBLIOGRAPHY

1. Marvin Weisbord, *"The Organization Development Contract", Organisation Development Practioner,* 5, no. 2 (1973), pp. 1–4.
2. *Abid.*
3. Edgar, H. Schein, "*Process Consultations: Its Role and Organization Development",* (reading, MA: Addision-Wesley, 1969), p. 82.
4. Roger Harrison's essay. *"Choosing the Depth of Organisational Interventions",* Journal of Applied Behavioral Science, 6 April-June 1970, pp. 181–202.
5. Wendill, L. French, Cecil H. Bell, Jr. and Veena Vorha; *"Organization Development",* Pearson, 2007, Sixth Edition.
6. Cris Argyris, *"Management and Organizational Development":* The Path from XA to YB, McGraw-Hill, New York, 1971.
7. Louis, P. White and Kevin, C. Wooten, *"Ethical Dilemmas in Various Stages of Organisation Development"*, Academy of Management Review, 8 (October 1983), pp. 690–693.
8. Tichy, N. and Hoernstein, *"Stand When Your is Called: An Empirical Attempt to Classify Types of Social Change Agents", Human Relations,* Vol. 29, No. 10, pp. 945–967.

CASE STUDY
IMPACT INDIA FOUNDATION

By
V.G. Kondalkar
(Based on the inputs from the Organization)

1. **Introduction**

Impact India Foundation (IIF) was established on 02 October, 1983 with the purpose of treating patients on a train called "Lifeline Express". Lifeline express consists of four coaches converted into a latest technology hospital. It consists of administrative coach, power generation coach, operation theatre and a general compartment where patients are detained before and after the operation. The hospital is fully self-contained and need not depend on the outside assistance. Patients from rural areas that cannot afford treatment are treated for various diseases. The Lifeline express moves to predetermined destination for treating patients on track. Once it completes its job of operations, it moves to the next location.

Objectives

2. The objective of the Impact India Foundation is to operate patients in the following diseases free of cost.
   (*a*) Split lips surgery.
   (*b*) Ear surgery. Patients having genetic problems leading to hearing loss are put under the corrective ear surgery. The foundation also provides hearing aids.
   (*c*) Polio corrective measures.
   (*d*) Eye (cataract) and implantation of lenses.

Concept

3. The foundation has the following noble concepts:
   (*a*) To work with people to bring awareness leading to prevention of diseases.
   (*b*) Generate own funds and run the organization. This is generally done though the voluntary organizations or corporate offices donating certain amount of funds.
   (*c*) Interplay of various organizations like railways, civil administration, corporate houses, and the charity organizations.
   (*d*) Rendering free of cost service to the humanity with particular reference to management of health of rural poor.

Conduct of the Services

4. Once a decision to avail services of the foundation is taken by the corporate house, NGO's like Rotary Club of India or any voluntary organization, civil administration is approached for their help. District collector is responsible to give wide publicity by distributing leaflets

in weekly haats and through the Grampanchayats. This will indicate venue of the Lifeline express, duration for which the services will be rendered, which is generally 20 to 30 days at any one place. Patients are collected at any one place as desired by the civil administration and put through the preoperative check ups. The list of patients is prepared with dates indicated for the operation by the Lifeline Express. The organizing NGO's/Corporate house then moves the patients to the Lifeline Express on daily basis. Collector bears the pre-operative and postoperative cost of the treatment. This is generally done through the existing chain of government hospitals/dispensaries. All administrative services like transportation; food is undertaken by the voluntary organizations as a social cause.

5. Each project costs about 18 to 20 Lakhs. Doctors from renowned hospitals like IIMS are invited for the operations. They do the service free of cost as they are considered on duty during the period of their stay with the Lifeline Express. Expenses incurred by them on travel, however is borne by the organizing agency. Success of the project largely depends upon the interest of the organization undertaking the project, level of involvement of the civil administration, local medical authorities and the services provided by the government hospitals before and after the operation. It also depends upon motivating affected people (patients), who are required to take journey from villages to the place where the Lifeline Express is parked on the railway track. Rajeev Gandhi Trust and Scindhiya Trust have undertaken two projects in the state of Madhya Pradesh recently. One of the projects was at Shivpuri railway station and was a grand success. The foundation has already been booked for the next two years by various agencies. The foundation has so far done 4,50,000 surgeries with 100 per cent success. The role-played by the local hospitals for the preoperative and the postoperative services cannot be under estimated.

Indian Railway's Contribution to the Foundation

6. Indian railways have donated four coaches for the project. Impact India Foundation has undertaken fittings for conversion into hospital. Indian Railways charges Rs. 17 per km for moving the hospital from one place to the other and Rs. 20 as parking charges per day. It should be remembered that the project is a fully social commitment. The success depends on the interest taken by various agencies and their commitment to the noble cause. Col R.S. Vishwen, an infantry officer of Sikh Light Infantry is in charge of Impact India Foundation. He undertakes and implements the projects in consultation with NGO's, corporate house, Indian railway, and local civilian administration and last but not the least The Impact India Foundation.

7. Since the earlier coaches have lived their life, and the same has now been converted into stationery hospital, Indian railways have now donated five additional coaches that have since become operational recently. It is called The New Life Line Express–Jeevan Rekha. It has the following facilities:

   (*a*) **Office:** This coach consists of drawing room, an office, a medical store, a dressing room and two modern autoclave machines for high pressure steam sterilization of instruments. It has a roof mounted air-conditioning unit.

(*b*) **Main operation theatre:** It has three operating tables. The operation theatre has a closed circuit TV camera. A recovery room with six beds is attached to the operation theatre.

(*c*) **Self-contained operation theatre:** This operation theatre has two operating tables and four recovery beds, a change room, store, air curtains, an autoclave machine for sterilizing instruments and an independent 75 KVA Diesel Generating set. This coach can be detached from the rake and used as a stand-alone operation theatre. This feature is of prime importance for uses in disaster management.

(*d*) **Auditorium and testing room:** The auditorium has a large LCD TV, public address system and closed circuit TV. It is air-conditioned and also has an Ophthalmic testing room, Laboratory, X-ray and a guard's compartment.

Achievements

1. Life Line Express has completed 92 × 5 weeks sponsored projects.
2. It undertook 4,50,000 operations in rural and remote areas where rail connectivity is available.
3. IIF is proud of having donated services of 75,000 surgeons, and medical practitioners from all over India and abroad, together with large number of volunteers.
4. Organization has won international and national acclaim. The original Life Line Express is now being converted into stationery hospital.

Conclusion

Impact India foundations is doing a great job of undertaking operations for the rural poor who cannot afford the cost of treatment. The project is required to be initiated by an organization well in advance. Civil administration is the key for the success of the project as it is under their ages that the project is conceived, wide publicity is given and affected people are put through the preoperation checkups. Once the operation is done, it is again the civil hospitals that have to take care of the patients. NGO's, social organizations, corporate houses should take the initiative and improve the life of the rural poor by involving themselves in social activities. The success of Impact India depends largely upon the coordination between the affected agencies, level of involvement of the civil administration, and the positive response of the affected people. We should learn the lesson from the impact India foundation and evolve identical social services platforms for improving the educational, social, cultural, and economical life of people staying in rural India.

Questions

1. Read the above case, and carry out SWOT analysis.
2. What all measures you can introduce in your village to improve the hygiene of the rural poor?
3. Take up a small project in your locality to improve social awareness of the residents.

CHAPTER 8

Team Building Interventions

CHAPTER PLAN

- *Introduction*
- *Understanding Teams*
- *Teams and Work Groups*
- *Types of Teams*
- *Characteristics of Effective Teams*
- *Team Building Interventions*
- *Process Consultation Interventions*
- *Techniques of Team Building*
- *Force Field Analysis*
- *Summary*
- *Text Questions*
- *Bibliography*
- *Case Study: Intelligent Tests for Indian Army*

INTRODUCTION

Team building interventions are one of the most commonly used methods of achieving organization effectiveness. Teams are very effective in globalized era where quality of product and services are of prime importance for sustainable growth for any organization. The purpose of having teams is (1) to make recommendations on specific issues (2) to conduct the affairs of the organization and (3) to carryout day-to-day operations. Teams represent groups of people who work together and are accountable for achieving the goals. Members in the team work in a coordinated manner utilizing their skills and are collectively responsible for accomplishment of task set by them. Performance level of a team is high, as they have achieved the synergy (synergy is a creation of a whole, which is greater than the sum of the individual efforts). Team members, because of their collaborative nature of operation are creative, remain flexible, adapt to change very fast and are able to operate within a flat structure. Cost reduction and innovation are chief benefits of the employment of teams in any organization. In this chapter we will study various types of teams and tools that are adopted for better performance of the work teams.

UNDERSTANDING TEAMS

1. Teams are composed of two or more than two people assigned to perform a well-defined job. The success of team performance depends upon the collaborative efforts put in by each individual. In reality most of the work is generally assigned to the team. Team efforts depend upon the content of the work that should be motivating, team cohesiveness, and rewards associated with assigned job. Individuals are interested more with the intrinsic rewards. The success of the team effort is assessed by the output that should be greater than the total of individual output. A team is a form of group, but has some characteristics in greater degree than ordinary group, including a higher commitment to common goals and a higher degree of inter dependency and interaction. Jon Katzenbach and Douglas K. Smith define team as follows: ***"Team is a small number of people with contemporary skills who are committed to a common purpose, set of performance goals, and approach for which they hold themselves mutually accountable."***[1]
2. A work group is a number of persons, usually reporting to a common superior and having some face-to-face interaction, which have some degree of interdependence in carrying out tasks for the purpose of achieving organizational goals (Wendill) [2].

TEAMS AND WORK GROUPS

"Team" is frequently used for any group, especially to get them to work together and to motivate them. Jon and Douglas differentiated team and work group. A work group's performance is a function of what its members do as individuals. A team's performance includes both individual results and what we call "Collective work products." A collective work product is what two or more members must work together. It reflects the joint, real contribution of team members. Comparative understanding of teams and the work group is given in Table 8.1 below:

Table 8.1 Comparison of team and work group

Teams	Work group
1. Plays a shared leadership role.	1. The work group has strong, clearly. Focused leader.
2. Team has individual as well as mutual accountability.	2. Individual accountability for the part of work he is doing.
3. Team has a specific purpose. It is a specific part of organization purpose.	3. Its purpose is the same that of the organization.
4. Collective work products.	4. Work group has individual work products.
5. Encourages open ended, active problem-solving meetings.	5. Work runs, effective meetings.
6. It measures performance directly by assessing collective work products.	6. Work group measures effectiveness directly from the (for example, financial performance of overall business).
7. The team discusses, decides, and works together.	7. It discusses, decides, and works individually.

(Reference Jon K.Kazenbach and Douglas K. Smith, "The Discipline Teams" Harvard Bussiness Review)

TYPES OF TEAMS

1. Cross functional teams: Cross functional teams are made up of employees from about the same hierarchical level, but from different work areas, who come together to accomplish a task. Cross functional teams are an effective way to allow people from diverse area within an organization (or even between organizations) to exchange information, develop new ideas, solve-problems and coordinate complex projects. Cross functional teams are also called 'natural teams' or 'formal work group'. They are commonly termed as "intact work teams" cross functional teams are widely used in the organizations and have been found to be largely effective. Cross functional teams are comprised of individuals who have developed expertise in a specific functional area what we call as functional home base *e.g.*, design, manufacturing, engineering, information technology and marketing etc. Individual representing various functions areas meet regularly at a specific time and solve problems that may be faced by the operations departments. Cross functional teams can be both permanent or temporary. Permanent teams tackle a problem by identifying root cause of the issue and then resolving it. The manager who wants to resolve a problem creates temporary teams. Once the problem is solved, they disband. It should be remembered that team members do the job in addition to their basic jobs. They are not exclusively detailed as members of cross functional teams. The duties are performed in addition to the main job that each individual is doing. Cross functional teams can of following two types:

(*a*) **Task force:** These are temporary cross functional teams.
(*b*) **Committees:** Composed of groups made up of member from across departments' lines.

2. Problem-solving teams: Problem-solving teams consists of groups of 5–10 employees from the same department who meet for few hours each week. The members share ideas and offer suggestions on the following issues:

(*a*) Improving quality, efficiency and work environment.
(*b*) Investigate causes of problems, recommend solutions and take corrective actions.

Self-managed Work Teams

A self-managed team includes collective control over the pace of work, determination of work assignments, organization of work hours in relation to short and long breaks, and collective choice of inspection procedures, they carryout self-evaluation, performance appraisal. These teams do their own scheduling, rotate jobs on their own, establish production targets, set pay scales that are linked to skills and do hiring if need arises. Self-managed teams, sometimes called autonomous work teams, are formally designated by management and can be made up of employees from all levels. Self-managed teams may make decisions and do the real work of the organization. These teams have no appointed manager. They do their own managerial functions.

Development of Self-managed Teams

Self-managed teams can be developed to a great extent. These teams should be made up of dedicated people who enjoy working together, who maintains high standards and demonstrate high productivity.

These teams should be monitored on a regular basis and evaluated in the following areas:

(*a*) Team mission
(*b*) Goal achievement
(*c*) Empowerment
(*d*) Open and honest communication
(*e*) Positive role and norms.

By controlling such key functions, self-managed teams can be effective and contribute to the performance goals of the organization. Effectiveness of the team can be achieved by considering following points:

(*a*) A proper training and development schedule should be planned well in advance.
(*b*) A facilitator (trainer) must be coopted with the team right from the beginning. Team members and facilitator should develop rapport. Facilitator should create an environment where individual member can clear his doubts without hesitation.
(*c*) Group goals should be set up in advance and required resources made available to the team. Processes should be well established.
(*d*) Decision-making, delegation of authority and extent of empowerment be clearly spelt out by the organization. Members should experience autonomy in the work environment.
(*e*) The group should be trained in various methods of group decision-making, intra group relations and have an adequate knowledge of various group functions.
(*f*) Intra group procedures involving setting up of meeting format, involving taking down of minutes of conference and progressing each point should be known to each of the members of the group.
(*g*) Team members should be so trained that they are self-managed.

CHARACTERISTICS OF EFFECTIVE TEAMS

Both Likert and McGregor[3] identified some of the characteristics of well functioning, effective groups (teams). McGregor's list of characteristics is as follows:

(*a*) The atmosphere tends to be relaxed, comfortable, and formal.
(*b*) The group's task is well understood and accepted by the members.
(*c*) The members listen well to each other; there is a lot of task relevant discussion in which most members participate.
(*d*) People express both their feelings and ideas.
(*e*) Conflict and disagreement are present but are centered on ideas and methods, not personalities and people.
(*f*) The group is self-conscious about its own operations.

(*g*) Decisions are usually based on consensus, not majority vote.

(*h*) When actions are decided upon, clear assignments are made and accepted by the members.

High Performance Teams

Katzenbach and Smith observed that the high performance teams have strong personal commitment to each other and commitment to the other's growth and success. Energized by this sense of commitment, high performance teams typically reflect strong extensions of the basic characteristics of teams: deeper sense of purpose, more ambitious performance goals, more complete approaches, fuller mutual accountability, interchangeable as well as complimentary skills.

Larson and Lafasto[4] found eight characteristics of high performing teams, these are as under:

(*a*) A clear elevating goal.

(*b*) A result driven structure.

(*c*) Competent team members.

(*d*) Unified commitment.

(*e*) Collaborative climate.

(*f*) Standards of excellence.

(*g*) External support and recognition.

(*h*) Principled leadership.

All the above characteristics are required for superior team performance, when anyone feature is lost, team performance declines. High performance teams regulate the behaviour of team members, help each other, and find innovative ways around barriers, and set even higher goals. Larson and Lafasto also discovered that most frequent cause of team failure was letting personal or political agendas take precedence over the clear and elevating team goals. High performance teams have the same characteristics that of effective teams. But the degree differs. Katzenbach and Smith say that strong personal commitment to each other commitment to the others' growth and success distinguishes high performance teams from effective teams.

Virtual Teams

The teams operate globally and have no face-to-face contact. This is a cost effective means of overcoming the constraints of time and space. They use Internet communication extensively.

Quality Circles

Quality circle comprises a group of eight to ten employees from different work areas. They meet once in a week during working hours to identify and solve-problems in work areas. They work continually, dealing with anticipated and potential changes in the environment and affecting required change. The team usually operates in consultation with the operating department and management. They operate as members of quality circle in addition to their basic job and consider it as privilege. The work is voluntary in nature and there is no reward associated with it. These teams have been very successful in Japan and US. Indian organization should adopt these based on feminine and collectivistic nature of our culture and norms. Team needs to be cooperative and share vital information on going basis and resolve misunderstanding and intra group conflicts to be effective.

They usually deal with the following issues:

(*a*) Problem related to production targets, quality and processes.
(*b*) Safety in the plant.
(*c*) Productivity and related issues.
(*d*) Assist in managing TQM.
(*e*) Evolves and recommends ideas to raise employee morals.
(*f*) Assist in training and development, employee productivity, salary administration and policies regarding employee empowerment.
(*g*) Job redesign.
(*h*) Resolving conflict and suggesting ways and means of reduction of stress.
(*i*) Assist both union and management in day-to-day functioning. The scope of their activities is unlimited.

Team Roles

Margerison and McCann (2001) have suggested that the teams have to carry out certain roles and maintenance functions. The team members play these **nine** useful roles:

(*a*) Creator-Innovators—person who innovates creative ideas.
(*b*) Explorer-Promoters—those who champion and applaud the intended ideas.
(*c*) Assessor-Developers—individuals who analyze the decision options.
(*d*) Truster-Organizers—members who provide the structure for the group.
(*e*) Concluder-Producers—persons who provide directions for, and follow up on activities.
(*f*) Controller-Inspectors—those who carefully check the details.
(*g*) Upholder-Maintainers—Individuals who act as gatekeepers and fight the external battles.
(*h*) Reporter-Advisers—individuals who seek complete information for decision-making.
(*i*) Linker—those who coordinate and integrate the work of the group.

TEAM BUILDING INTERVENTIONS

As studied earlier in this chapter, teams/groups may be classified into two types:

(*a*) **Formal group (Intact work teams):** It is composed of a leader and subordinates who are directly working under him. In formal group unity of command principle is well defined. Authority and responsibility phenomenon do exist that may hinder effectiveness of the group.

(*b*) **Special teams (Start up teams, special project teams, cross functional teams, parallel learning structure, etc):** It may be classified as start up teams newly constituted teams due to acquisitions and mergers. Intervention may be required due to organization structure changes or job redesign. Special teams may include plant start up teams, cross functional project teams and committees.

1. **Process of team building:** Team building interventions are generally applied in following steps:
   (*a*) Diagnostic meetings of team members.
   (*b*) Task accomplishment.
   (*c*) Interpersonal relationship between team members.
   (*d*) Review and improvement in team culture and managing organization processes.
   (*e*) Evaluation of roles being played.

Team building interventions are shown separately for formal groups and special groups in diagrammatic form.

Table 8.2 Team building interventions

Contents	Types of groups	Activities
Team building Activities	1. Formal groups (Intact work teams) 2. Special groups (Start up teams, special project teams, cross functional teams, parallel learning structure, etc.	A. Diagnostic meeting. B. Team building focussed on: • Task accomplishment, including problem-solving, decision-making, role clarification, goal setting, etc. • Building and marinating effective interpersonal relationships, including boss subordinate relationships and peer relationships. • Understanding and managing group processes and culture. • Role analysis technique for role clarification and definition. • Role negotiation techniques.

2. **Diagnostic meeting of all team members:** The need for diagnostic meeting arises due to failure on the part of the team members to function in a coordinated manner. This is observed by various "Battle Indications" — a fallout of the transactions. These may be in the following form:
   (*a*) Failure of managing conflict.
   (*b*) Lack of interest by team members in regards to identification of strength and weakness of the group.
   (*c*) Loosing track of team objectives leading to non-compliance in time.

(*d*) Inability of team members to cash on to the opportunities and achieve growth.

(*e*) Role conflict.

3. **Conduct:** The purpose of diagnostic meeting is to evaluate performance of the group and to identify why and where the group is going wrong. The meeting takes the following form:

(*a*) Team leader and consultant discussion of various issues that a team may be facing.

(*b*) Findings of the above meeting is conveyed to group members and assessing their reaction.

(*c*) Arriving at a conclusion as to what interventions are to be implemented if all the group members, group leader and the consultant arrive at a common solution (diagnosis).

(*d*) If (c) above is not possible, conducting a formal diagnostic meeting that may last for a day. This meeting is conducted in the following manner:

- **A full group discussion:** Using group decision-making techniques.
- **Discussion in sub groups** (if the group is large): Then the sub group reports back to the group about the outcome of their discussion.
- **Buddy system:** Forming a pair of two individuals who discuss their ideas with each other, each pair then reports back to the total group.

The formal group diagnostic meeting permits a group to critique itself and to identify its strength and problem areas, and allows everyone to participate in generating the necessary data. The data then forms the basis for planning future actions. Large volume of data is thus collected in the diagnostic meeting. The meeting should take minimum time and efforts. These meetings are generally held biannually. It must be noted that the focus of the diagnostic meeting is to identify issues and problems that should be worked on and to later decide "how" to take action step. The action step may call for a subsequent team-building exercise that may follow. In case of organizations that have come in existence due to mergers and acquisitions, similar meetings are generally required. The frequency may be higher due to problems faced by multi-culture nature of the organizations. The objective of such meeting is to pre-empt the problem. A key secret to the success of a short diagnostic meeting is the realization by all participants that the meeting is for the purpose of identifying problems and not for solving them in this stage.

4. **Team Building**

(*a*) Goals of team building: Team building generally has one of the following goals:

- Improvement of team effectiveness through better management of task demands relationships with superiors, subordinates and peer groups and management of various processes in the organization.
- Development of group's performance goals.
- Often the purpose is expressed in more general terms, like how can we develop ourselves as a better performance team? How can we do the job better?

The meeting takes place away from the place of work. A consultant is generally invited for the meeting. Three parties are involved in the team building intervention strategy implementation. Namely, (1) the group, (2) the leader of the group, and (3) the consultant. For the purpose of understanding let us consider the goal of the meeting being improvement of performance of the team. Usually the consultant interviews each of the members of the team and finds out the strengths and the problem areas that hinder the performance of the team. This is generally done before the formal meeting for team building interventions. He generally categorizes the data into various themes. The data thus collected is then presented to the team in the presence of the team leader. The group examines and discusses the issue for improvement of performance of the team in light with the factors identified and presented by the consultant. The team ranks them (issues) in order of their importance, examine the underlying dynamics of the problems identified, begins to find out solutions to the problems and initiates action plan to implement changes for higher effectiveness of the team. The follow up meetings are generally held to examine whether the action steps that were outlined were taken and to determine whether those steps had a desired effects. This flow of various activities constitutes the team building interventions. The meeting is generally held for the period of three days. In the course of the meeting, much interpersonal and group process information is generally generated; the group may also examine that in assistance with the consultant. The group thus works on two sets, (1) the agenda items and (2) the items generated as consequence of interactions of the participants. In the meeting important problems are discussed, alternatives are developed, and action plan is initiated. As a deviation, consultant may devote time on techniques of problem-solving, planning and goal setting methods, conflict resolution techniques and various methods of training and development of the group. This is generally undertaken at the behest of the team requirements.

It should be noted that the consultant interviews the whole group. He should preferably ask open-ended questions. The information obtained from the interview may be confidential or fit for public consumption. Due care must therefore be taken to maintain confidentiality as considered fit by the consultant. Treating information as public data helps to set a climate of openness, trust, leading to constructive problem-solving. On the contrary while dealing with confidential information, the consultant is careful to report the findings in a general way that does not reveal the source of information.

Purpose of team building: Richard Beckhard lists, in order of importance, the four major reasons/roles for team building meetings. These are as follows:

(*a*) To set goals and/or priorities.

(*b*) To analyze or allocate the way the work is performed.

(*c*) To examine the way the group is working, its processes (such as norms, decision-making, communications).

(*d*) To examine relationship among the people doing the work.[5]

He notes that often all four items will be covered in a single team building session. It is imperative that the *primary goal* be clear and accepted by all. He recommends that the consultant should also agree to the priorities drafted by the leader of the team and follow the same. It is often noted that the consultant will nominate examining relationship among the people doing the work, item (*d*) mentioned above as priority *one* item. But in reality it is not so. To set goals and/or priorities item (*a*) above stands *one* in priority. It should not be lost sight of that while examining item (*a*) above we are also dealing with some part of item (*d*). Hence, it does not stand to logic. Consultant therefore must tread a cautious line while dealing with modification to human behaviour interventions. Contradictions waste time and energy and do not lead to the fruitful conclusion.

PROCESS CONSULTATION INTERVENTIONS

Process Consultation (PC) is a team building approach. It lays stress on ongoing processes. The consultant works with the individuals to identify problems and assist them to solve. His role is only consultative. The consultant works with the individuals and groups to help them learn about human and social processes and learn to solve problems that stem from process events. Schein states the paramount goal of PC as follows:[6]

> The job of the process consultant is to help the organization solve its own problems by making it aware of organizational processes, the consequences of these processes and the mechanism by which they can be changed. The process consultant helps the organization to learn from self-diagnosis and self-intervention. The ultimate concern of the process consultant is the organizations' capacity to do for itself what he has done for it. Where the standard consultant is more concerned about passing on his skills and values.

Processes (some) that come under the scope of PC are as under:

(*a*) Communication
(*b*) Decision-making
(*c*) Delegating
(*d*) Problem-solving
(*e*) Group norms
(*f*) Group cohesiveness and growth
(*g*) Leadership and authority
(*h*) Inter group cooperation and competition
(*i*) Role of value in mergers and acquisitions
(*j*) Smoothing and promoting collaborations
(*k*) Negotiations.

Application of PC is carried out in four stages as under:

1. **Agenda setting:** PC basically deals with human and social processes pertaining to individuals and group of people. Agenda setting refers to forming of questions that are related to various processes of human behaviour pertaining to interpersonal processes and various topics that may relate to various groups. An appropriate agenda could be accordingly formulated.

2. **Feedback and observations:** Data of various meetings and observation is collected. Individuals are counselled during the regular work time/processes and/or after the meetings.
3. **Coaching/counseling:** Counseling could be considered as a apart of process intervention or it can even be considered as an independent interventions. Consultant answers to the questions posed by an individual like; what is scope of my improvement? How can I improve my performance? How do I go about to change my behaviour? Schein sees the role of consultant as follows:

   > "The consultant's role then becomes one of adding alternatives to those already brought up by the client, and helping the client to analyze the costs and benefits of the various alternatives which have been mentioned."

   Thus the consultant, when counseling individuals or groups continues to maintain the posture that real improvement and changes in behaviours should be those decided upon by the client. The consultant serves to reflect or mirror accurate feedback, to listen to alternatives and suggest new ones and to assist the client in evaluating alternatives for feasibility, relevance, and appropriateness. Consultant does not at any point of time suggest solutions to a problem. Consultant acts as an expert rather than resource.
4. **Structural suggestions:** Consultant suggests structural modifications, group membership issues, and may suggest work allocation. He may recommend modification to lines of command and control and communication networks.

TECHNIQUES OF TEAM BUILDING

Role Analysis Technique

Role Analysis Technique (RAT). Charles Hosford calls it as Role Analysis Process (RAP). All the members in the team should know their roles and create a synergy. Due to lack of awareness as to the expected behaviour misunderstanding may be created leading to stress or the conflict in the group where members are working. Role ambiguity therefore should be removed. RAT envisages adopting structured series of steps by an incumbent in cooperation with other team members. Role analysis is carried out so that every member is aware of what is his obligation in the smooth functioning of the team. This process is known as deciding on the **focal role.** Dayal and Thomas[7] have developed the RAT model. The model is in three steps as explained below:

(*a*) The **first step** consists of an analysis of the focal role initiated by the focal role individual. It envisages the role, its place in the organization, the rationale for its existence, and its place in achieving overall organizational goals. These are examined and discussed by the entire team. Behaviours are added or deleted until the team and incumbent are satisfied and they have defined the role completely.

(*b*) The **second step** examines the focal role incumbent's expectations of the others. The incumbent lists his expectations of the other roles in the group that most affect the incumbent's own role performance, and these expectations are discussed, modified, added to, and agreed upon by the entire group.

(*c*) The **third step** consists of explicating others' expectations and desired behaviour of the focal role, that is, the members of the group describe what they want from and expect from the incumbent in the focal role. These expectations of others are discussed, modified and agreed upon by the group and the focal role person.

The focal person draws out the summary of all the three steps mentioned above. The summary is known as **role profile.** Dayal and Thomas describe the role profile as under:

(*a*) A set of activities classified as to the prescribed and discretionary elements of the role.

(*b*) The obligation of the role to each role in its set.

(*c*) The expectations of this role from the others in its set. Viewed in toto, this provides a comprehensive understanding of each individuals "role space."[8] The role profile is viewed in the subsequent meeting before another focal role is analyzed. The outcome constitutes the role activities for the focal role person.

This intervention has a high pay off as it takes care of the mutual demands, expectations and obligations of the team members. It is a collaborative role analysis of the entire group. The entire exercise is or role profile can be shortened provided, there exists a rich organizational culture, high trust among all the members of the team and open communication. For example, if there is an overlap or the duplication in production managers **role profile** that conflicts with the supervisors role profile, the entire team can assemble together and carry out an open discussion on the blackboard. A revised list of the role profile can thus be drawn out that then be implemented.

Role Negotiation Technique

An OD intervention is planned to be applied once the diagnosis is carried out. When the causes of such diagnosis are related to the behaviour of the people working in the team, they seldom loose their power for loss of influence. "A role negotiation technique" has been evolved by Harrison to overcome such problems. **"A role negotiation intervenes in the relationships of power, authority, and influence within the group. The change effort is directed at the work relationship among members. It avoids probing into the likes and dislikes of members for one another and their personal feelings about one another".** It implies controlled negotiations between parties that are involved in the job environment. Each party gives in writing to the other party that it will modify its behaviour so that the other party can function effectively. Harrison states that the technique rests on one basic assumption: *"Most people prefer a fair negotiated settlement to a state of unressolved conflict, and they are willing to invest sometime and make some concessions in order to achieve a solution".* The intervention is carried out in the following four steps:

Step 1: Contract setting: Consultants sets the ground rules that states: (1) we are looking forward for work behaviours and not the feelings of the other party; (2) be specific in stating what you want others to do more of or do better, or to do less of, or stop doing, or maintain unchanged; (3) all expectations and demands must be in written form; and (4) no one is to agree to changing any behaviour unless there is a quid pro quo in which the other must agree to change also.

Step 2: Issue diagnosis: Each individual fills issue diagnosis form for the other person. On this form the individual states what he wants the other person to do more of, less of, or maintained unchanged so that his efficiency is improved. These forms are then exchanged among members and displayed on the board.

Step 3: Influence trade: Two individuals sit opposite and discuss the most important behaviour changes they want from the other and are willing to give the quid pro quo is required in this step. This is watched by the remaining members of the group.

Step 4: Implementation: The lists of modification to individual behaviour of both the groups are finalized and even may be published with every individual having a copy. It is a give and take exercise for improving group effectiveness.

The exercise takes a day or two for it to be completed. It is advisable to conduct another meeting after a month or so to evaluate whether the commitment made by the individuals are honoured and to assess the effects of he contracts on individual behaviour in the organization.

FORCE FIELD ANALYSIS

Kurt Lewin developed Force Field analysis. When a decision to implement change has been taken, it is necessary to identify and understand as to what forces are likely to push change and what forces are likely to restrain it. The process of identifying the number and strength of driving and restraining force is called the force field analysis. *Driving forces* are those forces affecting a situation that are pushing in a particular direction; they tend to initiate a change and keep it going. In terms of improving productivity in a work group, encouraging by supervisor, incentive earnings, and competition may be examples of driving forces. *Restraining forces* are forces acting to restrain or decrease the driving forces. Apathy, hostility, and poor maintenance of equipment may be examples of restraining forces against increased production. *Equilibrium* is reached when sum of driving forces equals to the sum of the restraining forces. If the analysis indicates that the restrained force is strong, steps may be required to reduce their strength or increase the strength of the driving force. This may be carried out by briefings sessions, meetings and conveying a point informally. The communication must be appropriately modulated. It is the responsibility of the leader to select appropriate leadership style to incorporate changes in organizational climate in general and group behaviour and attitude in particular. If the subordinates are not communicative among group members, participative style of leadership may be necessary. If the pattern of communication permits mutual consultations among subordinates, the autocratic style may mar the prospects of change. Modification may be required not only to the style of leadership but also to the 'change' itself. The implementation may start by introducing readiness of the group to proposed change and later introduce the required change. It is a gradual process and emotions, value, feelings, attitudes of employees need study in depth. Implementation of change in defence services is comparatively easier because people are customized to change and have achieved a higher degree of readiness to change by virtue of their professional climate.

Once you have determined that there is a discrepancy between what is actually happening and what you would like to be happening in a situation and have done some analysis on why that discrepancy exists the Force Field analysis becomes a helpful tool. Before embarking on any change strategy, it seems appropriate to determine how is the going for you in this change efforts (driving force) and what is likely to go against you (restraining forces). We have found that managers generally do not undertake such analysis and later face the adverse conditions and the change does not take place due to pressure of the restraining forces that had not been anticipated.

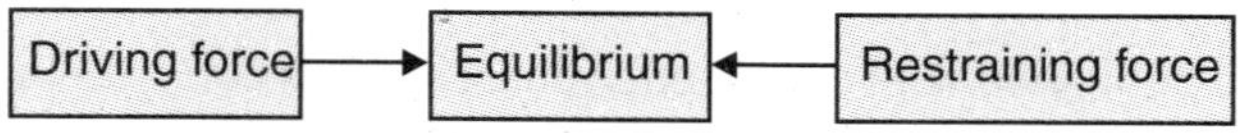

Figure 8.1 Force field analysis

Guidelines for Using Force Field Analysis

Paul Hersey *et al.*, have suggested the following guidelines for implementing Force Field Analysis:

1. If the driving forces far outweigh the restraining forces in power and frequency in a change situation, managers interested in driving for change can often push on and overpower the restraining forces.
2. If the restraining forces are much stronger than the driving forces, managers interested in driving change have two choices. First, they can give up the change efforts, realizing that it will be too difficult to implement. Second, they can peruse the change efforts, but concentrate on maintaining the driving forces in the situation while attempting, one-by-one, to change each of the restraining forces into driving forces or somehow to immobilize each of the restraining forces so that they are no longer factors in the situation. The second choice is possible, but very time consuming.
3. If the driving forces and restraining forces are fairly equal in a change situation, managers probably will have to begin pushing the driving forces, while at the same time attempting to convert or immobilize some or all the restraining forces.

SUMMARY

Team building interventions are one of the most commonly used methods of achieving organization effectiveness. The purpose of having teams is to make recommendations on specific issues, to conduct the affairs of the organization and to carryout day-to-day operations. "Team is a small number of people with contemporary skills who are committed to a common purpose, set of performance goals, and approach for which they hold themselves mutually accountable." Various types of teams are cross functional teams, problem-solving teams, virtual teams and quality circles. Self-managed teams can be developed to a great extent. These teams should be made up of dedicated people who enjoy working together, who maintains high standards and demonstrate high productivity. These teams should be monitored on a regular basis and evaluated for their mission, goal achievement, empowerment, open and honest communication and for positive roles and norms they observe in the team. Larson and Lafasto found eight characteristics of high performing teams; these are a clear elevating goal, result driven structure, competent team members, unified commitment, collaborative climate, standards of excellence, external support, recognition, and principled leadership. Team building interventions are generally applied in following steps:

(*a*) Diagnostic meetings of team members.

(*b*) Task accomplishment.

(*c*) Interpersonal relationship between team members.

(*d*) Review and improvement in team culture and managing organization processes.

(*e*) Evaluation of roles being played.

The need for diagnostic meeting arises due to failure on the part of team members to function in a coordinated manner. A full group discussion using group decision-making techniques. Discussion in sub-groups (if the group is large). Then the sub-group reports back to the group about the outcome of their discussion. Buddy system (Forming a pair of two individuals) who discusses their ideas with each other, each pair then reports back to the total group. Three parties are involved in the team intervention strategy implementation. Namely—(1) the group (2) the leader of the group and (3) the consultant. The meeting is generally held for the period of three days. In the course of the meeting, interpersonal and group process information is generally generated; the group may also examine that in assistance with the consultant. The group thus works on two sets: (1) the agenda items and (2) the items generated as consequence of interactions of the participants. In the meeting important problems are discussed, alternatives are developed, and action plan is initiated. Process consultation (PC) is a team building approach. It lays stress on ongoing processes. The consultant works with the individuals to identify problems and assist them to solve. His role is only consultative. Application of PC is carried out in four stages as under. Agenda setting, feedback and observations, coaching /counseling and structural suggestions.

Techniques of team building, first technique is Role Analysis Technique. Dayal and Thomas have developed the RAT model. The model is in three steps. The first step consists of an analysis of the focal role initiated by the focal role individual. The second step examines the focal role incumbent's expectations of the others. The third step consists of explicating others' expectations and desired behaviour of the focal role; the focal person draws out the summary of all the three steps mentioned above. The summary is known as role profile. Second team building is Role Negotiation Technique: "Most people prefer a fair negotiated settlement to a state of unresolved conflict, and they are willing to invest sometime and make some concessions in order to achieve a solution". Step 1: Contract setting. Step 2: Issue diagnosis. Step 3: Influence trade. Step 4: Implementation. The third model is Force Field Analysis. The process of identifying the number and strength of driving and restraining force is called the force field analysis. Driving forces are those forces affecting a situation that are pushing in a particular direction; they tend to initiate a change and keep it going.

TEXT QUESTIONS

1. Explain concept of teams.
2. What are various types of teams?
3. How will you carry out development of self-managed teams?
4. What are characteristics of effective teams?
5. Explain process of team building.
6. What do you understand by process consultation? Explain its process.
7. Explain various techniques of team building.
8. Explain with the help of diagram "Force Field Analysis".

BIBLIOGRAPHY

1. Jon, K. Katzenbach and Douglas K. Smith, *"The Discipline of Teams"*, (HBR, 71 March-April, 1993), p. 112.
2. Wendill, L. French, *"Human Resources Management"*, 4th Edition (Boston: Houghton Miffin, 1998), p. 111.
3. Douglas McGregor, *"The Human Side of Enterprise"*, New York; McGraw-Hill, 1960.
4. Carl, E. Larson and Frank, M.J. Lafasto, "*Team Work*" (Newbury Park, CA: Sage Publications, Inc., 1989).
5. Richard Beckhard, *"Optimizing Team Building Efforts"*, Journal of Contemporary Business, 1, No. 3 (1972), pp. 23–32.
6. Schein, 2nd Edition, 1988,Vol. 1, pp. 193–94.
7. I. Dayal and J.M.Thomas, *"Operation KPE: Developing Anew Organisation*", Journal of Applied Behavioural Science, 4 No. 4 (1968), pp. 473–507.
8. *Abid*, p. 488.

CASE STUDY
INTELLIGENCE TESTS FOR INDIAN ARMY

THE DEFENCE Research and Development Organization has developed a new method to assess the intelligence of the officers of the Armed Forces.

In future warfare, abilities like higher order mental function involving concept formation, attention ability and decision-making would be more crucial than simple intellectual abilities.

While earlier tests were confined to testing of reasoning capabilities, the prototype of the new method called Comprehensive Battery of Cognitive Assessment (CBCA) measures a wider spectrum of cognition including attention, memory, problem-solving, decision-making, reasoning and concept formation. The assessment test comprise of a set of sub-tests, which measure registration of a stimulus, processing of information and planning strategies and higher order functioning for application of that information.

A comprehensive cognitive profile can be generated through the CBCA within and hour and 15 minutes. (*Source*: HT-17, August 2007).

CHAPTER 9

Comprehensive OD Interventions

CHAPTER PLAN

- *Introduction*
- *Whole System in One Room*
- *Confrontation Meeting – Beckhard*
- *Text Questions*
- *Bibliography*

INTRODUCTION

Comprehensive OD interventions relate to the extent the whole organization is involved in the interventions and the depth of cultural changes applied while interventions are being practiced/implemented. In this chapter various such interventions will be discussed.

WHOLE SYSTEM IN ONE ROOM

The organizations have a large dimensions and are involved in manufacturing varities of products where the width being large. For example, Maruti Udyog Ltd. It has large span of products. It is therefore necessary that high level of coordination and collaboration is essential for higher productivity. "Getting whole system in one room" concept of Beckhard is related to this aspect only. It relates to conferences, deliberations for charting out the future course of action for evaluating the progress of the work in hand, problem-solving and policy formulation. Following the rationale of inviting all of the key actors of a complex system to meet together is congruent with systems theory and an extension of the assumptions underlying team building. If you get all the people with crucial interdependencies together to work on matters of mutual concern, good things can happen. [1] For example,

- All the departmental heads across the country are attending a conference at the corporate level to finalize the schedule of manufacturing a product.
- All the state heads are attending a disaster management conference at the national level to chalk out the plan as to how to meet the flood calamity.

CONFRONTATION MEETING – BECKHARD

Richard Beckhard introduced confrontation meeting OD intervention for overall development of the organization. It is quick, simple, and reliable way in which data about the organization is generated, which is later used for the action plan for organization improvement. This intervention is useful in the following situations: [2]

- There is a need for the total management group to examine its own workings.
- Very limited time is available for the activity.
- Top management wishes to improve the conditions quickly.
- There is enough cohesion in the top team to ensure follow-up.
- There is real commitment to resolving the issue on the part of top management.
- The organization is experiencing, or has recently experienced, some major changes.

Process of Confrontation Meeting

Steps of confrontation meeting are as under:

Step 1. Climate setting: The top manager introduces the session and states the goals of the confrontation meeting. It is stated that the whole meeting proceeding will be in open discussion and free from any action against any individual. The objective of the conference is to provide a quick and accurate means for diagnosing the organizational health and taking corrective actions without any prejudice. (Total time for this phase can be 45 minute to 1 hour).

Step 2. Information collecting: Groups of 7 to 8 members are formed. The basic principle in forming the group is that the bosses and subordinates are not put together in the same group. The groups carry out the following tasks and gather data as applicable:

- Identification of demotivators.
- Drawback in organizational policies, procedures, structures, goals and flows in implementation of the policies.
- Identification of problem areas relating to organizational culture, attitudes of the management, relationship and administrative lacunas.
- Identification of corrective measures. (Time 1 hour)

Step 3. Information sharing: Information gathered by various groups is classified in various categories and pasted on the wall, for the information of all the participants in the confrontation meeting. The objective of such a action is transparency and sincerity of the management to identify problem areas and come to some solution about the problems that may be faced by the organization. (Time 1 hour).

Step 4. Priority setting and action plan: The participant organizes themselves in the functional, natural work group of the organization. The top management is not the part of this group. The programme head puts the category number on each of the lists and distributes the same to each of the members of the confrontation meeting. This action is taken to achieve coordination and simplicity for ease of reference. The groups are asked to answer the following three types of questions:

- Identify and accord priority to various problems relating to their areas and suggest solutions with timeframe.
- They are asked to identify problems they think should be priority issues; the top management can handle.
- The groups are to determine how they will communicate the results of the confrontation meeting to their subordinates. (Time 1 hour and 15 minutes)

Step 5. Follow-up by top team: The top team meets separately to determine what actions should be taken on various issues raised in the confrontation meeting. The follow-up action plans are communicated to the rest of the management group in several days time. (Time 1 to 3 hours)

Step 6. Progress review: A decision is taken to conduct the follow-up meeting to review the progress and review the actions resulting from the confrontation meeting.

The steps represent the natural flow of various activities that may be involved to identify problem areas in an organization and seek solutions to them. Beckhard believes that the confrontation meeting provides a quick and accurate means for diagnosing organization health, promotes constructive problem identification and problem-solving, enhances upward communication within the organization, and increases involvement and commitment to action on the part of the entire managerial group.[3]

TEXT QUESTIONS

1. What is the objective of confrontation meeting?
2. Explain the concept of "whole system in one room."
3. What are various steps that are involved in conduct of confrontation meeting?

BIBLIOGRAPHY

1. Wendill, L. French, *Organization Development*, PHI, New Delhi, Sixth Edition, 2003, p. 190.
2. Richard Beckhard, *"The Confrontation Meeting,"* Harvard Business Review, 45 March-April. 1967, p. 150.
3. *Abid*, p. 153.

CHAPTER 10

Inter Group and Third Party Interventions

CHAPTER PLAN

- *Introduction*
- *Collaboration and Conflict*
- *Inter Group Operating Problems*
- *Transactional Analysis (TA)*
- *Strategies for Reducing Inter Group Conflict*
- *Stress Management*
- *Inter Group Team Building Interventions*
- *Third Party Peace Making Interventions*
- *Confrontation*
- *Organizational Mirroring*
- *Summary*
- *Text Questions*
- *Bibliography*
- *Case Study*

INTRODUCTION

Organization is a system that encompasses various sub-systems, departments, divisions and roles various people play. Effectiveness of a department is contingent on the support it receives from dependant departments. No organization can progress if it is dysfunctional due to conflicts, miscommunication between departments and individuals. If a department follows the policy of competing with the other departments instead of collaborating, it is certain that the organization is heading for a disaster. When two teams are working together misunderstanding or conflict may develop between them. Groups in conflict with one another spend a good deal of their time efforts and energy on the conflict resolution than on productivity. It is therefore necessary to evolve such organizational development strategies where groups work in harmony leading to excellent working conditions that will result in the growth of the organization. Every work team develops its own norms, goals and behaviours, and these forces contribute to the group's cohesiveness and morale. One key area in the improvement of the organization effectiveness involves the relationship between operating groups or departments. Organization tends to create situations of interdependence, where the performance of one group is contingent upon the other groups. Manufacturing depends upon engineering, production upon purchasing, marketing upon production, and so on. Consequently managers must operate and function in an interdepartmental environment. Boundrylessness must therefore be valued in functioning of an organization. Because of these contingencies, one of the most important dimensions in the organization development is the interface between operating groups. [1] It is the ability to work up and down the hierarchy, across functions and geographies, and with suppliers and last but not the least the customers. This is the key to success.

Because of these problems, one set of OD interventions aims specifically at improving interdepartmental interface and inter group operating problems. Such interventions attempt to bring underlying problems to the surface and use joint problem-solving and thus develop effective working conditions.

COLLABORATION AND CONFLICT

An organization is a large system consisting of various sub-systems. The sub-system has the internal boundary within which members exchange views, materials and information. The points of intersection between departments are termed **interfaces.** The organization requires cooperation among its departments and divisions if it is to be effective. Teamwork implies that all the members are contributing to an overall objective of the organization. In sports individuals play as a team and usually their degree of success depends on how well they cooperate and collaborate with each other on the sports field. The same is true of organizations. The climate of **collaboration and interface** between work groups often determine organization's effectiveness. Richard Beckhard notes, "One of the major problems affecting organizational effectiveness is the amount of dysfunctional energy expended in inappropriate competition and fighting between groups that should be collaborating. [2] The competition and conflict originate with differences in objectives, values, efforts and interests between groups. Some aspects of competition are consciously recognized and intentionally produced, whereas others are unconscious or unintentional. The interdependence is one major factor of conflict.

Conflict can be avoided by adopting the policy of being **boundary less.** It is a concept that promotes open, trusting, and sharing of ideas. A willingness to listen, debate, and then take the best idea and implement it. OD practitioner must be able to identify the interdependencies in the organization and obtain feedback while the departments interact. He should not fall prey to **open loop** phenomenon.

INTER GROUP OPERATING PROBLEMS

Operating problems stem from the following areas:

- Incompatible departmental goals.
- The extent to which the resources are scares.
- The degree of interdependence of the activities (There will be more conflict between groups when there tasks are interdependent). The potential for conflict is much higher for engineers and production managers or between sale people and credit managers. Because their level of dependency is much higher. See Figure 10.1 below:

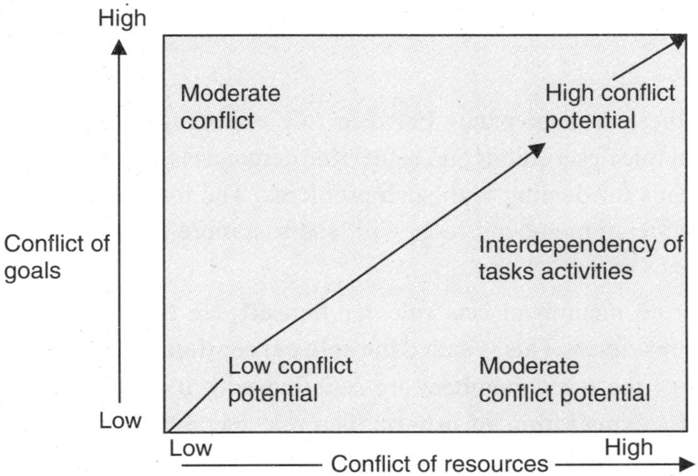

Figure 10.1 Factors involved in the potential for conflict

(Source: An experimental Approach to Organizational Development, Donald R. Brown and Don Harvey)

Sub-optimization

Sub-optimization occurs when a group optimizes its goals but loses sight of the larger organizational goals and displays **short sighting** effect. When the goals of the operating divisions are interdependent, optimization by one group may result in decreased goal attainment for other groups and the organization. Designer may design a product that is cost effective but may not meet the consumer requirements hence may not be sold in the market. The over all profitability will thus be low. Department should not be too autonomous. The objective of OD interventions is aimed at decreasing sub-optimization by increasing collaboration or integration between interdependent groups. Paul Lawrence and Jay Lorsch [3] found that effectiveness of any organization is closely related to degree of integration. One can hypothesize that sub-optimization or lack of integration, is contributory factor to decreased organizational performance.

Inter Group Competition

Intergroup problems are caused due to conflicting purposes or objectives of two different groups. The condition known as **inter groups competition** emerges when a group desires one goal while directly opposing the values of another group. Recently Indian Army has acquired helicopters for tactical air support in the battlefield. There is likely to be conflict as air force feels that air support falls within its jurisdiction. This defeats the over all objective of defending the borders.

Perceived Power Imbalance Between Groups

Organizations are adapting to mergers to remain competitive in the business. In such situations, there are occasions when the views of one group is generally considered for implementation. The other group therefore feels neglected and develops a sense of losing balance of power in the organization. The submissive group often feels compelled to revise the power balance. It may try to delay implementation of various jobs that would cause loss to the organization due to delayed schedule of implementation.

Role Analysis

Role conflict occurs when there is discrepancy between role expectations and role conception. Incongruence between formal role descriptions and actual role demands is another source of conflict. Role analysis provides a means for dealing with such problems. The intervention is based on the premise that agreement about team members' roles will lead to a more productive satisfied team. The steps in role analysis are as under:

1. **Role analysis:** The role incumbent sets role for himself. He lists the perceived duties, responsibilities and behaviours. This is called the **role perception.** The other team members modify it until rests of the team members are satisfied with it.
2. **The role incumbent's expectation of others:** The role incumbent lists his expectations of other group members. It describes expectations that affect the incumbent's role and impinge upon his performance. Again, rest of the team member modifies the list till they are satisfied.
3. **Role expectations by others:** The other members list their expectations of the role incumbent. This includes what they expect him to do. The rest of the members of the team again modify the list.
4. **Role profile:** The entire exercise is for drafting the role profile of the incumbent. He finalizes the list of his profile and distributes copies to all the members of the team.
5. **Repeat process:** The same exercise is followed for rest of the member of the team. That leads to having role profile of all the members of the team.
6. **Review:** The review of the duties, functions, and responsibilities is reviewed periodically and a suitable modification to role profile is carried out.

According to one study, role analysis is useful technique for reducing role ambiguity and increasing group effectiveness.[4] Another study found that where job demands were high, both high role clarity and high degree of latitude in decision-making helped individuals cope with work overload and job demands, but only in groups where there was supportive leadership.[5]

Role Ambiguity

Role ambiguity occurs when an individual or the members of the group are not clear about their goals, purpose and may be even objectives. Line and staff functions are examples of such situations.

HR manager may want to train employees of say production department, while the production manager may hinder the project. This will cause the conflict between two departments. This situation occurs due to role ambiguity. Organizations therefore, should have a detailed instructions in the form of standing orders in this respect, where roles of all the members are clearly spelt out, and that there is no room for any conflict.

Personality Conflict

This phenomenon is visible among the top managers where conflict arises for promotion or rewards. The conflict may result from conflicting functions, objectives, career aspirations and personalities. High degree of value perceived by both the parties reduces the chances of conflict.

TRANSACTIONAL ANALYSIS (TA)

"Transactional analysis is a technique to help people better understand their own and others behaviour, especially in interpersonal relationship." Another definition of TA, "which refers to a method of analyzing and understanding interpersonal behaviour. TA offers a model of personality and dynamics of self and its relationship to others that make possible a clear and meaningful discussion of behaviour."

Study of Awareness—Johari Window

Joseph Luft and Harry Ingham developed—The Johari Window model of inter-personal relationship as shown in Figure 10.2 below. It is a technique to analyze and improve inter-personal transaction.

	Information known to self	Information not known to self
Information known to others	Open self (public area) (1)	Blind self (blind area) (2)
Information not known to others	Hidden self (private area) (3)	Unknown self (dark area) (4)

Figure 10.2 Johari Window

The above figure indicates that there are four parts (*self*) in all of us that has been indicated by four quadrants. These are explained below:

1. **Open self:** Open self is known as **public area**. This quadrant indicates information about self is known to oneself and also to others. The information relates to feelings, motivation and behaviour of an individual, which he is willing to share with those whom he comes in contact. The individual behaves in a straightforward manner and is sharing. In an organizational setting, because of the openness of the individual the chances of conflict are reduced to minimum.
2. **Blind self:** This quadrant is related to information is not known to self but known to others, who interact with you, know more about you. This is known as **blind area**. It is important that an individual should reduce blind area to the minimum by interacting with people more intimately and by asking questions about self. For example, an individual may not be aware of the fact that he is extremely task oriented and employees do not like it. In other words, others know and perceive the individual as a hard taskmaster and dislike him because of

this. This is blind area that a person is blind to the fact that he interacts with others in a negative manner. This situation is likely to create an unpleasant atmosphere in the organization. Individual therefore should reduce blind area and increase public area. This will reduce conflict situations to a great extent in interpersonal behaviour.

3. **Hidden self:** Certain aspect of personality has formed this quadrant. Self knows information but others do not know it. There are certain aspects, which are private. Individual therefore does not want to share it with subordinates and wants to keep it hidden. The area is also called **Private Area.**
4. **Unknown self:** This area is characterized by facts unknown to the self and to others. This is **dark area,** which is not pregnable. There is nothing much that can be done about it. It should be an endeavour to improve upon oneself by obtaining feedback from others about self. Individual should carry out improvement and perceive one self correctly so that one perceives each person in right manner. These are certain factors to improve interpersonal relations (Public Area).

Principles of Changes in Awareness

Awareness in self is not static and subject to change. Quadrant to which Psychological state (information known to self and information known to others) is assigned also changes. Joneward has assigned eleven principles of such change.

1. Change in one quadrant will affect change in other quadrant and hence the changes in interpersonal behaviour can be noticed.
2. It takes energy to hide, deny or be blind to behaviour.
3. Threat tends to decrease awareness while mutual trust increases awareness.
4. Forced awareness (exposure) is undesirable and usually ineffective.
5. Interpersonal learning means a change has taken place. Therefore, when one quadrant enlarges the other becomes smaller.
6. A large enough area of free activity, more resources and skill facilitates working with others.
7. If No. 1 quadrant is smaller it is indicative of the poor communication.
8. There is universal curiosity about the unknown area due to customs, social training and diverse fears.
9. Sensitivity means appreciating the covert aspect of behaviours in quadrant numbers 2, 3 and 4, and desire of others to keep them so.
10. Learning about group processes help to increase awareness. It will increase quadrant number 1 for both group and individuals.
11. Value system of a group and its members may be observed in the way the group deals with unknown in the life of group itself.

Development of Inter-personal Relationship

1. **Develop positive attitude:** We have already studied attitude, perception and values and its relationship towards accomplishment of given task in OB. It should be an endeavour of every manager to look at the individuals, situations from positive point of view and remove distortions if any in a particular situation. Personal bias is dangerous and acts as bloc in improving relationship. If a manager is unbiased, have positive feeling towards his subordinates, advices them when in trouble and supports them in day-to-day functioning will develop a positive feeling about the workers, which will reduce blind area and convert it in to public area. This will bring an excellent work environment in the organization.
2. **Be empathetic:** Manager must look at from the employees' point of view. He should be able to identify subordinates need pattern and try and fulfill them. He should display high degree of sensitivity towards the subordinates and rise above the personal interests for the well-being of employees.
3. **Improve self-concept:** Every individual must improve his self-image. This is possible when work is assigned to an individual based on his skills, aptitude, experience, knowledge and qualification. In case there is distortion between the individuals' expectations and job requirement, a person is bound to develop frustration that would lead to the feeling of inadequacy (for a highly skilled person). In this situation a job rotation or even change of organization is recommended. This will bring to him new challenges, and have a greater degree of freedom of action and job satisfaction that will lead to increased degree of self-concept. **In nutshell, self-concept is achieved by achieving an ideal fit between individual competency and job requirement.**
4. **Communication:** Communication is an important factor in developing an ideal interpersonal relationship. All barriers of communication should be removed. Managers should conduct themselves in such a manner that the subordinates feel that the former is approachable. One must also be a good listener. Misperception should not be allowed to set in for want of communication. Subordinates should be kept posted about the latest ***happings*** in an organization so that they are prevented from imagining the situation that may distort perception. In the organization vertical, horizontal, diagonal communication is permitted. Formation of social clubs should be encouraged.
5. **Perception errors:** Common perceptual errors like stereotyping, halo effect, selective perception, attribution errors and distortion should be avoided. Managers must be able to lend credence to what they preach by practicing. This will enhance their image in an organization.
6. **Culture:** Development of organization culture emanates from top level. Work ethics, value based practices must be rewarded. Development of culture is a continuous process, which is unending. For short-term gains compromise on ethical practices will doom the best of the organizations.

Conflict Resolution Model

Conflict between parties can be resolved by five different modes. Parties involved may adopt any of the following solutions, which is explained in Figure 10.3 below:

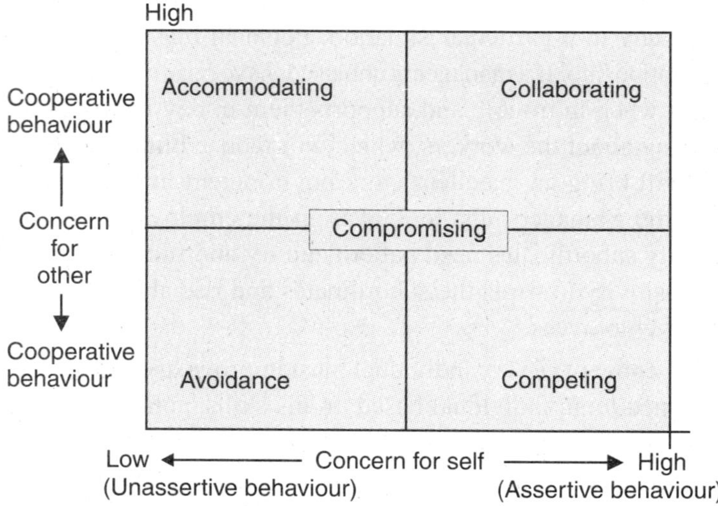

Figure 10.3 Conflict resolution model

Avoidance

One or both parties could ***avoid*** facing the conflict. The situation pertains to uncooperative and unassertive behaviour on the part of parties involved. A party may avoid facing B Party. When situation reaches a point of negligence by A Party, B Party may take advantage of the situation. By avoiding, the individual might side step, postpone or even withdraw from the conflictuating situation. This strategy is useful when issues involved in conflict are of a very minor nature or when more important issues deserve attention. This strategy suits a manager whose power base is very low and there is no chance of satisfying one's own concerns. Avoidance strategy should be applied when one feels that people in the organization should cool down so that the issue can be handled at a latter date in a better psychological environment. The issue can also be postponed if additional information is required to be obtained. Avoidance is a poor strategy hence if someone else is able to handle the situation of conflict more effectively, should be allowed to do so. Managers having high score on avoidance as a strategy of conflict management, may suffer from delayed decision-making and hence the loss to the organization. Those who have a low score on avoidance thereby wanting to attend to every single issue may spend lot of time on every trivial issue, hurt peoples feelings and stir hostility in the organization that should be taken care of.

Competing

This strategy may be adopted when other strategies of conflict resolution are not workable. Competing is also useful in emergencies where quick decisions are required. In this strategy power must be used unilaterally as a weapon when unpopular decisions like termination, pay cuts, layoffs, cost cutting and enforcing discipline are required to be taken. This strategy is based on win-lose principle of managing conflicts. The managers who are high on power base have an added advantage in using competing strategy because people from opposite side would not dare confront a person who is so powerful. There is a tendency that managers using this strategy should be careful about 'yes' men around them. They should identify conflicting situations and take bold decisions based on win-lose strategy. On the other hand, there are managers who are low on competing mode, are likely to feel powerless in many situations. Not realizing that though they have power but they are not comfortable using it. By trying to use power, one could enhance one's achievement. Another drawback in scoring low is that such individuals find it difficult to take bold stand on various issues concerning organizations. In situations when a manager is very low on 'concern for the people' may postpone vital decisions on matters pertaining to subordinates that may be detrimental to organizational effectiveness.

Collaborating

Strategy of collaboration involves attempt of one party to work with the other party in cooperative manner and find solutions to the problem for mutual benefits. The strategy involves identification of areas of disagreement, examining the issue in greater detail and a workable solution arrived at, which is for mutual benefit. This strategy signifies when two sets of solutions are important for both parties to be compromised. Hence finding integrated solution become imperative. This strategy signifies joint efforts, gain for both parties and integrated solutions arrived at by consensual decisions. Sekaran concluded that when people are *high* on collaborating, they have to be concerned about how they spend their time and other organizational resources. Collaboration is time and energy consuming. Not all situations need collaborative solutions. Over use of collaboration and consensual decision-making may reflect risk aversion tendencies or an inclination to defuse responsibility. When people score *low* on collaborating, they may fail to capitalize on situations, which would benefit immensely from joint problem-solving. Also by ignoring the concerns of employees, decisions and policies may be evolved, which make the organizational members both unhappy and uncommitted to the system. (Uma Sekaran). The strategy attempts a win-win solutions to their goals.

Accommodating

In accommodating mode a person scarifies his own interest for accommodating other person's interest. It is form of selfless generosity, obeying other person's point of view. This mode is usually adopted when other person's view is stronger, you want to achieve goodwill and indicate that you are reasonable. This strategy of conflict resolution is important when you want other person to give in at a later date when it favours you. Sekaran concluded that when people are *high* on accommodating score they might be differing too much to the wishes of others and pays very little attention to their own ideas and concern even though they may realize that they are not getting the attention they deserve. This might even lower one's self esteem in addition to depriving on the influence, respect and recognition from others, since it negates the potential contribution that individuals are capable of making to the organization. While individuals *low* on accommodating score, they should start thinking about whether they lack the goodwill of others and whether others perceive them as unreasonable, uncompromising, rigid and demanding (Uma Sekaran).

Compromising

In conflict situation, compromising is a mode when both parties try to find out some expedient, mutually acceptable solution that scarifies both the parties partially. In compromising there is no clear winner or loser. None of the party is fully satisfied as they ration the object of conflict and accept the solution, which is not complete to either of the parties. In compromising there is a possibility of an atmosphere of *'gamesmanship'* in the work environment. There is also a possibility of compromising on certain principles of behaviour, which is not desirable. Values, ethics, principles and long-term objectives of the organization must be protected while adopting compromising. When people are tough to compromise they find it hard to make concessions and land up in power struggle that must be avoided. Compromising policies can easily be adopted when competing or collaboration strategy fails. Research indicates that people have underlying disposition to handle conflict in certain ways. Especially individuals have preferences among the five conflict handling intensions. Their preferences tend to be relied upon quite consistently, and person's intensions can be predicted rather well from a combination of intellectual and personality characteristics. When confronting conflict situation, some people want to win it at any cost, some wants to find an optimum solution, some want to run away, others want to be obliging, and still others want to *"split the differences"* (Robbins Stephen P).

STRATEGIES FOR REDUCING INTER GROUP CONFLICT

Following strategies are used by the organizations to reduce inter group conflicts (Schein):

1. **Common enemy:** An outside object or group that both groups dislike, which brings the groups together.
2. **Increasing interaction among groups:** Increased interaction under favourable conditions tends to be associated with increased positive feelings and sentiments.
3. **Finding a super ordinate goal:** A goal that both groups desire to achieve but that neither can achieve without the help of the other.
4. Rotating members of the group.
5. Instituting some forms of training.

STRESS MANAGEMENT

Stress is an interaction between an individual and the environment characterized by emotional strain affecting a person's physical and mental conditions. [6] Stress refers to a reaction to situation and not to the situation itself.

Definition: ***"Stress may be defined as a pattern of emotional and physiological reactions in response to demands from internal or external sources".*** For example, working overnight is not a stress but reaction to it is a stress. Working over night is a stressor. Stressors are what cause stress. Stress requires two conditions. *One*, an external circumstance/event (stressor) and *two* emotional and physiological reactions such as fear, anxiety, fast breathing, muscle tension, increased heart beats and so on. [7]

Sources of Stress

1. **Technological innovations:** Technological changes in computer sciences have put employees to greater stress as the speed of work has increased many folds. Innovators must understand the physiological and psychological fall out of any inventions before it is introduced.
2. **Reorganization:** Changes in structure of the organization result in new work groups and changes in the way individuals work with one another. The structures may split up workers who have formed friendships.
3. **Competition:** There are fewer positions available for promotion due to reorganization and removal of middle level managerial cadre. The competition therefore has increased. This causes physiological and mental stress on the employees.
4. **Empowerment:** Empowerment offers disadvantage to the organization and also to the employees. Some employees' welcome empowerment that likes additional responsibilities while the others may dislike it, as they have little interest in the enhanced work responsibility. Some employees may even see group work stressful. These situations cause stress to the employees.
5. **Lack of participation in decision-making:** In the present environment, employees are part of decision-making that affect their work. Strategic decision-making is reserve domain of senior managers. Subordinates therefore feel that the decision is forced on them and that they are not the part of the decision making process. This suffers work and resultant growth apart from stress on the employees.
6. **Conflict with superiors in the work environment:** Organizations, by their nature, require people to work with one another. The current trend is for employees to be assigned to work in teams where they are more dependant on one another. Interaction with more people has higher chances of conflict leading to stress. Immediate supervisor has a pervasive influence on the organization's life. A study by Hogan, Gordon, and Hogan asserted that[8]

   > The reaction to inept leadership includes turnover, insubordination, industrial sabotage, and malingering. 60–75 per cent of the employees in any organization no matter what or where the survey was completed and no matter what occupational group was involved report that the worst or most stressful aspect of their job is their immediate supervisor. Good leaders may put pressure on their people, but abusive and incompetent management creates billions of dollars of lost productivity each year.

7. **Violence in the work place:** Acts of violence committed by employees and customers may be both the cause and result of stress. Recent violence for acquiring land for SEZs in West Bengal and Punjab states of India is a larger phenomenon of social justice being

neglected by the organization. It is an alarming state of affairs and the stakeholder must be taken in confidence before any action is taken.

Job Burnout

Job burnout refers to emotional exhaustion, depersonalization, and reduced accomplishment sometimes experienced by those who work with people or do "people work" of some kind. It is a response to the chronic emotional strain of dealing with other human beings, particularly when they are troubled and have problems. Under the stress of burnout, the individual can no longer cope with the demands of the job and becomes less and less willing to try. The symptoms include less interest, lack of responsibility sharing, leading to reduced participation and ultimately giving it up. The costs of job burnout, both to the organization and members suffering from burnout can be very high.

Stress Management Intervention Strategies

1. **Wellness programmes:** Wellness programme includes the following programmes:
   (*a*) **Employee assistance and lifeworks programme:** Help employees address personal issues and achieve balance between work and personal life. This includes childcare and old age care.
   (*b*) **Proactive health assessment:** Help employees assess their risk for certain health problems and solutions. This includes programmes on blood pressure control, moderation on drinks, fitness exercises, stress management capsules, diet control, control on smoking, etc. It even covers behaviour modification and counseling.
   (*c*) **Workplace health programme:** These programmes are carried out during the exercise of jobs on line. It ensures employee health and safety. The programme includes belt fitting on the job, safety against fire, accidents prevention and suggestion to keep fit.
   (*d*) **Wellness and fitness services:** Offer employees' additional opportunities like on-site fitness centers that address their health and wellness needs. Services of local NGO is generally taken to make programmes more attractive.
2. **Define objective for self:** Setting up of objective for self is a continuous process right from the childhood where parents generally decide as to the stream of learning, institutes and the like. When you join an organisation, it is important to study organizational structure, job involved and the prospects of growth. Every person must set for himself the object vis-vis the ability and skill one possesses. It is generally observed that individuals set high objectives for them to be achieved in short span of time. They inhibit inbuilt fear of failing. Setting up of high standards without analyzing resources available leads to stressful situation. People must modify their goals based upon various resources available, 'time' being the most important resource.
3. **Plan your life:** Work stress has an impact on personal life at home and at work place and vice-versa. It is therefore important to plan various aspects of life as is possible. This will include increasing professional competence by way of acquiring additional qualification

and skill, sound financial planning, home, children education and so on. Contingency plan must also be evolved in case of uncertainty. If this is done, a person is physically and mentally prepared for events to come. Investment in insurance for children education may make you free from 'stress' if it was planned well in advance.

4. **Social support:** A man is becoming isolated like an island in vast ocean due to breaking of joint family system, requirement of moving out of home for service purposes and thereby losing physical contacts with kith and kin. It is important to keep close rapport with relatives. At closer to work place develop friendship with fellow workers who can help in times of crisis, stress and strain. Social support can be easily built by adhering to social functions, norms and following religious activities at work place. This will enable individuals to regain sulking self-confidence and build self-esteem. People have resorted to GOD in old age. Old age homes, citizens committees etc. are signs of existence of stress and evolving of stress resolution strategies. The practice of confession to a priest in the Catholic religion is nothing but a way to eliminate stress caused by some action.
5. **Physical fitness:** Healthy body and mind are stress resistance. It has been conclusively proved that individuals, who exercise and so strengthen their endurance and cardiovascular system, are much less likely to suffer from certain types of stress related illness (Matterson, M.T. and J. Ivancevich). Regular physical exercises like walking, jogging, light gym exercises keep person fit and develop an ability to sustain greater level of stress. Soldiers are definitely more stress resistant as they keep themselves physically fit. They develop ability and mind to withstand worst of the situations. Appropriate daily diet helps individual to keep good health.
6. **Yoga:** Yoga is a methodology to integrate body and mind and achieve a required level of harmony with the God. This is achieved by physical exercises called Asana that stimulates various systems in the body like respiratory systems, nervous system, blood circulation system, etc. This brings a remarkable change into individual's physical capacity and mental ability to sustain through various stress and strain situations. Yoga is also considered as a process of attainment of ultimate peace. It is merely the physical exercises, which are aimed at healthy body and mind to counter stress.
7. **Time management:** Time management is one of the methods of reducing stress. Life has become very fast. Executives down to a common worker are pressed for time. Everybody has to play various roles in life. All the roles have to be performed in a given span of time. It is therefore necessary to plan time adequately. Time management can be for various events in life like education, marriage etc. At a day-to-day level, it is related to planning daily routine events. Every individual must maintain a diary in which work schedule and progress should be reflected when more than one job is required to be done at a particular time; priority should be accorded to comparatively important job. It is important to keep up to the schedule of events planned and ensure the same from the subordinates. This eases pressure on the work schedule and facilitates managing private/ personal work. It instills in an individual a habit of punctuality and a greater sense of responsibility and commitment to the organization.

8. **Live a simple life:** It is advisable that every person should leave a simple life free from cumbrances. Too much of issues being handled at any one-time saps individual's energy. One should not complicate issues rather provide simple, straightforward solutions. Do not ask your subordinates to wait for any decision or action on your part. Cases must be disposed off fast without loss of time. In personal life too simplicity of behaviour help individual resolve issues in time. This reduces tension and facilitates time management.
9. **Meditation**: Indian history is replete of examples of various saints having achieved salvation by meditation. Lord Gautam Budha had achieved 'nirwana' by meditation. Meditation involves sitting at quite place, closing eyes and concentrating on some symbol with uttering of simple world like 'OM'. It is aimed at total concentration thus forgetting routine situations. This technique also caters for synchronized breathing exercises aim being to block extraneous thoughts from one's mind. Meditation is combination of body, concentration of mind on a particular symbol, utterance of words, regulating of breathing thereby achieving a total concentration of body and mind to achieve a super natural personal power. If this is achieved, a person can comfortably handle stressful situation with ease. Meditation brings peace to the mind, develops tolerance power, improves personality and ultimately leads to sainthood.
10. **Biofeedback:** Biofeedback is the human ability to bring some of the bodily functions under voluntary control. It is the methodology designed to remove undesirable body responses through psychological transformation use of sophisticated electronics devices are designed to measure the level of stress in an individual. With subsequent relaxation or yogic exercises, the individual is brought back to normal standard situation by removing stress. The relaxation exercises are helpful to control heart attacks, acidity, and brain haemorrhage, blood pressure and muscle tension etc. Changes in these deceases are caused due to high level of stress, which an individual is not habitual to experience. Biofeedback takes care to control the effects of stress on voluntary basis by proper exercises. Biofeedback usually takes several weeks to several months. The course takes place in a clinic with trained technician and normally begins with the analysis of the person's stress points: work, family, and so on. Instruments that can measure brain waves, heart activity, temperature and muscle activity are connected to the person to measure physical reaction to stress. Biological feedback from the machines teaches a person, how to control nervous systems.

    Meditation and biofeedback are commonly used as relaxation techniques. The exercise is carried out at a fix time usually in the morning and in the evening. Person practicing meditation achieves control over his behaviour. Users of meditation often report higher energy and productivity levels. They have higher ability to get along better with others, lowered metabolic rates such as heart rate, and increased creativity.
11. **Career-life planning:** Some cases may need to be treated with career-life planning. The sessions may be one-to-one or in groups depending upon the requirement.

12. **Seminar on job burnout:** Seminars to help employees understand the nature and symptoms of job burnout are discussed. They are given insight about role ambiguity, roles to be played, communication and various techniques that promote good behaviour in the work place. The results of wellness programmes are found on several levels; some are quantifiable than the others. Medical research has shown the positive effect of exercise and the ability of healthy individuals to cope with increased level of stress. Evidence to date shows a strong positive relationship between fit employees and increased productivity, higher morale, reduced absenteeism, less turnover, fewer worksite accidents, and reduced health care costs to the employer. [9]

Organizational Level Strategies

Organization plays a decisive role in ensuring peaceful environment free of stress. Basically stress relates to two categories of events. *First* the organizational structure and policy and *second* personal development and growth that the job can provide. Following aspects must be carefully examined evaluated for its effectiveness and implementation.

(*a*) Organizational goals must be in realms of achievement. Too much high goals not only put the employees under undue stress but also creates unhealthy work environment.

(*b*) Organizational polices must be clearly defined with particular reference to training and development, promotion, leave, wage and salary administration, discipline, incentives, etc.

(*c*) Authority and responsibility must be clearly defined by setting up reporting channels. Principle of unity of command should be adhered to.

(*d*) Organizational structure, redesigning of jobs and improved communication reduces stress.

(*e*) Career plan for mangers must be developed and implemented in letter and spirit. Nothing discourages employees as bad developmental corporate policies; physical work environment should be suitable for higher productivity.

(*f*) An updated systems and processes increases efficiency.

(*g*) Management must create a healthy working environment.

(*h*) Programmes.

(*i*) Employees must be empowered. They should be provided with suitable time-to-time counseling by way of advice, reassurance, good communication, release of emotional tension, clarified thinking and reorientation is important to keep employees free of stress for increased productivity.

INTER GROUP TEAM BUILDING INTERVENTIONS

People have to achieve their group objective so that the organization objective is easily achieved. Organization objective is nothing but a sum total of individual and group efforts. The employees competing with other groups, displaying parochial independent point of view, spend significant time and energy. Misunderstanding of others point of view, misunderstanding and misperception is not uncommon in any group of people working together. Disparity in organization reward system adds fuel to the fire and the efficiency of employee's deteoriates with impunity. Inter group team building interventions are undertaken to smoothen the interpersonal relationship in work environment to promote organization effectiveness.

One set of activities developed by Blake, Shepard and Mouton are given below to reduce (if not eliminate) the hostile and strained relationship of people. [10]

Step 1: Leaders of two groups (conflicting) meet the consultant. Consultant asks them if there is any conflict among the groups, and if so, are they ready to resolve it with the help of the some mechanism, which may be applied by the consultant.

Step 2: The inter group intervention starts in this stage. The two groups meet in two separate rooms and prepare the following two lists; (1) Give their own thoughts, perceptions, feelings and attitudes about the other group. (2) In the second list they tries to predict what the other group is saying about them.

Step 3: Group A reads its list of how it sees group B and what it dislike about it. Group B also reads its list of how it sees group A and what it dislikes about it. No discussion is carried out and the consultant on both the groups imposes suitable restrictions. Later both the groups read out their respective list as to what is expected of each other.

Step 4: Both the groups disperse to their respective places and discuss what they have learned about themselves and about the other group during the preceding meeting. They identify areas of miscommunication, misperception, and disagreements. It is generally noticed that the problems are not as great as it was perceived before the meeting. These problems are solved by making lists of priority issues and handed over to each other.

Step 5: Both the groups come together and discuss the list and then prepare one common list of issues raised by both the groups. The items of greater importance are given priority for implementation. Together they generate action plan, and responsibilities are assigned to various members of the groups.

Step 6: A follow up meetings of both the group leaders are held periodically to assess the progress of the action plan. It is to ensure that the momentum of implementation is not lost and any problem that may have come up during the implementation stage are then resolved mutually. The meeting of all the members of both the groups are also held as and when desired.

THIRD PARTY PEACE-MAKING INTERVENTIONS

The basic feature of third party peace making intervention is **confrontation.** Both the parties involved in transaction must know that there exist a conflict and that it is bad for not only to them but also for the effectiveness of the organization too. The third party must be able to diagnose conflict situations. Walton [11] presents a diagnostic model of interpersonal conflict based on the following four principles:

1. The conflict issues.
2. The participating circumstances.
3. The conflict relevant acts of the principals.
4. The consequences of the conflict.

Walton states:

> A major distinction is drawn between **substantive and emotional conflict.** Substantive issues involve disagreements over policies and practices, competitive bids for the resources, and differing conceptions or roles relationship. Emotional issues involve negative feelings between the parties (*e.g.,* anger, distrust, scorn, resentment, fear, rejection).

CONFRONTATION

Confrontation refers to process in which the parties directly engage each other and focus on the conflict between them. This intervention is implemented in the following manner:

1. **Ensuring mutual motivation:** Each group needs an incentive to resolve the conflict. This may entail arranging for the organization to offer reward for participating group. This is done to encourage participation.
2. **Achieving balance in situational power:** Both the parties should enjoy the equal situational power. But there may be situation when one party is stronger than the other. In this situation a neutral party is invited to support the party, which is weak. The party so invited help achieve equilibrium in the conflict resolution process.
3. **Coordinating confrontation efforts**: A less motivated group may perceive a higher motivated group as weak and willing to capitulate. The third party therefore protracts the discussion or encourages the more motivated group to moderate its enthusiasm. The aim being win-win for both the parties.
4. **Develop openness in communication:** The third party helps to establish norms of openness, provide reassurance and support, and decrease the risks associated with openness.
5. **Maintaining appropriate level of tension:** Threat and tension inhibit the parties to take initiative to resolve issues. It is the duty of the third party to ensure peace is maintained during the discussion. The third should therefore provide objective intervention for confronting or resolving issues between the two disputing parties. It must be understood that conflict situations are often tense and emotion laden. The third party aids in identifying conflict factors and then helps facilitate changes in the relationship.

ORGANIZATIONAL MIRRORING

Organizational mirroring is an intervention technique to assess and improve organization's effectiveness by obtaining feedback from the organizations it is interacting. When an organization experiences difficulties working with other organizations, it can seek assistance from these organizations. The process of organization mirroring is as under:

1. Representative from outside organizations like suppliers, government organizations with whom host organization is facing problems are invited for mirroring or reflect back their perception.
2. Consultant generally interviews the people attending the meeting in advance of the scheduled meeting.
3. Consultant in the interview identifies the magnitude of the problem the host organization is facing.
4. Meeting continues in which groups/sub-groups identifies problems faced by the host organization and suggest solutions.
5. Host organization should be genuine in wanting to resolve problems it is facing with the external organizations, and then only, the organizational mirroring can be of use.
6. Host organization should implement the action plan developed during the meeting.

SUMMARY

Organizations are today undergoing a metamorphosis. Whether one thinks of it as downsizing, rightsizing, flattening, or becoming a learning organization. It is simply a "transformation", a new phenomenon that has started in the 21st century, yet unknown! In this environment group is required to play a very decisive role. Hence a OD intervention that deals with avoidance of conflict among groups and role played by third party in catalyzing. One of the most important dimensions in the organization development is the interface between operating groups. The climate of collaboration and interface between work groups often determine organization's effectiveness. Inter group operating problems stem from, (1) incompatible departmental goals, (2) the extent to which the resources are scares, and (3) the degree of interdependence of the activities. Role conflict, perceived power imbalance between groups, role ambiguity and personality conflict make the situation worst for managers to handle.

Transaction analysis is a technique to analyze and improve interpersonal transaction. Joneward has assigned eleven principles of such change.

Development of interpersonal relationship can be achieved by developing positive attitude, by being empathetic, improving self-concept, communication, perception and culture. Conflict resolution model has been recommended for resolving conflict between parties. Parties involved may adopt any of the following solutions; avoidance; Competing, collaborating, compromising and accomodating strategies for reducing inter group conflict.

1. Schein has suggested the following strategies that can be used by the organizations to reduce inter group conflicts. He has suggested that both groups should identify common enemy so that the concentration is to face the situation away, increasing interaction among groups, and finding a super ordinate goal for themselves. This will keep groups away from the conflicting situation and that they will concentrate to achieve higher goals. Rotating members of the group and instituting some forms of training can also be considered towards reducing conflict among the groups.

2. Inter group team building interventions has been suggested. The concept behind this model is that both parties believe that there exist the conflict and they are ready to resolve it by mutual understanding. Six-step model has been suggested in this respect. Third party peace making interventions presents a diagnostic model of interpersonal conflict based on the following four principles:
   1. The conflict issues.
   2. The participating circumstances.
   3. The conflict relevant acts of the principals.
   4. The consequences of the conflict.

Confrontation

Confrontation refers to process in which the parties directly engage each other and focus on the conflict between them. This intervention is implemented by ensuring mutual motivation, achieving balance in situational power, coordinating confrontation efforts, develop openness in communication and maintaining appropriate level of tension. Organizational mirroring is another intervention technique that assess and improves organization's effectiveness by obtaining feedback from the organizations it is interacting.

Stress is another factor that the OD practitioner's should care and take remedial actions. Stress requires two conditions. One, an external circumstance/event (stressor) and two emotional and physiological reactions. Sources of stress are technological innovations, reorganization, competition empowerment, and lack of participation in decision-making, violence in the work place and job burnout. Job burnout refers to emotional exhaustion, depersonalization, and reduced accomplishment. Stress Management Intervention Strategies includes wellness programmes, meditation and biofeedback, and career-life planning,

TEXT QUESTIONS

1. Explain the internal environment of organization in the present era.
2. "Collaboration and interface between work groups often determine organization's effectiveness". Explain the above statement.
3. What are various operating problems? Explain with the help of a diagram.
4. What are various factors that multiply conflicting situations?
5. Explain the concept of Transactional Analysis (TA). Drawout a diagram of "Johari Window" and explain how awareness can be improved.
6. What are various principles of improving awareness?
7. List out various strategies to improve interpersonal relationship.
8. Explain conflict resolution model.
9. Schein has recommended various strategies for reducing inter group conflict. Explain the same with example.

10. Chronologically give out various steps that are involved in inter group team building OD interventions.
11. Explain third party peace making interventions.
12. Explain, what are the various sources of stress and suggest remedial measures?
13. Write short notes on the following:
    - Confrontation
    - Organization mirroring
    - Collaboration
    - Role ambiguity
    - Job burnout.

BIBLIOGRAPHY

1. Tjosuold, D., *"Cooperation Theory and Organisations"*, Human Relations, 37, No (1984).
2. Richard Bekhard, *"Organisation Development; Strategies and Models",* (Reading, Mass, Addison and Wesley, 1969), p. 33.
3. Paul, R. Lawrence and Jay, W. Lorsch, *"Organisation and Environment Managing Differentiation and Integration",* (Boston: Harvard University, Graduate School of Business Administration, 1967), p. 40.
4. I. Dayal and J. Thomas, *Operation KPE: Developing a New Organisation,* "Journal of European Industrial Training, Vol. 6, No. 7, 1982, pp. 25–27.
5. Paul, D. Bliese and Carl Andre Castro, *"Role clarity, Work Overload and Organisational Support: Multi Level Evidence of Importance of Support",* Work and Stress, Vol 14, no. 1 (Jan. 2000), p. 65.
6. Richard, S. DeFrank and John M. Ivancevich, *"Stress on the Job: An Executive Update",* Academy of Management Executive, Vol. 12, no. 3, August 1998, pp. 55–67.
7. Bruce Cryer, Rollin McCraty, and Doc. Childre, *"Pull the Plug on Stress"*, Harvard Business Review, Vol. 81, No. 7, (July 2003), pp. 102–08.
8. R. Hogan, J.C. Gordon and I. Hogan *"What we Know about Leadership: Effectiveness and Personality"*, American Psychologies, Vol. 49, No. 6, 1994, p. 494.
9. Chris Riush, *"Wellness can Mean a Trim Bottonline"*, Business Week August, 1993, p. 112.
10. This discussion is based on R. Beckhard's work.
11. *Abid.*
12. R.E. Walton, *"Interpersonal Peace Making: Confrontations and Third Party Consultation"*, (Readings Mass, Addison-Winsley, 1969).

CASE STUDY*

Mrs. Batra has been working in the Administration Department of a hospital in Mumbai for the last 20 years. She is highly dedicated to her job and has a very good rapport with her superiors and co-workers. About eight months ago, she was promoted into the upper ranks of management and was assigned to the supply department of the hospitals as a manager. Everybody was happy for her and congratulated her on her promotion. The employees in this new department welcomed her and promised her all the cooperation. Mrs. Batra finds the job very challenging and psychologically rewarding.

She is a very good manager and an interesting person. Everyone in her department likes to come to work because Mrs. Batra makes the day interesting. Since she became the manager, absenteeism is down by over 20 per cent. She has very pleasant personality and is always available to help her subordinates. She is efficient, responsible and responds to all communication in timely manner. She attends all meetings fully prepared to discuss all issues under consideration. This is, she was, at least until last month.

During the last month, she seems to have changed considerably for the worse. Both her superiors and her subordinates find her behaviour strange. She is not as polite and amicable as she used to be. Last week she missed a very important meeting of the top administrators. She was requested to research an issue and prepare the material to present at the weekly meeting. She did not do so. She is often late to work and does not take much interest in the communication, she receives from superiors and other departments and does not respond to the memorandums in a timely manner. She has become aloof and seems tired most of the time.

The Director of the hospital, Mr. Verma, noticed this change in her behaviour early and has been covertly monitoring her behaviour for the last three weeks. Early today, Mr. Verma had a talk with one of the in-house psychiatrists explaining Mrs. Batra's changing work behaviour patterns. The psychiatrist, Dr. Rekhi suggested that perhaps she has been over-working herself and takes the job too seriously. Mr. Verma suggested to Dr. Rekhi that he should talk to Mrs. Batra and find out if there were any difficult situations at home that might be affecting her behaviour. Mrs. Batra has been married for over 20 years and has no children. Mr. Verma is concerned that Mrs. Batra ought to get help before she suffers a total collapse. Dr. Rekhi promised to do so.

Questions

1. What are some of the symptoms of overload? Does, Mrs. Batra seem to suffer from over-working conditions? Explain your reasons.
2. Given this information, do you think that there may be marital problems at her home that are affecting her work? Could it also be that her work is affecting her family life that is further affecting her work? Justify your speculations.

(Based upon: Richard M. Hodgetts, Organizational Behaviour, Macmillan Publishing Company, 1991, adopted from "Organizational Behaviour", 3rd Edition, 2005. Edited by Jit S. Chandan, Published by Vikas Publishing House, New Delhi).

Mrs. Batra

CHAPTER 11

Structural Interventions

CHAPTER PLAN

- *Introduction*
- *Job Redesign*
- *Quality of Work Life*
- *Quality Circles*
- *Management by Objective (MBO)*
- *Difficulties in Managing MBO Concept*
- *Six Sigma*
- *Total Quality in Human Resources Management*
- *Re-engineering*
- *Systems Approach to Management*
- *Benchmarking to Improve Competitive Performance*
- *Summary*
- *Bibliography*
- *Cast Study: Voltas Limited*

INTRODUCTION

In this chapter, we will study structural interventions. These are aimed at achieving organizational effectiveness through changes in the tasks, structural, technological, and goal processes in the organization. In particular this includes study of the following aspects:

(*a*) Job redesign.

(*b*) Quality of work life.

(*c*) Quality circles.

(*d*) Management By Objective.

(*e*) Six sigma.
(*f*) Total quality in human resources management.
(*g*) Re-engineering.
(*h*) Systems approach to management.
(*i*) Benchmarking to improve competitive performance.

JOB REDESIGN

Herzberg introduced a concept of work design. He concluded that workers were happier on their jobs based on intrinsic value of the job itself. Such as personal growth, recognition, higher responsibility sense of achievement and recognition. He stressed that work motivation and higher productivity can be achieved if appropriate changes are incorporated in the job design.

The recent changes in technology have seen a progressive use of technical devices and increasing dependence on technology. This has led to decrease in and erosion of the human component. To keep the morale high and simultaneously meet the organizational objective, redesign of work is necessary. Redesign aims at higher productivity, optimum utilization of skills and experience of the employees. Various benefits of redesign are as under:

(*a*) Relationship between people and job: Job redesign alters the relationship of people and the job assigned to him. Every job must be interesting, challenging and accord happiness to the worker. Job has an everlasting influence on employee motivation. The job must provide intrinsic value to the employee for which he must be proud of certain component of job that needs modification should be altered keeping in mind the employee job satisfaction.

(*b*) Job and human behaviour is directly related to each other: While redesigning a job, it must be kept in mind that employee who is likely to be assigned the job should have positive attitude and therefore display a creative and favourable attitude towards the group in which he is working. If the job contents are not favourable and employee is likely to display resistance, stress symptoms and even involve him in conflict situation that is more dangerous to the organization. It should be borne in mind that employee behaviour is more important in an organization than any other elements of management.

(*c*) Work redesigns open avenues and enhanced opportunities to employees in various departments in the organization they are serving. It is likely to invite changes in various areas of operation. Work redesign exercise must ensure workers participation so that they accept the change willingly. The process can later enlarge and also cover other areas.

(*d*) Management of resources, processes and keeping work force satisfied are the major responsibilities of manager. An experienced manager can easily handle former two aspects, however creating and an enhanced level of satisfaction in employees is a crucial job. Work redesign brings among people a feeling of worth, facilitates personal growth and makes them psychologically and technically fit to handle higher responsibilities. Organizational policies should cater for training and development that brings each individual worth for holding one up higher responsibility at all times. This is also possible by way of work redesign.

(i) *Job simplification:* In this technique, jobs are broken down into very small parts where a fragment as task is repeatedly done over and over again by the same individual. Thus the worker achieves high level of proficiency, quality of the product and high volume is produced in a limited time frame. Employee therefore is paid higher rewards. On the organizational side, the productivity is high. Since the individual is doing the job repeatedly, he achieves proficiency and training cost to the organization is practically negligible. However, there are certain disadvantages also. Because the task is very repetitious, a worker is likely get bored and remain absent frequently. Quality and quantity may also suffer in the long run due to frustration caused. Organization may have to attract workers by offering higher wages.

(ii) *Job enlargement:* Job enlargement, where two or more simple tasks are combined and allotted to a employee, as in the case of vehicle driver, who apart from driving can also undertake the maintenance of the vehicle. In this situation, it adds more tasks to a job so that the worker has variety of simple tasks to perform. This also adds to acquiring additional proficiency. Dissatisfaction of employees cannot be avoided after a prolong period, because it still has a tendency to set a boredom in an employee.

(iii) *Job rotation:* Job rotation refers to a technique where the employee is periodically rotated from one job to another within a work design. It involves moving employees among different tasks over a period of time. In this system workers do not get bored and problem of job enlargement is automatically taken care of. In job rotation workers get opportunities to do different jobs within a span of few weeks/months as he is rotated from one job to another. Thus company achieves specialization among the work force. However people who desire to do something challenging are likely to develop frustration as rotation involves very restricted exposure to job variety.

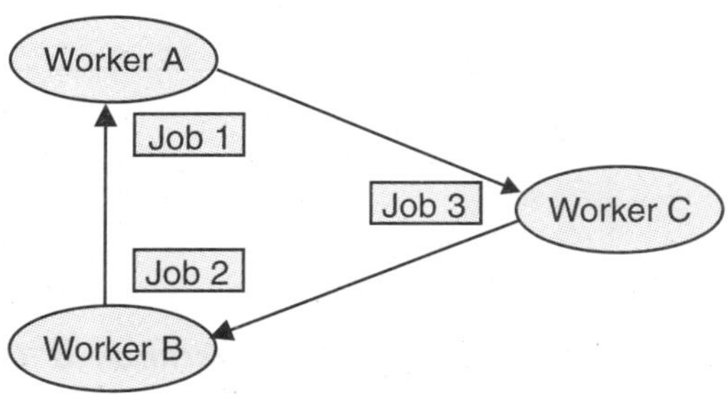

Figure 11.1

In the Fig. 11.1 above, workers A, B and C are performing different jobs within a specific period of time.

(iv) *Job enrichment:* Job enrichment refers to the technique of job design in which variety of skills is required to be possessed by the individual. Job enrichment entails, skills development and a challenge to the idle. It entails inbuilt motivation, absolute control over the job, opportunities for growth and learning. Enriched jobs offer an intrinsic value to the worker and promote motivation among the individuals doing the job.

There are five core job characteristics:

1. Skill variety: It denotes the degree to which a job requires utilization of variety of skills, abilities and talent of an individual doing the job. If the job is enriched, obviously the worker will achieve job satisfaction and provide him the challenge in accomplishment of the same.

2. Task identity: It is the degree to which the job requires completion of "Whole" identifiable unit of work. The job involves, involvement of an individual from beginning to the completion of a piece of work, which he should be able to see in its entirety. This gives an individual a sense of pride, job satisfaction and desire to improve upon the present standards. Job identity gives an individual an identity in the group he belongs to and provides him an intrinsic reward.

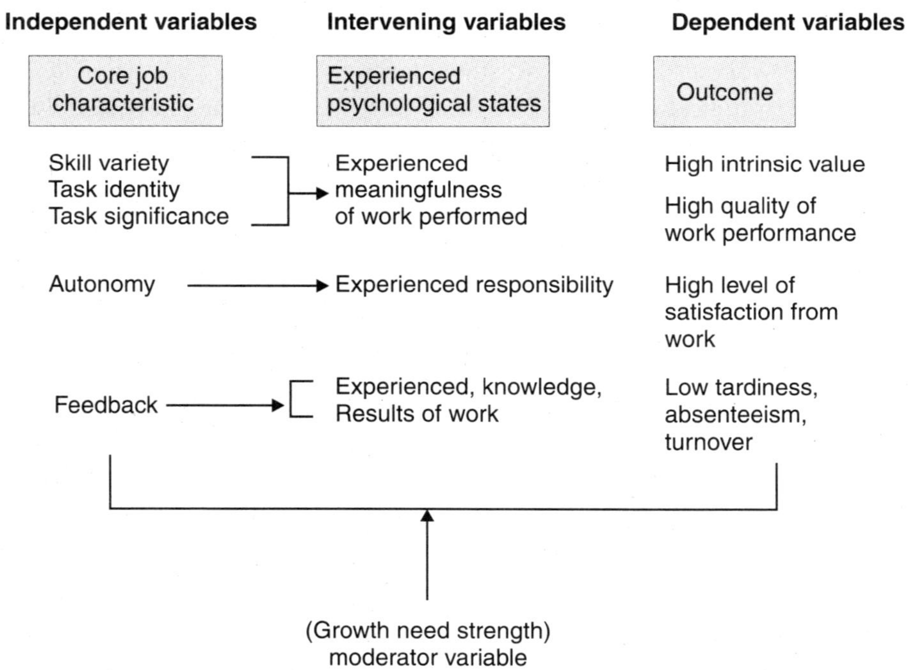

Figure 11.2 ***Job design model of Hackman & Oldham***

3. Task significance: It refers to the meaningfulness or significance of the impact on the lives or work of the other people both inside and outside the organization. In DRDO where tanks are being assembled, the manager states that a worker is putting nuts and bolts on a tank that will defend the territorial integrity of our nation, to a worker. The task significant in this case is of a very high order than putting nuts and bolts on a car through the skill requirement for both the jobs is the same.

It is this part that motivates the employees. The managers must ensure that the people are doing worthwhile and significant jobs, which is beneficial to society.

4. Autonomy: Anatomy reflects the extent to which job provides an individual freedom of work, independence in decision-making and full discretion in scheduling procedures in its execution. If the job content caters for the above factors, obviously an individual will take pride in completing the same. Greater the degree of autonomy more the person feels " in control" of the work in hand. In such situations people are motivated and display a great sense of belonging and job satisfaction.

5. Feedback: It is a core dimension of achieving direct feedback from the work itself as to how well a person is performing. Are the things going in the right directions? This is a conscious phenomenon, a person experiences while doing a job. If you are painting, one would definitely get to know if the paints are reflecting the image one desires, are the colours being mixed appropriately? This will indicate performance standard of the individual.

QUALITY OF WORK LIFE

Quality of work life refers to high level of satisfaction an employee enjoys by virtue of job design in the organization. Quality of work life is measured by factors like job involvement, job satisfaction, competence, job performance and productivity. People must ensure that the job they are doing is central to individuals' life and they display maximum involvement. Studies indicate that challenging jobs which have skill variety, influence employees to get involved in their jobs. Correlates of job involvement are personality characteristics, high achievement and high work ethics (Ref. Sekaran 1981, Robinowiz and Hall, 1977).

QUALITY CIRCLES

Quality circles is one of the recent concept of group job design. It consists of a group of 7–10 employees from a unit or across units who have volunteered to meet together regularly and analyse and make proposals about product quality, investigate cause and corrective actions. The recommendations of quality circles are later forwarded to coordinating or steering committee. A meeting of quality circles is held once in a week or when need arises which are chaired by supervisors or any of the group members. Leaders are encouraged to create high degree participation within the group. Group members are trained in group communication skills, product quality and problem-solving techniques. This concept develops a sense of belonging, boosts employee moral, accords job security and develops 'we' feeling among group members and enriches organizational culture.

MANAGEMENT BY OBJECTIVE (MBO)

The concept of 'Management By Objectives' was introduced by Peter Drucker in 1954 and later developed by various writers like John Humble, Dale McConkey, Edward Schleh and Douglas McGregor. It is significant to note that even many years before 1954, classical management writers like Fayol, Urwich and Barnard emphasized the concept of objectives. However in the recent years MBO has become a philosophy to manage organizations. The concept was being practiced in few of the organizations but has failed to make the mark due to various reasons. MBO is both a philosophy and approach of management. It is process whereby superiors and subordinates assess the contribution of each other and integrate individuals with the organization so as to make best use of organizational resources. MBO is a system of integrating managerial activities.

Definitions

MBO is a comprehensive managerial system that integrates many key managerial activities in a systematic manner, consciously directed towards the effective and efficient achievement of organizational objectives (Koonz, 1992).[1]

John Humble defined MBO as a dynamic system, which integrates the company's need to achieve its goals for profit and growth with manager's need to contribute and develop himself.

According to George S. Ordiorne, the system of management by objectives (MBO) can be described as "a process whereby the superior and subordinate managers of an organization jointly identify its common goals, define each individuals major areas of responsibility in terms of measures as guides for operating the unit and assessing the contribution of each of its members."[2]

Chakravarty (1976) has suggested integration of individual and organizational objectives through MBO. He has defined MBO as follows:

"MBO is result centred, non-specialist, operational managerial process for the effective utilization of material, physical, and human resources of the organization by integrating the individual with the organization and organization with the environment."[3]

Chabra (1999)[4] has explained that MBO is a comprehensive management planning and control technique and is bound to affect the entire organizational structure, culture and style. Management by objective calls for regulating the process of managing in terms of meaningful, specific and verifiable objectives at different levels of management hierarchy. Management by objectives moulds planning, directing and controlling in number of ways. It stimulates meaningful action for better performance and higher accomplishment. It is closely associated with the concept of decentralization because decentralization cannot work without the support of MBO.

Features of MBO

1. **Operational technique:** MBO is highly practical concept. The goals should be quantifiable. Peter Drucker puts it, "Objectives must be operational, and they must be capable of being converted into specific targets and specific assignments. They must be capable of becoming as basis, as well as the motivation for work and achievement."
2. **Comprehensive technique:** MBO provides the stimulus for introduction of new techniques of management and enhances the relevance of existing ones. MBO envisages the joint application of a number of principles of management and works as an integrating device, MBO represents comprehensive tool of management. MBO is concerned with realization of objectives at each level of organization.
3. **Result oriented:** MBO is also known as management by results and goal setting approach. McCokey has preferred the term "management by results". He has explained it as an approach to management planning and evaluation in which specific targets for a year, or some other length of time are established for each manager on the basis of the results which each must achieve if the overall objectives of the company are to be realized. At the end of the period, the actual results achieved are measured against the original goals, *i.e.,* against the expected results, which each manager knows he is responsible for achieving. The approach concentrates on ends rather than means and is diagnostic rather than punitive in nature.
4. **Participative management:** MBO is characterized by objective setting and performance evaluation by managers and subordinates. Each manager sets objective for himself in consultation with subordinates, and evaluates the same after a specific period of time. It is a joint relationship with peers, superiors and subordinates for setting of goals, evaluation of achievement, identification of problem areas and taking corrective actions. Workers experience a sense of autonomy in work culture. MBO is not merely a meeting of minds, but joint authorship of goals and their joint implementation.
5. **Systems approach:** MBO attempts to integrate the individual with the organization and the organization with its environment. It seeks to ensure the accomplishment of both personal and enterprise goals by creating goal congruence. It provides guidelines for appropriate system and procedures. Resource allocation, delegation reward system etc., are determined on the basis of objectives. It is a comprehensive field of system implementation.
6. **Concentration on "Key Result Areas" (KRA):** The emphasis on MBO is on performance improvement in the areas, which are of critical importance to the organization as a whole. By identifying KRA, MBO ensures that due attention is given to the priority areas which are crucial for good performance and growth of the organization.

Process of MBO

Process of MBO: MBO is a system to achieve organizational objectives (long-term and short-term) through employee involvement and optimum utilization of resources. Factor of accountability is inbuilt in the concept of MBO. Organization on its part has to ensure total commitment to employee training and development and enhancement of practical skills so that individual and organizational objectives are met. The process of MBO is given in Figure 11.3 below:

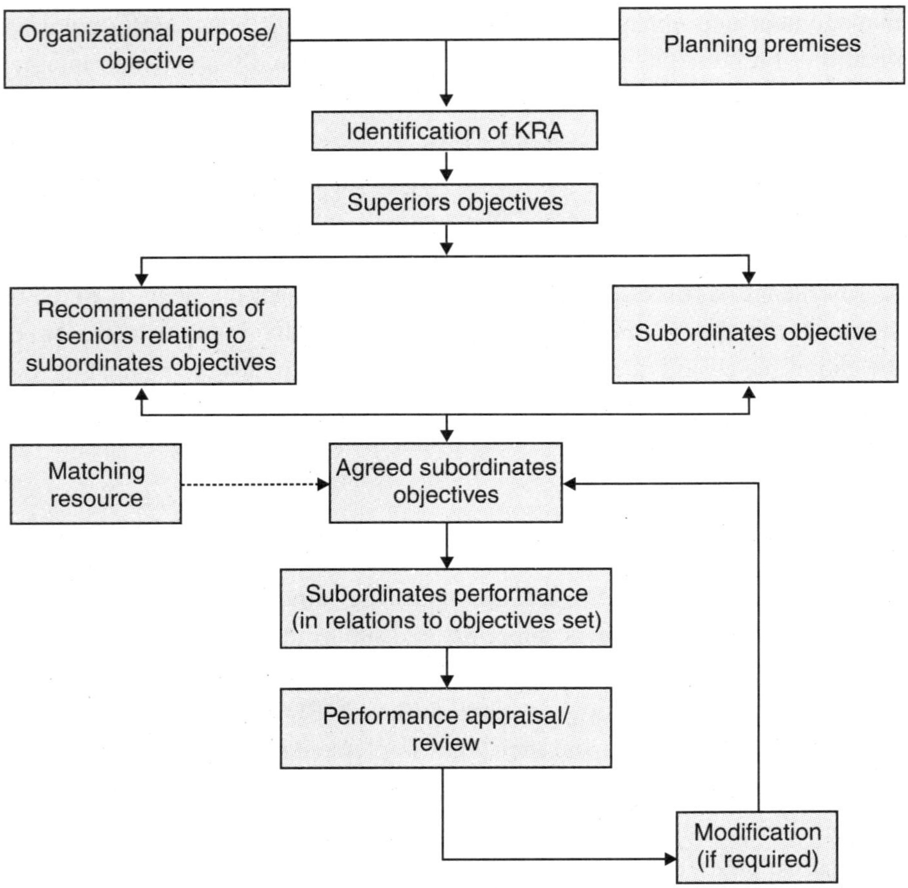

Figure 11.3 Process of MBO

1. **Organizational purpose/objective:** The first step in the process of installing MBO in any organization is to establish verifiable objectives for the organization as a whole. In order to set the objectives for the enterprise a detailed study and assessment on the following points is required:
   (*a*) Conduct market survey to know what type of goods and services are required by the society.

(*b*) Scanning of external environment.

(*c*) Identification of customer needs etc.

(*d*) Market forecasts.

(*e*) Resources available vis-a-vis requirement.

(*f*) Level of employee expertise available/ needed.

Detailed analysis would lead to identifying of desired objectives, both short and long-term. An attempt should be made to set specific goals in various key areas on which survival and growth of the organization depends. The goals should be specific and attainable. Too much or ambitious goals are not desired as these may not be attainable.

2. **Planning premises:** Top management should consider planning premises. These are fallouts of overall objective of the enterprise. This involves determination long-range strategic perspective of the business. This includes various factors like

(*a*) Achievement of growth.

(*b*) Deciding of right product mix.

(*c*) Vertical integration envisaged.

(*d*) Level of skill existing/ required.

Organizations and planning premises together provide basis for identification of Key Result Areas (KRAs).

3. **Establishing key result areas:** KRAs are developed from the expectations of stakeholders, strength of the organization, market analysis and the level of cohesiveness of the employees and their tolerance. It indicates the present of the organization and top management's perception. KRA is expressed in terms of project, market share, and R&D achievements with particular reference to innovations. Employee performance and the social obligations the organization is to meet. KRAs should be reviewed periodically. MBA calls for periodic review between managers and subordinates to evaluate the progress of the work done. Standards of performance should be laid down for evaluation. KRA analysis should be reduced in writing and contain the following details:

(*a*) Overall objectives of the job of subordinates.

(*b*) Result that an individual is expected to achieve vis-a-vis the objective set for himself.

(*c*) Priorities of various tasks.

(*d*) Assistance that may be required in terms of information and logistic support.

(*e*) Performance evaluation and reward system.

4. **Formulation of objectives:** The major activities of every enterprise are divided on some basis of departmentalization. The top management must determine the objectives of every department. At this stage, the top management should discuss the objectives with departmental managers so that a statement of agreed objectives may be evolved. Each department sets

its long range and short-range objectives that are approved by the top management. The process of setting objectives is repeated at lower levels of management. At each level, objectives are set in verifiable units where possible so that performance of every department and individuals may be reviewed.

5. **Performance appraisal and review:** Performance of the individual is evaluated against the standards, agreed upon by both the subordinates and superiors. Generally performance of all employees of an organization is reviewed after every six-month/year. This will depend upon the policy laid down by the organization. Informal advice, appraisal is done by superior on a daily basis in the work environment. Under MBO, the superior does not evaluate the individual but apprises him of his performance and suggests ways for its improvement. Performance of every section, department, division and the organization as a whole is carried out periodically. Based on this exercise, suitable changes are implemented. This is necessary to respond to the changes in the environment. The system of MBO is also integrated with organizational design, process and practices of the organization.

DIFFICULTIES IN MANAGING MBO CONCEPT

1. MBO is a philosophy rather than a mere technique. Though the process appears to be simple but difficult to actual implementation, some of the weaknesses are given below:
   (*a*) **Difficulty in setting up of individual objective:** Measurable or verifiable objectives can not be set for the individual. Hence performance cannot be effectively measured. This leads to non-implementation of MBO.
   (*b*) **Time and cost:** Implementation of MBO is not simple as it appears. Sometimes managers get frustrated due to additional workload of MBO. The concept involves lot of paper work, organizational resources and time. There is also a communication overload in initial stages. However, these problems are of temporary nature. Once employees understand the concept it becomes a part of organizational culture.
   (*c*) **Emphasis on short-term objective:** There is a tendency to set short-term goals usually for a year of even for a lesser period of time to facilitate working at individual level. This leads to overlooking long-term goals. In the process, eventually long-term goals do not correlate with short-term goals. This is an unhealthy practice for organizational effectiveness. People concentrate on short-term goals as their performance is measured based on six-month/year.

2. **Resistance to change:** Implementation of MBO requires far reaching changes in thinking and practices. In practice, it is resisted at each level of the organization. Changes in organizational structure, departmentation, goal setting, job redesign, appraisal systems, wages and salary based on performance are major impediments in implementation of MBO.

3. **Lack of training:** Systematic training is required in the organization for disseminating the concept and philosophy of MBO. People should be apprised as to why the organization wants to implement the concept. There is a general lack of training on the part of supervisors in implementing the programme. Training in MBO concepts, skills, attitude change is necessary for it to be successful. Lack of training may have adverse effect on employee morale and initiative.

4. **Rigidity:** Since goals are set for short-term of six-month to one year, the superior may not modify them in between for fear of resistance by the subordinates. Need for revision of goals therefore be handled skillfully by the manager.

5. **Follow up:** Once the MBO programme is accepted to be implemented, a ruthless follow up at each level is generally absent. It has an adverse effect on employee productivity. In such situation neither old programme is implemented nor new (MBO) programme is effective. An utter confusion at various levels prevails that is detrimental to growth.

6. **Time and cost effectiveness:** MBO is time consuming setting up of objective, feasibility of subordinate's willingness to implement, laying down of standards; evaluation of performance and its appraisal is time consuming. It requires great deal of analysis for which executives do not have adequate patience and sufficient time.

Implementation: For successful implementation of MBO, the following guidelines should be followed:

(*a*) **Top management support:** Effective participation of top management to this programme is essential for its implementation. If the top management adopts MBO and follows it in their day-to-day functioning it is bound to have salutary effect on subordinates.

(*b*) **Goal setting:** Goals have to be measurable. Subordinates and superiors should set goals jointly. Face-to-face communication and free flow of information is necessary. Managers should be in full known of individual/ group capabilities, availability of resources, organizational/departmental goals and based on this input individual goals should be set. Review of goal achievement if considered necessary should be carried out.

(*c*) **Decentralization:** The subordinates who have accepted challenging assignments through discussion with superiors must be given adequate authority to accomplish their goals. A greater degree of delegation of authority is required for the success of MBO concept in an organization. It is "delegation" that is feared by seniors as they perceive loss of control and power. Decentralization of authority will facilitate accomplishment of subordinate goals. Ineffective delegation of authority may lead to non-compliance of individual and organizational objectives leading to failure of MBO philosophy and resultant lack of growth.

(*d*) **Education about MBO:** As stated earlier the organizational members must be adequately educated in the philosophy of MBO. Before implementing MBO philosophy, an organization should clearly define the purpose and objectives to be achieved. Set goals for the organization, down the ladder to the individual goals with timeframe in mind. Delegate authority. This is possible when everybody in the organization is aware of MBO philosophy in details. A consultant may also be invited to educate employees. A special attention should be paid to executive's training as they are the people who will actually implement MBO.

(*e*) **Integration:** MBO programme cannot succeed in isolation. It should be integrated into existing systems, processes and organizational programmes. Due attention should be paid to human recourses planning and control, product planning and development, financial planning. R & D efforts and host of related issues. MBO concept is very wide and demands individual involvement, initiative, vision, hard work, dedication, skill, innovation and desire to do better every time. It should be interactive at each level of hierarchy.

SIX SIGMA

Six sigma is a statistical concept that measures a process in terms of defects. Achieving six sigma means organizational process having only 3.4 Defects Per Million Opportunities (DPMO). Sigma (the Greek letter) is a term that measures standard deviation. The objectives of six sigma is as under:

1. Eliminate errors to 3.4 per million.
2. Reduce cost.
3. Satisfaction to customers.
4. It is an organizational philosophy.
5. A symbol of quality.
6. A methodology.

Operating anything less that six sigma levels is not desirable because of higher probability of delivering defects. Figure 11.4 below indicates probability of defects of different sigma levels:

Sigma level	Defects per million opportunities
2	3,08537
3	66,807
4	6,210
5	233
6	3.4

Figure 11.4 Probability of defects of different sigma levels

Six sigma was first introduced as a quality goal of Motorola in 1980s. During that time technology was becoming very complex and the traditional ideas about defects were not acceptable. In 1989 Motorola announced a five-year goal—a defect rate of not more than 3.4 parts per million (six sigma).

Six Sigma Methodology

Six sigma methodology uses statistical tools to identify the vital few factors that matter most for improving the quality of processes. It consists of following five phases:

(*i*) Define the project, the goals, and the deliverables to customers (internal and external).

(*ii*) Measure the current performance of the process.

(*iii*) Analyze and determine the root cause of the defects.

(*iv*) Improve the process to eliminate defects.

(*v*) Control the performance.

It should be noted that six sigma methodologies is flexible. Air academy of USA uses the concept as PCOR (priorities, characterize, optimize and realize). This set of tools to assist employees to understand and improve upon critical processes.

Six sigma focus on the following concepts:

(*i*) Defect

(*ii*) Variation

(*iii*) Critical to quality (CTQ)

(*iv*) Process capability

(*v*) Design for six sigma.

(*a*) Six sigma focusses on defects and variation. It begins its work by identifying areas that are CTQ and concentrate on the attributes that are most important to customers. It analyzes the capability of the process and aims at stabilizing it by reducing or eliminating variations.

(*b*) Six sigma philosophy is about tying quality improvement directly to financial results.

(*c*) It goals are to link internal processes and systems management to end consumer requirements.

(*d*) It is scientific approach driven by data. The concept does not have place for opinion.

(*e*) It does not believe on management fads like "zero defects" or "magic pills".

(*f*) It relies on hard work, factual data and problem-solving approach.

(*g*) It aims at transformation of people and processes at all levels.

(*h*) Six sigma practitioners use computers extensively and statistical software to take advantage of speed and knowledge.

Culture

To achieve that level of quality it needs cultural changes in the organization. Six sigma approach is rigorous and demands full commitment from top management level down to bottom line employee. For six sigma to be successful, it requires a tolerance and a sense of urgency an understanding to promote profitability and customer satisfaction.

TOTAL QUALITY IN HUMAN RESOURCES MANAGEMENT

The concept of Total Quality Management (TQM) essentially revolves around the effective use of the available human resources. Hence emphasis on training and continuous personal improvement is essential. TQM means that an organization's culture is defined by and supports the constant quest for customer satisfaction. This involves continuous improvement of organizational processes, resulting in high quality products and services (Kreithner and Kinicki, 1995).[5]

Deming's Pioneering Work

Pioneering work in TQM was done in Japan through the efforts of W. Edward Deming. He stressed the need for all the individuals involved to work in a cohesive team, keeping in mind the fulfillment of the given objectives in time. Training in statistical process control techniques is necessary for all so that quality control of the product being manufactured is maintained in accordance with the standard laid down and corrective measures are taken while the product is being manufactured. In other words, TQM is not just a technique that can be turned on when quality improvement is required. TQM is rather a philosophy that requires active participation on part of both the management and the employees. TQM is an on-going process that is to be approached from the standpoint of continuous improvement by incremental stage. The ability to ensure the quality of a product or a service is, therefore, dependent on the quality of the working relationship between the human beings at the work place. It involves the dynamics of the behavioural processes. For the six best companies of Europe, TQM means continuously improving processes and performance by involving people so as to delight customers (Binney, 1992).[6]

Deming's framework of Total Quality Management is aimed at improvement in the quality of the product, reduction in the cost of production, gaining an increased market share, thus ensuring the prosperity of the business. Deming was fully aware of the potential of human beings and knew that TQM could be achieved only by changing the nature of the organization, stressing the importance of leadership and the need to reduce variations in the organizational processes. Deming proposed 14 principles of TQM:

1. Create consistency of objectives and plans.
2. Adopt a new philosophy of quality.
3. Cease dependence on mass inspections.
4. End the practice of choosing supplies based solely on price.
5. Improve the system constantly and continuously.
6. Institute training on-the-job.
7. Strengthen leadership.
8. Drive out fear.
9. Breakdown barriers between departments and units.
10. Stop requesting improved productivity.

11. Eliminate work standards that prescribe numerical quotas and quality standards.
12. Remove barriers to pride in workmanship.
13. Institute vigorous education and self-improvement programmes.
14. Put everyday in the company to work to accomplish the transition to total quality.

(Shani and Lau, 1996), TQM is an approach that fosters quality leadership, quality production and full utilization of organizational resources. It can transform an organization's culture.

Based on the above 14 points, Deming coined the following four practical policies of TQM :

1. Do it right the first time so as to eliminate costly rework.
2. Listen to and learn from customers and employees.
3. Make continuous improvement an everyday matter.
4. Build teamwork, trust and mutual respect.

Though Deming's Total Quality Management revolved around ensuring quality products and services, he nevertheless paid full attention to developing individuals and the organizational culture. This is evident from the fact that of the 14 factors he enumerated, ten pertain to the human beings in the organization that is involved in providing quality products and services. He laid stress on training and development of subordinates, which he believed, was the key for Total Quality Management, as it relates to the improvement of the human resources. Removing barriers to pride in workmanship and improvement of various systems in the organization were other humans research suggestion given by him.

Juran's Framework of TQM

Joseph Juran, an electrical engineer was Deming's collaborator in Japan. He suggested ten principals of TQM.

1. Build awareness of the need to improve.
2. Set goals for improvement.
3. Organize so as to reach the goals.
4. Provide training.
5. Conduct projects to solve problems.
6. Report progress.
7. Give recognition.
8. Communicate results.
9. Keep score of progress achieved.
10. Maintain the momentum by making annual improvement part of the regular.

    System and process of the company: Juran too laid stress on the human resources of an organization. He firmly believed that human resource development by various techniques could help bring about Total Quality Management in a company. Selection and maintenance of personnel is not the important pre-requisite for any organization. What is important is that all personnel should keep the company's objectives as the focus of all their activities and identify ways to accomplish them. Further, the objectives or goals for each department or unit and all resources including the personnel should be deployed for their attainment. Efforts to improve human performance should be taken up as an on-going process.

Training and development, therefore, merits the serious attention of the management. Training must be progressive in nature, realistic and preferably done on the job to be of real value. Freedom of action should be encouraged among the trainees and the bogey of zero defects should not be flauted during training. The trainer should encourage discussion and full participation in a free environment, so that contributions from all the participants enrich the contents of training. Once the stage of tutorial discussion is over, the inputs should be tried out by subjecting the trainees to various exercises and later to practical cases. Their reactions should be observed and corrected by the facilitator. No compromise should be allowed. Those found fit should be allowed to go up. Psychological testing, especially of managers, during the recruitment stage is recommended. It should be the endeavours of each head of unit to ensure that all employees are trained in such a way that they are capable of undertaking jobs one step above the existing one, without losing time and without any additional efforts. This will ensure higher performance and job satisfaction for each individual.

Steps must be taken to relate performance to recognition. Recognition fosters job satisfaction and promotes a sense of belonging in the organization one is serving.

Juran's teachings emphasize the idea of managing for quality and getting it "right the first time", rather than inspecting things into finished products (Thiagrarjan and Zairi, 1977).[7]

Philip B Crosby's Approach

If Deming and Juran are credited with jump starting the quality movement in Japan, Crosby can be credited with the quality awakening in the United States through his 1979 bestseller.

Quality is free: The art of making quality certain: Croby's approach to quality is based on management commitment to quality goals, prevention of defects and respect for employees and their efforts. Crosby advocates zero defects as the quality performance standard for everyone in the organization. This calls for a change in the culture of the organization.

Crosby lists four new essentials of quality management, which he calls "the absolutes".

1. Quality is defined as conformance to requirements.
2. Quality is achieved by prevention not by appraisal.
3. The quality performance standard is zero defects.
4. The cost of lack of quality is measured by the price of non-conformance.

The key points which are derived from the absolutes are: The need to understand customer requirements; a management commitment to satisfying the customer; communicating customer requirements to the workforce; training the workforce to produce to customer requirements; prevention of errors by a proper understanding of the process involved in producing products and services;

doing things right the first time as a management performance standard; creating an enabling environment to achieve such standards; and measuring and publicizing the cost of rejects, reworks and waste. Crosby talks about the three stages in the evolution of a total quality culture: first, the conviction that quality is an asset; next a commitment to implement quality as a way of life; and finally, the conversion of the entire organization to this way of life.

Leadership

The top management is the main driver of TQM (Zairi, 1992).[8] Therefore, the most important factor in TQM is leadership. What is expected of a leader is first to know his subordinates, their social background, their financial status, the number of their dependents, and the level of their dependency on the employee. This will enable a leader to judge what job to assign to each individual and how much to expect from him. Secondly the leader must be professionally competent, so that subordinates can look up to him as a person who has solutions to the problems they face. He should display an ability to adjust to changing situations and to different people. A leader should be able to work effectively in adverse circumstances and not show signs of creaking up. He should display professional honesty and be known for integrity. This is essential to obtain the willing obedience of subordinates and to accomplish his mission. Hence a leader should adopt a code of conduct for him and for the organization.

People have been concerned about the nature of leadership, so as to identify the difference between leaders and non-leaders, and between successful and unsuccessful leaders. Research suggests the six most important characteristics that a leader should possesses are:

(*i*) A high level of personal drive.

(*ii*) A desire to lead.

(*iii*) Personal integrity.

(*iv*) Self-confidence.

(*v*) Analytical ability.

(*vi*) Knowledge of the job and of the organization.

Apart from these factors, charisma, creativity and flexibility are highly desirable qualities in a leader. Finally successful leadership depends more on appropriate behaviour skills and action and less on personal traits. The traits only provide the latent potential and the behaviour is the successful release and expression of this potential. Leadership of this kind is indispensable to build up an organizational culture suitable for Total Quality Management.

Appraisal and Recognition

Performance appraisal has assumed great significance. It is the measure of the effectiveness of an individual, a barometer for furtherance of one's career. An individual's performance must measure up to the objectives assigned to him. He must accomplish his job at least in the given time, since time management is a key factor in any job. The attainment of quality standards is a necessary element in effective performance appraisal. Besides a person displaying innovative ideas should be recognized and facilities should be accorded to him to show his worth. Outstanding performance must be recognized in public. This has a strong motivational effect on all the employees. Remuneration must also be compatible with the job and merit should be the sole consideration for promotion. An award system should be introduced and fairly implemented. All these actions on the part of the leadership are bound to bring about an organizational culture conducive to Total Quality Management.

TQM in human resource management should be looked upon as a central company police. It should originate at the highest level and percolate down to last person doing his job. It should be treated as a movement. However, this is possible only when autonomy is accorded to leaders at various levels in the performance of their jobs. Mutual trust and respect for each other's ideas is most helpful. If Total Quality Management is undertaken in an organization, then, reengineering and quality control at various stages becomes outdated as all these factors are at the very core of the TQM concept.

Organization itself can be a sub-system of even larger system like society and society a sub-system of environmental system. Since the entire sub-systems/systems they are interdependent and must function with great precision and coordination. Each of the system must contribute positively as they are influenced and get influenced by other sub-systems/systems. What in effect emerges as an outcome of this interaction is called emergent system.

The emergent systems remain valid and operative as long as these are no change in the environment. Once there are changes in environment factors like technology, marketing variables, social changes etc., the emergent system take a new form. It is a continuous process therefore we say change is a constant phenomenon.

RE-ENGINEERING

Michael Hammer has coined the concept of re-engineering. Re-engineering is the fundamental rethinking and radical redesign of business processes to achieve dramatic improvements in critical, contemporary measures of performance such as cost, quality, service and speed. Re-engineering involves total redesign of the job. The process of re-engineering begins with a clean slate and a job is planned from beginning till the end. The objective of re-engineering is to improve efficiency, performance and overall productivity.

Steps in Re-engineering Process

Under the re-engineering process, employees are important element; they must understand the new way of carrying out the task.

1. **Mission:** The first step of re-engineering is managements rethinking of identifying the basic mission of the organization and deciding what business they are in and what they want to do. This facilitates the desired approach to carry out various processes to attain mission.
2. **Process:** Top management will play an active role in leading the process, thus ensuring the overall cooperation from the personnel.

3. **Creation of sense of urgency:** An atmosphere of urgency among the personnel regarding the need for re-engineering is necessary. This will ensure commitment of efforts to the case of re-engineering.
4. **Identification of customer needs:** Identification of customer needs for re-engineering efforts to be successful is essential. To know the customer needs and wants and then creating an organizational structure and team work providing it.
5. **Organizational support:** When needs have been identified an organizational support of various department is essential so that the processes and systems are modified for higher efficiency and increased productivity. Sight of the mission and fulfillment of customer needs is the focus.

There are number of examples of re-engineering efforts *i.e.,* conduct of online interviews, examinations and declaration of results of various technical institutes, introduction of E- business and transfer of money etc.

SYSTEMS APPROACH TO MANAGEMENT

Kast and Rosenzwing, [9] defines system as **"an organized, unitary whole composed of two or more interdependent parts, components, or sub-systems and delineated by identifiable boundaries from its environmental suprasystem."** From the above definition following aspects stands out.

(*i*) A system has several parts. These are dynamic in nature and therefore interact with each other.

(*ii*) The parts or systems are interdependent and interrelated.

(*iii*) The interdependence is required due to specialized nature of job, division of labour, sharing of limited resources and scheduling of activities.

(*iv*) Creating various departments carries out the work in the organizations, sub-departments and sections.

(*v*) Work is carried out by teams and groups who performed specialized task to accomplish overall organizational objective.

(*vi*) Change in one department affect the other departmental work.

A system is therefore composed of several sub-system and sub sub-system. Every system or sub-system has its own objective and various processes. Personnel employed to manage the system have to play their roles and work under a systems that are open. Katz and Kahn include importation of energy, throughput, output, phenomenon. Organization import resources, energy and information from environment, transform them into product and services and export it to the environment where society uses the same. Organizations do not export all that they produce but retain certain portion for its survival and growth. Organizations carry out modification and improvement based on performance feedback. Organization must also develop the ability to absorb the shocks and influences from the environment by developing inbuilt flexibility and responses.

In order to obtain clarity of this concept, take an example of soft drink bottling plant. The plant is a system. Filling plant, marketing of bottles, advertisement may be considered as sub-systems of bottling plant. Collection of empty bottles from the consumers, washing the bottles and making then ready for refilling may be considered as sub sub-system. All the systems, sub-system and sub sub-systems are interdependent and intertwined. Without the support of each of the sub-system and sub-sub-system, soft drink bottling plant cannot function effectively. If empty bottle collection sub sub-system fails, the bottle plant will come to a virtual halt. The plant draws raw material, technical know how, machinery, human resources, land and plant from the environment, transform it into soft drink bottles and export product and services back to the environment, retaining a part of it for survival and growth. A strong bottling plant has to receive shocks from other bottling plants in the form of price war, shortage of raw material and yet ensure survival and growth by using various business strategies. There can be several ways of classifying systems and one may follow any basis. Broadly speaking, Carzo and Yanouzas gave three kinds of sub-systems in an organization as a system-technical, social and power. The technical sub-system represents the formal part of organization and the remaining two, the non-formal one.

Technical Sub-system

When an organization is formed, there is only a technical sub-system, which is nothing but an entire formal organization. Organization is structured based on technology, product and market that one is required to serve. There is a given layout. Policies, rules and regulations are framed, span of management is created and authority and responsibilities is delegated based on need. Appropriate engineering, information technology and other considerations are laid down. The organization imports necessary resources from the environment, transform them and export the finished product/services to the environment. In the process, decision-making, communication control measures are implemented. Administrative system ensures balance in the organization so that no department becomes powerful while carrying out the job. Due care is taken about the status, norms, attitudes and behavioural pattern of employees. The whole arrangements are synchronized, all details are tied up and everybody knows as to what he has to do to achieve the organizational object. Therefore, this sub-system is called technical sub-system, which exists in all the organizations irrespective of product/services they produce.

Social Sub-system

Social sub-system provides social security and social satisfaction to its members. Enrolment of human resources is carried out to match the requirement of job. Individuals have varying degree of interests, capabilities attitudes, beliefs, likes, dislikes. Based on these they join group of like-minded employees to meet their social aspiration even by cutting across hierarchical barriers. It has often been noticed that employees join various social organizations groups, sports club to enhance their image in the work environment. The employees thus seek a power base to meet the social needs. The process thus leads to emergence of social groups who have their own objectives, structure and role to play. These groups develop a pattern of social norms, image in the society and subsequently exercise immense power in the society. Member of Rotary or a golf club are some of the examples.

Power Sub-system

Every job is important in the organization. People have to be not only dependent on others, but also interdependent so that the individual, group and ultimately the organizational objectives are met in given time. Specialization has become an important aspect in organization. Individuals display power behaviour based on the ability, skill, importance of their job, the critical appointment they hold and lastly the proximity to the decision-making authority. Some people have more influence areas than others while those who do not care for organizational norms engage themselves in politic king and play opportunistic games. Power sub-system takes its firm root based on personality traits, dominant nature, relationship with superiors, ability to influence others, the success story and the like. Therefore, the power-holders enjoy extra privileges, status and turn the situation in their own interest.

Technical, social and power sub-systems do not function independently there is an overlap. In fact, they are intertwined to a great extent. Individual behaviour is displayed and guided by these sub-systems. On occasions individual may behave in such a way that it is different to make distinction between various sub-systems. These sub-systems are a part of larger system say organization as system. Organization itself can be a sub-system of even larger system like society and society a sub-system of environmental system. Since the entire sub-systems/systems are interdependent and must function with great precision and coordination. Each of the system must contribute positively as they are influenced and get influenced by other sub-systems/systems. What in effect emerges as an outcome of this interaction is called emergent system?

The emergent systems remain valid and operative as long as these are no change in the environment. Once there are changes in environment factors like technology, marketing variables, social changes etc., the emergent system take a new form. It is a continuous process and therefore we say change is a constant phenomenon.

BENCHMARKING TO IMPROVE COMPETITIVE PERFORMANCE

Benchmarking is the art of learning from companies that perform certain tasks better than other companies. There can be as much as a ten fold difference between the quality, speed, and cost performance of a world-class company and an average company. The aim of benchmarking is to copy or improve on "best practices", either within an industry or across industries. Benchmarking involves seven steps:

1. Determine which functions to benchmark.
2. Identify the key performance variables to measure.
3. Identify the best-in-class companies.
4. Measure performance of best-in-class companies.
5. Measure the company's performance.
6. Specify programmes and actions to close the gap.
7. Implement and monitor results.

How can companies identify best practice companies? A good starting point is asking customers, suppliers, and distributors whom they rate as doing the best job.

(*Source*: Robert C. Camp, Benchmarking, the Search for Industry-Best Practices that Lead to Superior Performance (White Plains; NY: Quality Resources, 1989.)

SUMMARY

(*a*) Job redesign
(*b*) Quality of work-life
(*c*) Quality circles
(*d*) Management by objective
(*e*) Six sigma
(*f*) Total quality management
(*g*) Re-engineering
(*h*) Bench-marking.

Jobs should be redesigned on a regular basis. The objective being to create enthusiasm, interest, and ensuring development of skills of the employees. Quality of work-life plays an important role in the life of the employees. The layout of the work place, availability of tools, literature, advice of seniors and the total work environment must be conducive to higher productivity leading to organizational effectiveness. Due to advancement of technology and the multiplicity of skills involved, the jobs are being done in groups. It lends itself to greater autonomy and freedom of action with particular reference to sequencing the jobs on the part of employees. It gives them the sense of greater job satisfaction and the employees feel that they are doing a productive work. Management by objective is a concept that has not succeeded in India because of non-involvement of the management people, and due to the fear of loosing control over the events. MBO basically deals with selection of jobs by workers, setting up of objectives for themselves, undertaking the job as per the schedule, carrying out self-evaluation and resultant modification. This involves self-appraisal, empowerment and autonomy in work culture. Six sigma philosophy is about tying quality improvement directly to financial results.It relies on hard work, factual data and problem-solving approach. It aims at transformation of people and processes at all levels. Six sigma practitioners use computers extensively and statistical software to take advantage of speed and knowledge. Six sigma methodology uses statistical tools to identify the vital few factors that matter most for improving the quality of processes. Michael Hammer has coined the concept of re-engineering. Re-engineering is the fundamental rethinking and radical redesign of business processes to achieve dramatic improvements in critical, contemporary measures of performance, such as cost, quality, service and speed. Re-engineering involves total redesign of the job. A system is composed of several sub system and sub sub-system. Every system or sub-system has its own objective, and have various processes. Personnel employed to manage the system have to play their roles and work under a systems that are open. It includes importation of energy, throughput, and output, phenomenon. Organization imports resources, energy and information from environment, transform them into product and services and export it to the environment where society uses the same. Organizations do not export all that they produce but retain certain portion for its survival and growth. OD heavily depends on these processes. It is important for organizations to achieve highest efficiency to be competitive.

BIBLIOGRAPHY

1. Harold Koonz, Cyril O'Donnell, and Heinz Weihrich, *Management*, Tokyo: McGraw-Hills International, 1992.
2. Ordiorne, Geroge S., *Management by Objectives*, Pitman, New York, 1965, p. 26.
3. S.K. Chakravarty, *Management by Objectives*, New Delhi, MacMillan, 1976, p. 5.
4. Chabra, T.N., *Principles and Practice of Management*, Dhanpat Rai & Co. (P) Ltd., New Delhi, Sixth Edition, 1999.
5. Kreither Robert and Angelo Kinicki (1995), *"Organisational Behaviour"*, Third Edition, Chicago; Irwin.
6. Binney George (1992), *"Making Quality Work"*, Lessons from Europe's Leading Companies. London: The Economist Intelligence Unit.
7. Thiagrajan, T. and Zairi, M. (1997), "*Understanding the Fundamentals of TQM in Productivity"*. 3 (1), pp. 87–102.
8. Zairi M. (1992), "*Managing User – Supplier Interactions",* Management of R & D Activity in Management Decision, 30.
9. Kast, F.E. and J.E. Rosenzwing, "*Organisation and Management",* McGraw-Hill, New York, 1979.)

CASE STUDY
VOLTAS LIMITED

From being the top player in the branded air-conditioner market in India, with a market share ranging between 30 and 40 per cent in 1992–93, Voltas Limited became a relatively minor player by 2000–01 with about a 7 per cent market share. The air-conditioner market of late has been growing at about 20 per cent. The company realized that to achieve higher volumes, prices needed to be lower. This, in turn, could only be achieved if they brought down the costs due to economies of scale. One of the first initiatives dealt with focussing on the household air-conditioning market (the retail segment), revamping the product range and improving the technology. For this purpose, the company, based on a manufacturing joint venture with a leading room air-conditioning company in the U.S. called Fedders International, launched a series of technologically improved models catering to different market segments. Relocating the manufacturing plant to get tax shield, globally sourcing the components, and improving the manufacturing processes helped in reducing costs significantly. Voltas Limited invested in IT solutions to make the backend robust. In addition, the service infrastructure was strengthened to include over 2,000 service personnel equipped with fully loaded toolkits, mobile phones, mobiles vans, scooters, and other support facilities. The company also revamped its distribution systems; non-performing dealers were weeded out, new dealers and distributors were appointed to improve the reach, new standards for sales and service were set, and training and development inputs were provided to channel partners. Brand communication also underwent a change with new themes for communicating with the target audience. The brand now spots a new tagline—"India ka dil, India ka AC". These initiatives seem to have borne fruit– 'Voltas' market share improved from a low 7 per cent to a healthy 16 per cent in about 4 years.

CHAPTER 12

Training and Development Interventions

CHAPTER PLAN

- *Introduction*
- *T-group Training*
- *Behaviour Modeling*
- *Coaching and Mentoring*
- *Instrumented Training*
- *Career Anchors*
- *Summary*
- *Text Questions*
- *Case Study:*
  1. *Training Skill Sets*
  2. *Succession Planning—Keeping the Seat Warm*

INTRODUCTION

Training and development is a continuous process. It is the responsibility of every individual to ensure that his subordinates are professionally sound, technically expert and possess adequate skills of a job for which they have been employed. HR manager is responsible to organize training of all the employees every year so that the quality of human skills is maintained. It has now become mandatory to ensure professional excellence every year so that the quality of human skills is improved in globalised environment. Training and development is a HR function, all organizations have a schedule worked out for it. When we talk about training and development from OD angle, what we are doing is to modify individual behaviour and implement change of a permanent nature. OD interventions diagnose the cause, select appropriate intervention and implement it till desired results are achieved. It could be repetitive in nature. Its base is to understand human behaviour and modify various organizational processes for desired results. In this chapter, we are not discussing conventional training, development training, modules like on the job training; classroom training, seminars; workshops conferences etc. We are trying to explain certain concepts for individual and group behaviour modifications.

T-GROUP TRAINING

Kurt Lewin, Kenneth Benne, Leland Bradford and Ronald Lippitt have pioneered T-group (T for training) in the year 1946. It was an outcome of laboratory training exercises that was practiced in Britain. Laboratory training was essentially an unstructured small group exercising in which participants learn from their own experience interacting with other members of the group. It is basically a group dynamics experience. T-group as it aims at developing individuals skills that unfolds OD efforts for personal growth and development. At team levels it is more diagnostic, issue oriented, problem-solving and has an organizational focus. T-group is generally conducted for a group of 10 to 12 people under a professional trainer who may be called a facilitator who acts as a catalyst for the period of few days to couple of weeks. Group member in a particular situation given by the trainer interact with each other. During the process large volume of data is collected. The data relates to various actions, reactions, interactions and feelings displayed by various members. The main learning relates to the group experience. The programme may cover various topics like communication skills, interpersonal relations, personality, theories and group dynamics.

In an early work, Benne, Bradford, and Ronald Lippitt have outlined the following goals for T-group:

1. Increased awareness of and sensitivity to emotional reactions of participants.
2. Ability to perceive and to learn from the consequences of individual reaction and also learning from the others' behaviours. Utilizing feedback to modify own behaviour.
3. Development and clarification of values in line with democratic and scientific approach to decisions and actions.
4. Development of concepts and theoretical insights that will serve as tools in linking personal values, goals, and intentions to actions. Inner value etc. and its linkage with the situation is an important contribution of T-group training. Laboratory programmes normally focus on the development of behavioural skills to support better integration of intentions and actions.
5. All laboratory programmers foster the achievement of behavioural effectiveness in transactions with ones environment. Learning—the learning of concepts, the setting of goals, the clarification of values, and even the achievement of valid insight into self, are at sometimes far ahead of the development of the performance skills necessary to expression in actual social transactions.

The T-group can give individuals the basic skills necessary to work effectively in the organization. T-group is a powerful learning laboratory where individuals gain insights into the meaning and consequences of their own behaviour, the meaning and consequences of other's behaviours, and the dynamics and process of group behaviour. These insights are coopted with growth of skills in diagnosing and taking more effective interpersonal and group action (French & Bell). Mentoring, coaching, counseling, and consulting skills can be enhanced significantly by T-group experiences. In the T-group setting, people typically learn to listen more carefully to pay more attention to emotional content and feedback.

BEHAVIOUR MODELING

Behaviour modeling is a social learning theory based on the modeled behaviour that is observed by the client group. The process is as under:

Step 1: The facilitator announces problem situation. A brief discussion is later undertaken. For example, correcting absenteeism.

Step 2: Videotape is shown to the group. This video programme of identical situation is prepared in advance as training material.

Step 3: Trainer discusses the behaviour skills displayed in the videotape.

Step 4: Individual carries out role-play by depicting the present situation (the situation mentioned in step 1).

Step 5: Feedback from the trainer and the other group members.

Step 6: All participants role-play the situation.

Step 7: These skills are practiced in real situations in the coming weeks.

Step 8: Feedback is given in the next session. In case improvement is required an additional practice in role-playing is given before taking a fresh problem.

COACHING AND MENTORING

Coaching is generally carried out by immediate superior online and is related to job performance. Coaching is related to job contents and various processes. In production unit it is related to the product, its features and quality. In-service organisation, it may be related to taking care of customer, his needs and providing him highest possible satisfaction. Mentoring is a broader term and focusses on general career and personal development. Immediate superior does not fill the role of a mentor. It is filled by someone other than the immediate superior who is comparatively senior in rank and has enough experience in the field of OD. Mentoring is conducted individually on one-to-one basis or in a small group of four to six people. Various topics that a mentor can undertake are effective communication skills, leadership styles, good listening as an approach to learning and various aspects of behaviour modification. Coaching and mentoring skills are of a great importance for an effective teamwork. Various team members can also undertake mentoring mutually.

INSTRUMENTED TRAINING

OD practitioner extensively uses instruments in various organisations to implement OD strategies. Self-diagnosis surveys are interesting and useful in instrumented training field. Individuals would like to know more about themselves. The knowledge adds to self-awareness. If there is seemingly conflict among team members, it is related to various organisation processes like delegation of authority, empowering employees or leadership style used by the leader and even the level of preparedness of the team members to accept change. Various instruments are available, say to judge the level of delegation and freedom of work employees enjoy. Leader can apply the instrument and can judge for himself the style of leadership and required style. The gap can be breached by behaviour modification to the style of leadership on the part of the leader. This is only possible once the instruments are applied. Advantages of using self-diagnostic instruments are probably greater in the context of training programmes involving strangers or individuals from different organizations.

CAREER ANCHORS (The Text is Based on the Work of Edgar S. Schein)

A person's career anchor is his self-concept of (1) self-perceived talent and abilities, (2) basic values, and most important, (3) the evolved sense of motives and needs as they pertain to career. Career anchors only evolve as one gains occupational and life experience. However, once the self-concept has been formed, it functions as a stabilizing force, hence the metaphor of "anchor," and can be thought of as the values and motives that the person will not give up if forced to make a choice. Most of us are not aware of our career anchors until we are forced to make choices pertaining to self-deployment, family, or career. Yet it is important to become aware of our anchors so that we can choose wisely when choices have to be made.

The self-concept around which the career anchors are formed are as under:

1. Autonomy/independence
2. Security/stability
3. Technical-functional competence
4. General managerial competence
5. Entrepreneurial creativity.
6. Service or dedication to a cause*
7. Pure challenge*
8. Life style*.

First 5 anchors were studied in 1970's (* These were added later.). As careers and lives evolved most people discover that one of the eight categories is **the anchor**, the thing the person will not give up, but most careers also permit the fulfilling of several of the needs that underlie different anchors. For most of the 1970's and 1980's when career anchor were applied, the self-analysis exercise obtained fairly consistent results with roughly 25 per cent of population anchored in "general management," another 25 per cent" in technical/functional competence," 10 per cent each in "autonomy" and "security" and the rest spread across the remaining anchors (Schein).

Security/Stability

Individuals anchored in security/stability experience the most severe problems because of the shift in organizational policies from guaranteeing "employment security" to touting "employability security." This shift implies that only the career occupant can really expect of an organization is the opportunity to learn and gain experience, which presumably makes him more employable in the base of security and stability has to shift from independence on the organization to dependence on oneself. Self-reliance and self-management are becoming dominant requirements for the future career management. Therefore, individuals who oriented themselves initially to finding a good employer and staying with that employer for the duration of their careers have to develop a new way of thinking about themselves and locate new external or internal structures on which to become dependent. Security is no more an anchor; it is self-employability that will count. Down sizing and flattening of organization is an example for people not to be complacent. Similarly, the government bureaucracy as a lifetime employer can no longer be relied upon as pressures mount towards decentralization, reducing the size of the government, and making government more efficient. It is not at all clear where the security anchored person of today can find his or her niche.

Autonomy/Independence

Individuals anchored in autonomy find the occupational world an easier place to navigate. The autonomy anchor is aligned, at least at the present, with most organizational policies of promising only employability. The self-reliance that may be needed in the future is already part of the psychological make up of this group of people. They may well become the role models for future career incumbents. In tracking our various populations it is also evident that for many people, as they age, their autonomy needs *increases,* leading to fantasies of doing something of their own once they retire from the main stream thus reducing their dependency on a particular organization.

What is not clear is whether the ability to be autonomous depends upon a baseline of security that we take for granted. The retiree with a good pension can afford to think creatively about the next steps, but the laid off mid-life worker or manager without adequate life savings or well endowed retirement programme may continue to seek secure positions even though his anchor is autonomy.

Technical/Functional Competence

People in the organization are becoming self-conscious and want to get into management to climb the ladder. The world will always need craftsman and experts in specific functions and, as technological complexity increases, the need for technical experts will increase. But, as technologies in all the functions themselves change more and more rapidly, experts will become obsolete more and more rapidly. In other words, to remain technically/functionally competent will require constant updating and relearning in an organizational world that will not bear the costs in terms of money and time for this updating process. Individuals will have to plan their career or alternatively government and organizations will jointly share the responsibility of training the younger employees. Old employees may not be preferred by the organization, as they would not be able to keep pace with the speed of change of technology. It is very easy to say that the future organizations will be knowledge based. But it is equally difficult as to how the organizations will be able design knowledge based jobs in rapidly changing environment.

General Managerial Competence

This anchor category continues to attract its share of career occupants who understands what is really involved. The position attracts high status. The technically/functionally anchored person recognizes that the skill set and emotional make up that is needed for such jobs is fundamentally different. Organizations are changing their structure to more flat organizations. The skill of general management *i.e.,* analytical, interpersonal and emotional competence will therefore be needed at lower and lower levels. Team managers, project managers, and programme managers will have to have general management and leadership skills above and beyond their technical understanding of the task at hand. General management, like leadership, may cease to be a role or a position, and become more of a process skill that will be needed in all kinds of roles and positions. The career occupant with general management anchor will be forced to examine once again what he is really after power, glory, responsibility, accomplishment of a task, the ability to build and manage a team, or various combinations of these.

Entrepreneurial Creativity

More and more people are drawn to the idea that they can develop their own business and, as the world becomes more dynamic and complex, the opportunities for individuals with this anchor will increase dramatically. The need for new products and services deriving from information technology, biotechnology, and yet unknown new technologies will continue to increase. The increasing mobility that is available in the world today will make it more feasible for the entrepreneur to go to whatever part of the world is most hospitable to his ideas. The dynamic complexity of industry will put a premium on creativity, and it is creativity that is at core of this anchor.

Service/Dedication to a Cause

The number of people showing up with this anchor is increasing. More and more young people as well as mid-life career occupants report that they are feeling the need only to main an adequate income, but to do something meaningful in a larger context. As the world becomes more conscious of large-scale problems such as the environment, the growing gap between the developed and underdeveloped world, the problems of race and religion, product safety, privacy, overpopulation and social responsibility issues around health and welfare, new kinds of organizations and careers are being created to address the new issues. The information technology explosion has made all the world's problems highly visible and thus drawn the attention of the more service oriented. The service anchor combined with the entrepreneurial anchor is already creating new organizations devoted to recycling, to privatizing health care and welfare, to managing the environmental problems through the products that use less energy, to waste management and so on. Such organizations will, in turn, absorb a lot of the technologically unemployed as well as attracting some of the best and brightest of the generations.

Pure Challenge

There has always been a small group who defined their career in terms of overcoming impossible odds, solving the unsolved problems, and winning out over one's competitors. There will not be a shortage of challenges to be met, so long as this group is willing to become active learners as well since the nature of these challenges will itself evolve rapidly with technological change.

In summary, what we have seen so far is that each of the anchor categories still attracts a set of people, but that the working out of a given anchor can become problematic as the world of work and organizational structure become more turbulent. The main effect is that people will have to become more self-reliant and figure out where their particular anchor best fits into the emerging occupational structure. The ability to analyze oneself as well as the ability to figure out what kind of job is available and how that job will evolve become crucial skills.

Life Style

Initially job security anchor was broken into two parts: (1) economic security and (2) geographic stability. Most people in this anchor group thought of economic security but a few talked of stabilizing their life pattern by settling into a given region and refusing to be moved by their company every few years. In the subsequent studies it became evident that these two components aιe really two different anchors. There are still who were in dual career situations and who therefore defined their career as being part of a larger "life system". They had to integrate two career and two sets of personal and family concerns into a coherent overall pattern, best described as a particular life style. Employees preferred to choose the jobs that provided them the life style of their own. The trend towards autonomy and life style is a welcome change and healthy development around the world. The situation today is becoming more organization oriented, organizations owe less and less to their employees. Organizational positions and advancement is increasingly defined in terms of what one knows and what skills one possesses and based less and less on seniority or the loyalty. They are becoming less paternalistic. More and more employees are therefore equipping themselves in dual career paths to suit their life style.

SUMMARY

Kurt Lewin, Kenneth Benne, Leland Bradford and Ronald Lippitt have pioneered T-group (T for training) in the year 1946. It was an outcome of laboratory training exercises that was practiced in Britain. Following goals are achieved by conducting T-group training:

1. Increased awareness of and sensitivity to emotional reactions of participants.
2. Ability to perceive and to learn development and clarification of values.

3. Development of concepts and theoretical insights.
4. All laboratory programmers foster the achievement of behavioural effectiveness in transactions with ones environment.

Behaviour modeling is carried out in eight different steps.

Coaching and mentoring, instrumented training, and career anchors are other methods of undertaking development of employees.

Career Anchors are evolved as one gains life and occupational experience. However, once the self-concept has been formed, it functions as a stabiliging force, hence the term "anchor". Edgar Schein has identified eight anchors. These are as follows:

- Autonomy/independence
- Security Stability
- Technical/functional competence
- General management
- Entrepreneurial creativity
- Service
- Challenge
- Life style.

TEXT QUESTIONS

1. Explain T-group training model.
2. Write short notes on the following:
   (*a*) Coaching and mentoring.
   (*b*) Instrumented training.
3. Explain the concept of Career Anchor as recommended by Edgar S. Schein. What is your Career anchor? Discuss.

CASE STUDY 1
TRAINING SKILL SETS

JS Capital Management Pvt. Ltd. believes that today a major constraint in industry is the lack of quality manpower. Hence after hiring people they have to train them to suit their needs. Since the company has a linear-staffed organization, this kind of HR exercise does not get the due time and attention that it usually demands. One major shortcoming faced at the lower level is the rapid spread of the concept of 'learning by doing' attitude that can actually cost investor heavily.

For such impediments JS Capital ensures intensive employee training modules designed to suit their requirements. They send their people to institutes like the London School of Economics, Harvard Business School etc. to learn strategies related to the industry. Then, they conduct a number of in house training programmers. They also "throw them into the water" to investigate and evaluate their imbibed skills and talents. Employees of the company have to pass the certificate test, which is separate from the one, which the company has for its distributors.

Questions

1. Do you think such an extensive training is really necessary?
2. How can we determine the cost effectiveness of such programmers?
3. After making so much investment in human resource, if the employee leaves the organization, how will the loss be accounted for?

(Source: Gupta, Shashi K. and Joshi, Rosy; Human Resource Management, Kalyani Publishers, New Delhi, 2007).

CASE STUDY 2
SUCCESSION PLANNING-KEEPING THE SEAT WARM

We have all seen it happen. The company reins passing from one generation to the next. But if there is no heir apparent, organizational heads are groomed from within the organization after a hectic round of talent scouting. Times however, are changing and company owners are becoming more professional. These days even Chief Operating Officers (COOs) could be hired for a fixed tenure. This trend can be observed within industry, verticals and is often fuelled by the unprecedented growth in the entire industry. The trend is more prevalent in IT and management consultancy companies rather than in traditional brick and mortar companies. "Where a company has been growing at a steady pace it makes sense to hire from within. Rewarding deserving employees is very motivating for others. It also helps in retaining top management talent" informs the CEO of a prestigious Infotech company.

What works best in which situation is ultimately up to the company to decide. The important thing is that the decision should be communicated properly to all stakeholders. However, if you have someone who fits the bill internally, ethics demand that you give this person the first chance. Hiring externally must be considered as the last option. Good management practice favours internal growth.

According to Dr. C.S. Venkatratnam, Director, International Management Institute, "An exception can be made only when a company is diversifying into unrelated fields where there is a real crunch of in house talent. The other exception is when a company is doing so badly that it desperately needs external help from a person who can think out of the box and turn the company's sagging fortunes around."

In such a situation, a CEO will bring a fresh perspective. His lateral thinking and his ability to take objective decisions can propel the company towards a new growth path. Some attrition may result from external hiring but in certain circumstances, this is unavoidable. Eventually, it depends on the CEO as to how he responds to these challenges with a clear vision and knowledge of the best practices drawn from his rich and diverse experience. In such situations, the need of the hour is to set clear targets and give the new incumbent a free hand.

"An ideal succession plan is thus, based not on a "what if" scenario but on well designed future leadership plans. Anticipating organizational growth and keeping a pipeline of future talent ready are the best strategies to adopt in terms of succession planning. Organizations that prepare people for higher responsibilities on a regular basis do not have to go to the drawing board every time a problem raises its head. For them such events represent opportunities not threats."

Questions

1. "Promoting from within or brought from outside" which in you opinion is the best practice.
2. How suitable temps can be for an important position like that of a COO of a company?

(Source: Gupta, Shashi K. and Joshi, Rosy; Human Resource Management, Kalyani Publishers, New Delhi, 2007).

Chapter 13

Empowerment

CHAPTER PLAN

- *Introduction*
- *Definitions*
- *Factors Favourable for Empowerment*
- *Why Empowerment?*
- *Process of Empowerment*
- *Factors Contributing to Empowerment*
- *Redesigning Organizational Structure*
- *Team Based Work Environment*
- *Types of Empowerment*
- *Model of Empowerment*
- *Benefits of Empowerment*
- *Barriers of Empowerment*
- *Career-Life Planning*
- *Summary*
- *Text Questions*
- *Bibliography*
- *Case Study: People Power at Jet Airways*

INTRODUCTION

1. There is a growing concern about achieving excellence by the organizations. Various methods are being practiced so that higher job satisfaction and productivity is achieved. Most organizations are able to introduce latest technology and modern processes to achieve growth. Those organizations are likely to survive that has excellent, skilled, experienced and

dedicated manpower. To achieve this end, organizations should empower their employees in the turbulent times. Empowerment is an effective management tool to achieve maximum potential of employee. The old order of bureaucracy proposed by Max Weber is no more valid in the present times. To achieve greater degree of involvement and responsibility a process of empowerment is necessary. Empowerment is the process of passing authority and responsibility to individuals at lower levels in the organizational hierarchy to enhance feeling of self-efficacy and a sense of owing a job. Managers are encouraged to allow a high degree of workforce participation, group involvement and autonomy, and to develop self-managing work teams. These management styles are to empower employees and thereby to increase workplace environment, in turn, are intended to result in empowerments in work performance and good citizenship behaviours as well as quality of work life (Brief and Motouridlo, 1986; Cohen *et al.*, 1997). The degree to which empowerment, participation, autonomy to subordinates is accorded depends upon the judgment of the manager.

2. To achieve empowerment, managers must be sure that employees at the lowest hierarchical levels have the right mix of information (about process, quality, customer feedback and events), knowledge (of the work, the business and the total work system), power (to act and make decisions about the aspects of work) and rewards (tied to business results and growth in capability and contribution), to work autonomously or independently of management control and direction (Lawler, 1992; Lawler 1994; Lawler *et al.*, 1989).

DEFINITIONS

(*a*) **"Empowerment is a process of delegating authority to subordinates to shoulder additional responsibility based upon their ability, knowledge, experience and power to achieve autonomy, independence and quality of work-life for organizational effectiveness."**

(*b*) **"As a process which enhance their intrinsic work motivation by positively influencing impact, competence, meaningfulness and choice."**[1]

(*c*) Brown and Brown defines the process of empowerment as **"The reorientation of forces, values and beliefs, which determine human behaviour in organizations so that they support and liberate the individual rather than reduce their range of thought and action."**

FACTORS FAVOURABLE FOR EMPOWERMENT

1. **Technology:** Hi-tech tools are now facilitating manager to undertake larger volume of work. In financial sector, it will be seen that all executives function independently and take operational decisions. It has been possible because of fast track communication due to technological development.

2. **Customers:** Customers are deposing greater trust and faith in the employees who come in contact with them. The later have to take on the spot decisions relating product, its cost, after sales service and payment schedules etc. Organization therefore supports employees by delegating sufficient functional authority to the employees. Markets have become competitive and global enterprises are now adapting to flexible production systems. Products are now customized and variety models of one product are available. In such situation there is no alternative but to make subordinate take their decision within the overall policy of the organization that calls for empowerment.
3. **Organizational structure:** For greater effectiveness organization structure is becoming flatter. Targets and production quotas is the order of the day. Quality control is inbuilt in the organization culture. The workers possess greater knowledge, knowhow, and desire to participate in decision-making. To enable better organizational climate and to achieve greater efficiency, empowering employees is essential.
4. Lorenz (1992) described his vision on an empowering structure as follows:
   (*a*) Instead of series of levels, which command and control the one immediately beneath them, power and information in many issues must be delegated, decentralized and diffused.
   (*b*) Trust must be established among superiors, peers and subordinates.
   (*c*) Information should be shared as accessible through networking.
   (*d*) Fewer managers should be appointed with wider responsibilities. The span of empowerment of well above 20, in which the manager's role shifts from controller to coach and mentor (Drucker, 1989; Lorenz, 1993). [2]
5. **Organizational culture:** Empowerment is implementing a change that must be proactive in nature. Culture plays a vital role that recognizes the need to change autocracy into participation and cooperation. Structural changes do not matter and what matter in empowering employees is to understand dynamics of change, employee willingness and the rich culture the organization has.

WHY EMPOWERMENT?

1. Empowerment is considered necessary due to following reasons:
   (*a*) To stimulate commitment and innovation from the employees.
   (*b*) To achieve competitive advantage by producing goods and services that meet customer needs/requirements.
   (*c*) There is a need to organize enterprises around a flexible production system rather than around the criteria of mass production. Empowering employees best achieve this.
   (*d*) To implement change and stimulate decision-making from everyone where there is no precedence.
   (*e*) To promote entrepreneurship and higher degree of risk.

PROCESS OF EMPOWERMENT

1. Dobbs suggests that there are four prerequisites of empowering people. These are participation, innovation, access to information, and accountability. Empowering by multi-skilling giving people more authority and full responsibility from the inception to completion of the job. Empowerment is more than delegation. It is related to genuinely involving people in decision-making process. Randolph[3] believes that is not just "giving people the power to make decisions." He holds that they already have the power to make intelligent decisions to help the company operate more effectively. Thus, at its most practical level, ***he defines empowerment as recognizing and releasing into the organization the power, which the people already have in their wealth of useful knowledge and internal motivation.*** An empowering authority has to follow the process of empowerment as under:

Process of Empowerment

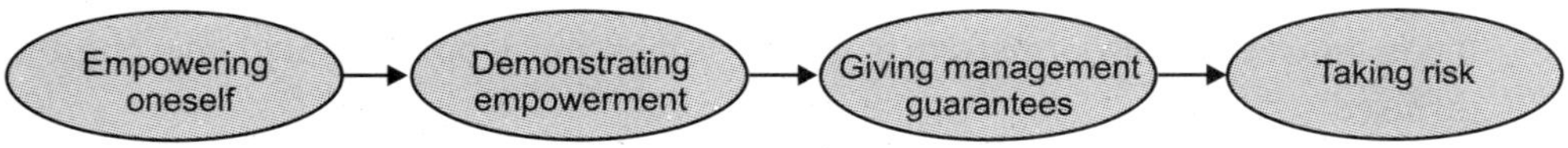

Figure: 13.1 Process of empowerment

Empowerment involves releasing the authority and making employees more authoritative and responsible in their work. It involves management commitment. Manager must feel more powerful and enlarge the scope of his functions. He must demonstrate to his subordinates the authority and power (of operation) that he possesses. It involves transforming the way of doing things from bureaucratic system into empowering system. It is a tough job as it involves transforming and leading people to feel empowered and function in that manner. It should be understood that management would require undertaking by the employees that the empowerment mission would lead to growth of the organization. The leaders in empowered environment are able to mobilise employee skills and produce goods and services at lowest cost, better quality and reduce process time.

FACTORS CONTRIBUTING TO EMPOWERMENT

1. Employees dedicate themselves to the organization. They want to be aware of the things going on in the organization. It is the responsibility of managers at various levels to keep their subordinates posted about the following aspects:
   (*a*) Goal to be achieved.
   (*b*) Long-term and short-term plans of the organization.
   (*c*) Financial position of the company.
   (*d*) New ventures.

(*e*) R & D facilities.

(*f*) Administrative changes.

(*g*) Feedback on performance.

(*h*) Transparent company polices.

(*i*) Reward policy.

(*j*) Promotional parameters.

2. It must be understood that informed employees take greater risk and additional responsibility. Awareness about financial positions leads employees to take steps to generate additional revenue. If the position of the company is critical, employees give fresh ideas for rejenovation. They develop a feeling of having an additional power that leads employees to be creative and generate innovation. It leads to building "trust" between the owner and the employees. The bogie of "no defect" is not good for growth-oriented organizations. Employees would learn from their mistakes. If mistakes were critcised, no one would venture to innovations. An empowering culture must be promoted at all cost.

3. Information should be shared at individual, department and organization levels. It must be allowed to spread as wild as possible. The mangers must guard the fear of loosing control over events. Goal must be challenging. Achievement of such goals should be rewarded. This will lead to empowering individuals leading to taking higher challenges. Sharing of information will kick start the process of empowerment? It is only the beginning.

REDESIGNING ORGANIZATIONAL STRUCTURE

1. The people generally resist change. In organizations, people are used to working effectively under the traditionally organized culture where there is hierarch and unity of command principle is implemented in letter and spirit. In such environment employee depend more on their superiors for advice and a culture of participative or supportive leadership prevails. This situation does not promote empowerment. Hence the structural changes are recommended. These changes involve the following:

(*a*) **Vision:** Vision statements are nothing but tall statement made by the organization. Vision statement has a meaning as they are broken down to the goals and objective of the department, group of people and that of the individual. At lower levels objectives must be realistic and measurable and linked with the vision of the company. Managers are supposed to work as guide, mentor and facilitator to guide, advice and develop and empowering partnership with the employees.

(*b*) **Decision-making:** Empowerment starts with the group decision-making. Empowerment is something larger than the authority of decision-making. Employees should be made party in decision-making process. They should feel that they have made decisions that would lead to implementation obligations. Bottom up approach should be adopted in this regard. It is clarified that strategic/tactical decision-making shall always rest with the management. Subordinates are required to make operational decisions within the domain of their work. For example scheduling of work, improvement in better customer care, making of sales calls etc. Subordinates are expected to take their own decision and implement the same.

(*c*) **Goal setting:** For empowerment to be more effective, individual should set his personal goal. Individual goals should give us departmental or group goals leading to organizational goals. This must be monitored as each level. Goals must be achievable, and contribute towards achieving organizational goals. Collaborative efforts are required in this process. Commitment of employees not only in goal setting but implementing and achieving the same is as important.

(*d*) **Performance appraisal/feedback:** Every individual desires to know about his performance. The managers should prepare appropriate self-appraisal format. In addition time-to-time feedback on performance shall be introduced. 360° performance has its own drawbacks as it keeps an employee under tension. This does promote liberty of action in performing the job. Performance appraisal should include the following:

(*i*) Performance planning.

(*ii*) Implementing revised plans/goals.

(*iii*) Focus on collaboration between managers and subordinates.

(*e*) **Leadership:** Empowerment cannot be left to chance. The transition of empowerment is a top-down phenomenon. Implementation of empowerment needs strong leaders who is dedicated and can show path to the employees, teach them new skills and clarify on different parameters of empowerment. The leader must be more of a task-oriented leader. He must state the basic parameters of empowerment and ensure its implementation. Bold actions, self-confidence, desire to self-growth, achievement orientation type of leadership is best suited for empowered organization.

(*f*) **Training and development:** Training and development plays a decisive role in installing the concept of empowerment. People have to be trained in the following concepts:

(*i*) Group decision-making.

(*ii*) Management of stress.

(*iii*) Management of conflict.

(*iv*) Negotiations.

(*v*) Skill development.

(*vi*) Development of technical competence.

(*vii*) Handling of redefined job boundaries, promotion of trust, attitude and behaviour modifications.

(*viii*) Introduction of modified culture. Mindset of the employees needs to be developed that align with the new (changed) way of implementing a task.

(*ix*) Managing teamwork.

(*x*) Functioning under collaborative work culture.

TEAM BASED WORK ENVIRONMENT

1. Various organizations are now pruning down their organizational structure and reducing tiers of operations, gradually leading to more flat organizational structure. This phenomenon has created a vacuum in middle management level, either this position has become redundant or lost its effectiveness on one hand and requirement of guidance, promotion of empowered culture, appraisal and measurement of accountability on the other. Work now is assigned to the team that involves implementation and feedback. These teams are accountable for the outcome. These self-managed teams take decisions about manpower requirements, source of employment, process of employment, work schedules, budgeting and other related decisions. Middle level managers play an important role in assisting the team leader and the team in the above areas.
2. Introduction of empowerment in an organization is a critical journey as it involves change from bureaucratic management style to participative management style. It involves introduction of development of skills, guidance and human behaviour modification. Hesitation on the part of management to part with delegation, decision-making and more authority to the employees on one hand and fear of success of changed synergy for managers on the other makes the journey more fearful. A strong and achievement oriented leader will be able to implement new strategy and lead the employees to new way of doing things. Banks have been able to implement the strategy of empowerment successfully. They are able to sell various financial products single handedly. It is with great satisfaction that one notes subordinate staff taking great financial decisions thus rendering excellent social service to the people. It is applicable to the insurance sector. For empowerment to be successful good personal policies is however a prerequisite.

TYPES OF EMPOWERMENT

Robert Quinn and Gretchen Spreitzer[4] found two vastly different views of empowerment:

(*a*) **Mechanistic view of empowerment:** It is a top-down delegation of decision-making with clear boundaries and strict accountability that increases managerial control.

(*b*) **Organic view of empowerment:** It is a bottom-up approach and is less controlling. They describe the organic view: "The other group of executives saw empowerment much differently. They believed that it was about risk-taking, growth, and change. Empowerment meant trusting people and tolerating their imperfections. The most important contrast between the two views involve the implicit but potentially volatile assumptions people make about trust and control." Authors believe the organic view, with its emphasis on risk-taking, personal initiative, and growth, is more useful perspective. But both views contain valid ideas. For example, the organic approach unleashes talent and energy in people that are best channeled by providing clear guidelines and boundaries. Quinn and Spreitzer concluded: "Empowering them, is not something that management does to employees but rather a mind-set that employees have about their roles in the organization."

MODEL OF EMPOWERMENT

Belasco believes that:

1. Only massive changes will suffice to keep organizations viable in the future.
2. People will not naturally embrace the needed changes. Is the key to getting people to want to participate in change
3. Empowerment is the key to getting people to want to participate in change. Belasco's four step model of empowerment is given in Figure 13.2 below:

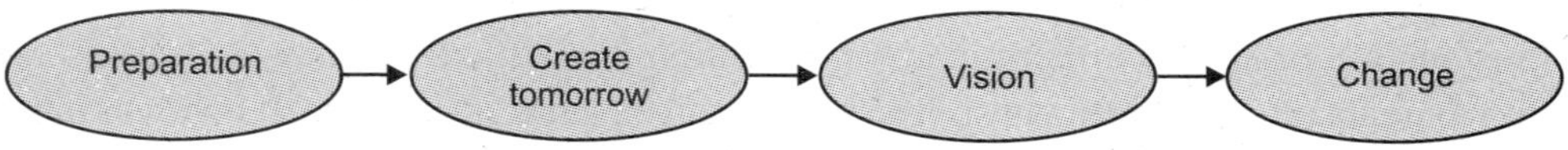

Figure 13.2 Model of empowerment

Developing a clear vision, devising a strategy to achieve the vision and unleashing the intelligence and energy of the workforce to accomplish the vision are what empowerment is all about[5].

BENEFITS OF EMPOWERMENT

1. Empowerment benefits the organization itself by creating an environment that encourages proactively problem-solving, accepting challenge, innovation, continuous improvement, optimum utilization of employees, a high degree of employee motivation and enhancement of business performance.
2. For employees, empowerment provides a sense of high self-esteem, high degree of involvement and participation, a learning environment opportunity for personal growth and development and greater sense of achievement. Replacing the 'fear and greed' hierarchy with network of empowered workers creates benefits like faster responses, loyal customers, high quality-lower costs, greater productivity and employee orientation (Carter, 2000).

BARRIERS OF EMPOWERMENT

1. The literature indicates that there are varied barriers to empowerment, which can hampers empowerment efforts in organizations. The barriers are as under:

(*a*) Incongruence between empowerments goal of inclusion and organizational culture.

(*b*) Low need for autonomy among people.

(*c*) Managerial fear related to distribution of power.

(*d*) Need for high power among managers.

2. It is suggested that the organizations must determine before hand the extent to which they have to apply empowerment by assessing its pros and cons. The suggestion is based on contingency approach to empowerment.
3. While management can create a context that is more empowering, employees must choose to be empowered. They must see themselves as having freedom and discretion; they must feel personally connected to the organization, confident of having an impact on the system in which they are embedded.

CAREER-LIFE PLANNING

Career-life planning is the process of choosing occupational, organizational, and career paths. There are several approaches to career-life planning. All of them use the idea of goal setting and achievement motivation to gain greater control over one's future career development.

Peter Drucker advocates that individuals take responsibility for managing their own future.[6] The broad intervention revolves around the following three factors. Namely (1) determining where you are now, (2) deciding where you want to go and (3) developing plans. Career-life planning can be carried out in a workshop (working in a pair-participant and consultant) and involves following steps:

Step 1: Preparation by the individual the list that includes the career goals. This may have a larger scope of inclusion of goals relating to professional, social, personal and environmental goals (List 1).

Step 2: Consultant in collaboration with the participant examines the list for its feasibility and accords priority to the goals mentioned therein.

Step 3: Each participant in this step indicates his past achievements or happenings including peak experiences and satisfactions (List 2).

Step 4: Consultant now compares both lists and identifies conflicting areas and incongruencies. Based on this observation practitioner now calls for the third list from the participant. This list is considered to be the final list for career life planning intervention.

Step 5: Participants in consultation prepares an action plan of how the goals set are to be achieved. The intervention is then implemented.

Career planning can provide employees with information that will enable them to make better career decisions. Career goals need to be redefined often due to change in individual's objectives and opportunities change over time. The result of OD intervention is indicative that individuals who were committed to both individual and organizational goals reported high job satisfaction. They felt more empowered than the other employees.

SUMMARY

1. Organization is likely to survive that has, skilled, experienced and dedicated manpower. To achieve this end, organizations should empower their employees in the turbulent times. Empowerment is an effective management tool to achieve maximum potential of employee. To achieve empowerment, managers must be sure that employees at the lowest hierarchical levels have the right mix of information.
2. "Empowerment is a process of delegating authority to subordinates to shoulder additional responsibility based upon their ability, knowledge, experience and power to achieve autonomy, independence and quality of work life for organizational effectiveness." Factors favourable for empowerment are technology, customers, organizational structure, vision, and organizational culture. Process of empowerment contains **empowering oneself, demonstrating empowerment, giving management guarantees,** and **risk taking.**
3. Redesigning organizational structure needs vision, decision-making, goal setting, performance appraisal, feedback and leadership. Training and development is an important factor for introducing empowerment. Team based work environment should be created in all the departments. Introduction of empowerment in an organization is a critical journey as it involves change from bureaucratic management style to participative management style. There are two types of empowerment as suggested by Robert Quinn and Gretchen Spreitzer. These are **Mechanistic View** of Empowerment and **Organic View** of empowerment. Authors believe the organic view, with its emphasis on risk-taking, personal initiative, and growth, is more useful perspective. But both views contain valid ideas. Organic approach unleashes talent and energy in people that are best channeled by providing clear guidelines and boundaries. Quinn and Spreitzer concluded: "Empowering people, is not something that management does to employees but rather a mind-set that employees have about their roles in the organization. Belasco has suggested four step model of empowerment, the steps involved are **preparation, create tomorrow, vision,** and **change.** Management must ensure that the factors causing resistance are handled carefully and that the efforts gone in for empowerment bear resultant growth and organization achieve effectiveness.

TEXT QUESTIONS

1. Explain the concept of empowerment.
2. Define empowerment.
3. Explain with the help of flow chart the process of empowerment.
4. What are various factors that contribute for successful empowerment?
5. Explain the model of empowerment as suggested by Quinn and Spreitzer.
6. Explain mechanistic and organic views of empowerment. Which view, in your opinion is better suited for empowering organizations?

BIBLIOGRAPHY

1. Thomas, K.W., Velthouse, B.A.: *Cognitive Elements of Empowerment*, Academy of Management Review 1990; 666–81.
2. Peter Drucker, 1989. (Full source not known)
3. Randolph, W.A., *Navigating the Journey to Empowerment.* Organisation Dynamics spring 1995, pp. 19–32.
4. Robert, E. Quinn and Gretchen, M. Spreitzer, *The Road to Empowerment*: Seven questions every leader should consider: Organizational Dynamics, 26, No. 2, 1997, pp. 37–49.
5. James, A. Belasco, *Teaching the Elephant to Dance:* The manager guide to empowering change, Plume Publishing, NY, 1990.
6. Peter, F. Drucker, *Managing Oneself*, Harvard Business Review, Vol. 77, No. 2, March 1999, 64–75.

OD IN PRACTICE
L & T INFOTECH LTD.

1. L & T IT Ltd. believes in learning organization, where learning in room for those driven by the zeal to surpass their peers and most importantly, themselves.
2. L & T IT mix and match intensive training with equal thrust on job skills and behavioural development. Group therapies and seminars are organized to ensure professional rapport and keep employee morale running high. The company realizes the value that people add to the organization and formulate policies that take into consideration individual needs and benefits.
3. Some of the activities that make learning a continuous process at L & T Infotech are:
   (*a*) An extensive orientation-cum technical training programme for Software Engineers Trainee at the well-equipped Training Centre.
   (*b*) Conduct focussed management development programmes at premium management development centers.
   (*c*) Continuous skill up gradation on new emerging technologies.
   (*d*) Behavioural training programmes offered to enhance personal and professional effectiveness of the project groups viz. customer orientation, teamwork, communication and self-development. The company engages the best faculties in the field of management like IIM, administration staff college etc.

(Source: Human Resource Management by Biswajit Patnayak, PHI, Third Edition, 2006.)

CASE STUDY
PEOPLE POWER AT JET AIRWAYS

Selection and placement are two most critical decisions that all organizations make. Like other organizations, various inputs such as competence tests, personality assessment, letters of recommendations, interviews, and so on lead Jet Airways also to the final decision. Besides, Jet Airways follows a unique and unconventional selection process. One classical example of such process is the case of a highly qualified experienced pilot, who was interviewed for the position of cockpit in the late 1990s. He was duly certified to fly all of the aircrafts in the Indian Territory or inventory. He enjoyed quite good letters of recommendation as well. He had an excellent and impressive interview with a panel of six pilots from Jet Airways, Air India and Indian Airlines. The panel gave him Consensus rave review. The promising pilot assumed his competence and expertise along with his relationship with peer group constitute his power base.

Jet Airways has a unique organizational culture where all people regardless of job description and roles are considered important. For example, unlike other organizations, having a personnel department, Jet Airways has a "people department". People in Jet Airways have their own influence over selection decisions.

For that matter, The Travel Agent who booked the pilot's flight from Calcutta to Mumbai had his input into the final decisions in pilot's selection. Similarly, the coordinator who arranged the pilot's interviews also contributed to his input into the final decision. The receptionist who receives the pilot at Bombay for his scheduled interview had her own say in the final decision of pilot's selection. What it does mean is power at Jet Airways is in the hands of the people working in it.

However, the pilot failed to obtain the job at Jet Airways despite his recognized competence as a pilot, his strong recommendations, and quite high grade awarded by the panel of six pilots. These factors were undoubtedly very much in his favour. But he was rude to the travel agent who booked his air ticket from Calcutta to Mumbai. He was not polite to the coordinator who arranged his schedule of interviews in Mumbai. Finally he failed to be polite to the receptionist when he arrived for his interview in the head office of Jet Airways at Mumbai. What happened? Three strikes and he was out.

Questions

1. What made the pilot fail the job in Jet Airways?
2. What lesson, as a prospective job seeker, will you draw for yourself from this case?

Source: S.S. Khanka, Organisational Behaviour, Third Revised Edition, S. Chand & Co., New Delhi., 2005.

CHAPTER 14

Normative Re-Educative Strategy

CHAPTER PLAN

- *Introduction*
- *Examination of Various Strategies*
- *OD is an Applied Behavioural Science*
- *Summary*
- *Text Questions*
- *Bibliography*
- *Case Study: Managing the Mind*

INTRODUCTION

Organization development is achieved by implementing changes in the organization Chin and Benne[1] has described three types of strategies to implement change. These are as follows:

(*a*) **Empirical rational strategies,** based on the assumptions that people are rational, will follow their rational interests, and will change once they realize that the change is to their advantage.

(*b*) **Strategies normative re-educative,** based on the assumptions that norms form the basis for behaviour, and change comes through re-education in which old norms are discarded and supplanted by new ones.

(*c*) **Power coercive strategies,** based on the assumption that change is compliance of those who have less power with the desires of those who have more power.

EXAMINATION OF VARIOUS STRATEGIES

Chin and Benne further states that

> ***"A second group of strategies we call normative re-educative. These strategies build upon assumptions about human motivation different from those underlying the first strategy. The rationality and intelligence of men are not denied. Patterns of action and practice are supported by socio-culture norms and by commitments on the part of the individuals to the norms. Socio-cultural norms are supported by the attitude and the value systems of individuals—normative outlooks which undergrid their commitments. Change in pattern of practice or action, according to this view, will occur only as a person involved are brought to change their normative orientation to old patterns and develop commitments to new ones. And change in normative orientation involve change in attitudes, values, skills and significant relationship, not just changes in knowledge, information, or intellectual rationales for action and practice."***

Take an example of Polio eradication campaign launched by the Indian Government at the national level in which polio dose is served on each child below the age group of 5 years. A massive advertising campaign is also launched so that every parent from villages go to the primary health centers close by in their village or to the neighbouring village where primary health center is functioning. In urban areas apart from the existing medical centers, temporary polio booths are opened where polio dose is administered to the children. The mission is to eradicate polio disease from the country. This involves change in perception and attitude of the masses. Because people still feel that the polio dose, if administered in excess, the child may have adverse effects like paralysis.

Empirical rational strategy suggests that all rational, self-interested people will take the polio eradication campaign as their own campaign; they will not only take their child to polio booth but that of the neighbours too. The aim of the government would be to inform the public about the dates of vaccine.

If you believe in *normative re-educative strategy* of change, you would do additional things like educating people, assisting the people in taking their children to the polio booth, reminding them of the next dose, and even maintaining the records of affected children. It must be understood that the behaviour of the people are deep rooted on socio-cultural beliefs, norms, value system, knowledge of the latest inventions and the benefits to the people. People will change their behaviour (administer the drugs) to their children if their belief, faith is there in the invention (of polio) and positive attitude to take the national mission to eradicate the polio patients to a successful end.

If you believe in *power coercive strategy*, the Job of the government would be very simple. It will pass a law that all children below five years will take a polio dose every month. Those fail to do so will be punished; and the punishment would be made known to all the people on mass media.

The point here is that different strategies are available for affecting change, and OD is based primarily on normative re-educative strategy and secondarily on a rational empirical strategy. Chin and Benne identified following implications for implementing change through application of normative re-educative strategy:

(*a*) The client system members define what changes and improvements they want to make, rather than the OD practitioner.

(*b*) The practitioner intervenes in a collaborative way with the clients, and together they define problems and seek solutions.

(*c*) Anything hindering effective problem-solving is brought to the light and publicly examined; that is doubts, anxieties, and negative feelings are surfaced for "working through".

(*d*) Solutions to problems are not a priori assigned to greater technical information but may reside in values, attitudes, relationships, and customary ways of doing things.

The client system members generally decide the norms to be changed and the form of re-education. This gives the client a considerable control over the OD system and thus they can implement appropriate OD intervention with collaborative efforts. It should be understood that norms are socially accepted beliefs that are held by the groups; for a change to be effective the target group of change has to be the group and not the individual. In this respect Burke writes:

> ***If one attempts to change an attitude or the behaviour of an individual without attempting to change the attitude or behaviour in the group to which the individual belongs, then the individual will be a deviate and either will come under pressure from the group to get back into line or will be rejected entirely. Thus, the major leverage point for change is at the group level; for example, modifying a group norms or standards.***[2]

OD IS AN APPLIED BEHAVIOURAL SCIENCE

'Pure' sciences are related to the theory: imparting education to the group of people. While technology refers to applied science. OD refers to application of knowledge to the practical problems. In organizations, certain symptoms indicate that there is something wrong or incorrect is going on. Say for example, the sales are falling. This causes disequilibria in the organization; to say production levels are disturbed, stocks are piled up, cash flow is reduced and a general level of satisfaction of the employees is low. The problem areas cannot be identified because of complexity of the situation. It is the duty of the OD practitioner to diagnose the main cause and apply suitable OD interventions so that the desired change is achieved and the production levels are improved. In case an OD intervention does not bring the desired results, a redignosis is carried out and the OD practitioner to correct the problem areas adopt a revised approach. The cause of fall in the sales may just be low levels of wage structure to the sales persons. If an OD practitioner is expert and is able to identify the cause; just by improving the salary structure may lead to improvement in the sales; thus implementing the OD intervention that will pay rich dividends. Other causes mentioned earlier may be redundant. The two things involved in the process are—diagnosis and the treatment. The diagnostic typology allows the practitioner to know what category of situation he has examined; the treatment typology allows him to know what remedial measures (interventions) to apply. Finally, he must in collaboration with the client system carry out the evaluation of the success achieved. OD thus is a "applied behavioural science".

SUMMARY

Organization Development is achieved by implementing change in the organization. Chin and Benne has described three types of strategies to implement change. These are Empirical rational strategies, Normative re-educative and power coercive strategies. Different strategies are available for affecting change, and OD is based primarily on normative re-educative strategy and secondarily on a rational empirical strategy.

TEXT QUESTIONS

1. Explain the concepts of empirical—rational strategies, normative re-educative strategies and power coercive strategies.
2. With the example, explain normative re-educative strategy.
3. "Different strategies are available for affecting change, and OD is based primarily on normative re-educative strategy and secondarily on a rational empirical strategy." Visit an organization of your choice; examine as to which strategy the organization is following to implement change.

BIBLIOGRAPHY

1. Robert Chin and Kenneth D. Benne, *"General Strategies for Effecting Changes in Human Systems"*. The Planning of Change, 3rd Edition (New York: Holt, Rinehart, and Winston, 1976).
2. Warner Burke, *Organisation Development*, p. 151.

Case Study
MANAGING THE MIND

By
V.M. Wabgaonkar
Senior Vice President, Strategic Planning, DRAFTFCB India,
(Business Standard, 14 August, 2007)

Hard working, vivacious Kiran is an MBA with a good standing, but she is still single. Her plump figure brings proposals she doesn't like. She doesn't get down to dieting or exercise, either. A soft, meditative MBA, Aniket is very bright in writing. However, his presentations are shy and subdued. He often carries meditative moods to social situations. The result: a lacklustre love life. Introverted Anamika, a topper, writes well but the quantum of her output is a far cry from her true potential. She is easily hurt, it makes her tired, sour from inside, and this attitude leaves much to be desired in her work.

They are all MBA as engaged in consultancy work at a reputed multinational. However, their business schools never taught them "brain management". Brain management refers to managing the mind not only for incremental effectiveness, but also for magical results — as practiced by Milton Erickson, Richard Bandler and so on. Their writings bear names like NLP, time-lien therapy and hypnosis. When any stimulates stops changing, our nerves stop sending its signals to the brain. Without such evolution, we would have remained consciously aware of our bodies even in the middle of activities that need absorption, such as sleep. Similarly, to keep a feeling alive, we have to keep it circulating inside. With some practice, we can become aware of the paths that prominent feelings follow in our bodies. Imagine touching the depths of tranquility, romance, and ego-getter mood at will, as required.

Language is a wonderful example of a skill that we learn consciously, but practice enough to make it an unconscious process. Otherwise, just imagine the inconvenience of consciously locating every letter, every word and its required arrangement right in the middle of a communication process. It is the unconscious mind that manages the heartbeats as you walk faster. For that matter, the unconscious mind controls every single body process of every single cell. The most magical and sweeping results of "body-mind management" and "brain management" come about by establishing communication with the unconscious. In my example above, Kiran will benefit tremendously if she can do that. Analogously, so will thousands of corporate managers who suffer from blood pressure, acidity and ulcers because of their fear of failure and high stress levels. B-schools are doing a great job of handing over a gate pass to aspiring young boys and girls for their entry into the corporate world. However, as yet, they are leaving the tougher job of honing up the body and the mind for maximum effectiveness to the youngsters themselves.

Questions

1. How do you think to manage brain by adopting one of the above strategies of change?
2. Examine conscious and sub-conscious changes that take place with an individual.

CHAPTER 15

Management of Organization Change

CHAPTER PLAN

- *Introduction*
- *Understanding Change*
- *Organizational Growth as a Factor of Change*
- *Forces of Change*
- *Force Field Analysis*
- *Change Process*
- *Seven Stage Model*
- *Levels of Change*
- *Types of Change*
- *Steps in Managing Change*
- *Change Agents*
- *Resistance to Change*
- *Managing Resistance to Change*
- *Summary*
- *Text Questions*
- *Bibliography*
- *Case Study: Magic Kingdom*

INTRODUCTION

Change is inevitable. Nothing is permanent except the change. It is the duty of the management to manage change properly. Organizations must carefully observe the environment and incorporate suitable changes the situation demands. Change is a continuous phenomenon. Organization must be proactive in affecting change. Even in most stable organizations, change is necessary just to keep the level of stability. The major environmental forces that make the change necessary are technology, market forces and socio-economic factors. Resistance to change is not desirable. It is counter productive for growth and destructive in nature. Managers must evolve policies to affect change. According to Barney and Griffin, "The primary reason cited for organizational problems is the failure by managers to properly anticipate or respond to forces for change."(Barney and Griffin, 1992. [1]

UNDERSTANDING CHANGE

Change refers to any alteration that occurs in over all work environment of an organization. It may relate to change in technology, organizational structure, working processes; work environment, organizational policy and even the roles people play. Introduction of change in one part in an organization forces change in other part. Introduction of computers in the organization has literally threatened the very continuation of some employees in the organization. If the change is beneficial people accept it willingly. If it is not desirable, there is great resistance. If it is of no consequence to the people, they may adopt an attitude of indifference. If they consider the change detrimental to their growth and prosperity, they may resist through counter pressure. This reaction is based not necessarily on the reality or facts but on their perception. The change therefore should be sufficiently strong enough to overcome the counter pressure. Due to advancement of technology, and social environment change has become a necessity. If the change takes place, a balance or equilibrium is achieved by the organization. Thus people learn to expect various environment relationships within the organization. They learn adaptation. The essence is that when people feel that there is need to change, and when they change, they actually are adjusting to changed situation thus equilibrium is achieved with the changed environment. This process carries on and is never ending because change takes place continuously.

ORGANIZATIONAL GROWTH AS A FACTOR OF CHANGE

Greiner's model is explained in Figure 15.1 shown Greiner has evolved a theory of change by considering 'growth' as a factor for change. He has identified various problems at each stage of evolution. The solution to the problem brings about the change. To illustrate, he quotes an organization that desires to achieve 'growth'. Initially growth is achieved through creativity of a founder who is usually entrepreneurial oriented but that creates a problem of leadership. To tie over the problem of leadership, management hires top class managerial personnel who take charge of the situation. Over a period of time it comes to the notice that excessive leadership creates a situation of concentration of power in the organization. With the effect the subordinates have to wait for the decision on a trivial issues.

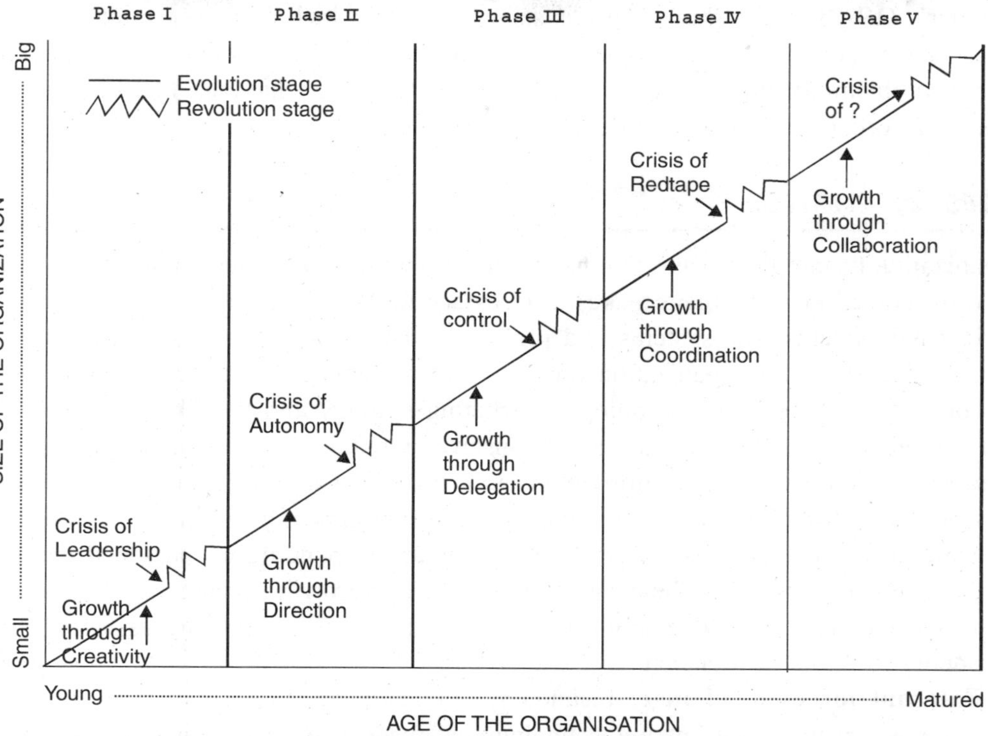

Figure 15.1 Growth as a factor of change (Greiner's Model)

Therefore, a change is necessitated and that leads to delegation of authority to subordinates. This leads to another problem based on autonomy at group level and control becomes difficult. Since the organization has already changed from concentration to delegation a new change is envisaged to exercise adequate control over the group. The change is in the form of issuing fresh orders and detailed instructions on each of the perceivable issue so that while individual enjoys autonomy in work culture, he still has to work within the framework of rules and regulations. It was later noticed that excessive rules and regulations brought with it the red tapism. This problem leads to change of philosophy to collaboration. In this changed situation individual employee, work teams and work groups perform job. It will be seen that for achievement of organizational growth, the organization had to change its strategy beginning from entrepreneurship, leadership, delegation, autonomy of work groups, collaboration leading to the strategy of self-control, self-discipline and individual work ethics. It is important to understand each change that takes place is associated with unforeseeable problems. It will also be seen that change is necessary at every stage. If that was not implemented the organization will not be able to achieve growth.

Greiner's (1972) model shows various stages through which an organization is likely to go during its growth period. The potential issues and problems between various stages are highlighted. The major problem should also be seen as one of managerial behaviour, that is what managers have to do in order to overcome these crises in relation to time span.

FORCES OF CHANGE

An organization is an open system that has to interact with environment and is solely dependant on it. Any change in environment makes it necessary for the organization to incorporate change in the internal systems, sub-systems and processes. This change has a chain reaction on the other internal elements of organization for example, any change in consumer preferences, may change product feature, cost, technology, marketing strategy and the like. Organization must interact with external environment in order to survive. Organization gets input from environment (men, material, process, finance information etc.), transform it and export output (product and services) to the environment. Organization takes what environment gives and in the process passes on what the environment wants. Thus organizations are responding to the social requirements. If the response is positive, then the change takes place and growth is achieved. If on the contrary response is negative, it will adversely affect the growth. So there are various factors that must be considered to implement change.

1. **External forces of change:** Technology is a major external force, which calls for change. In the recent times information technology has made a remarkable impact on the ability of managers to use information to arrive at a decision. Storage, retrival of information and its utilization are important parts of technology. Where human being cannot operate, robot has been replaced to work for and on behalf of human beings. Financial decisions, operations, product features, new product development market potential and marketing strategies are changing at a fast speed and organizations must carry out appropriate change in time otherwise one will be left behind in the race. Because of liberalization market has become one entity though its size is large. Organizations have to be highly sensitive to the changes in the external environment. External environment is task related and general in nature. Task related environment has a direct influence on the health of the organization. It consists of customers, competitions, suppliers, labours and stakeholders. All these factors induce change in the organization. General environment consists of political, legal, economic, socio-cultural and technological forces. Change in government polices or fiscal policies have a direct impact on the organization. A change in needs, expectation and desires of society for housing has changed a financial sectors outlook and loans are easily available to all sections of society.
2. **Internal forces of change:** Once the organization adapts to an external change, the mangers have to take appropriate steps as far as internal systems are concerned. Change of process, modification to human behaviour, training and development of work force based on new technology and adopting new polices which are beneficial to the organization. Due to current social changes where women are taking jobs in greater numbers, childcare, more

and frequent rest periods and flextime may be necessary. Workers are more educated and are aware of their duties and rights. This may necessitate change in corporate policies towards wage and salary implementation, promotion policy and management obligations towards them. Customers, shareholders, board of directors and employees may bring about changes in internal environment. These however, have to be in line with the external factors and not arbitrory. Change that is deliberately designed and implemented is a 'planned change'. This is carried out to counter threats and encash opportunities. "Reactive changes" are unknown and cause as a response to sudden surprises like change in price of a particular product etc. It is therefore necessary that the management must be 'proactive' in incorporating change with fewer surprises. It must build on into strengths and take appropriate preventive actions as is necessary to be competitive in the market place.

FORCE FIELD ANALYSIS

When a decision to implement change has been taken, it is necessary to identify and understand as to what forces are likely to push change and what forces are likely to restrain it. The process of identifying the number and strength of *driving and restraining force* is called the **force field analysis**. If the analysis indicates that the restrained force is strong, steps may be required to reduce its strength or increase the strength of the driving force. This may be carried out by briefing sessions, meetings and conveying a point informally. The communication must be appropriately modulated. It is the responsibility of the leader to select appropriate leadership style to incorporate change. Knowledge of organizational climate in general and group behaviour in particular is essential. If the subordinates are not communicative among group members, participative style of leadership may be necessary. If the pattern of communication permits mutual consultations among subordinates, the autocratic style may mar the prospects of change. Modification may be required not only to the style of leadership but also to the 'change' itself. The implementation may start by introducing readiness of the group to proposed change and later introduce the required change. It is a gradual process and a necessary care needs to be taken of emotions, values, feelings and attitude of employees. Implementation of change in defences services is comparatively easier because people are customized to change and have achieved a higher degree of readiness to change by virtue of their professional climate.

CHANGE PROCESS

Kurt Lewin[2] proposed three Stage Model of the change process for moving the organization from present position to the changed position. This is as under:

Stage 1: **Unfreezing:** Creating motivation and readiness to change through

(*a*) disconfirmation or lack of confirmation.

(*b*) creation of guilt or anxiety.

(*c*) ensure employees of psychological safety.

***Stage 2:* Changing through cognitive restructuring:** Helping the client to see things, judges things, feel things differently based on new point of view obtained through

(*a*) identifying with a new role model, mentor, etc.

(*b*) scanning the environment for new relevant information.

***Stage 3:* Refreezing:** Helping the client to integrate the new point of view into

(*a*) the total personality and self-concept.

(*b*) significant relationship.

1. **Unfreezing:** Process of unfreezing makes individuals ready for change. Lewin believes that employees must be informed in advance of impending change and that they should not be surprised. Unfreezing entails unfreezing the old behaviour or situation. Edgar Schein[3] took this excellent idea propagated by Lewin and improved by specifying psychological mechanism involved in each stage of the model. Unfreezing involves creating motivation and readiness to change by creating an environment of disconfirmation of existing psychological safety in the changed pattern of behaviour. This can be achieved by making announcements, meetings and promoting the idea throughout the organization via bulletin boards, personal contacts and group conferences. The unfreezing process basically cleans the slate so that fresh behavioural patterns, customs, traditions can be imprinted which can then become a new way of doing things.

2. **Moving:** Once unfreezing process is completed, moving takes place. Moving is incorporating change. Persons undergo cognitive restructuring. The process is carried out by the following three methods as proposed by Kellman.[4]

   (*a*) Compliance: Compliance is achieved by introducing rewards and punishments. It has been established that individuals accept change if rewards and punishment system exist in an organization. Appropriate reinforcement strategies may be introduced by the organization to facilitate change.

   (*b*) Identification: Members are psychologically impressed upon to select their role model and modify behaviour. If a leader can act as a role model the change is easier.

   (*c*) Internalization: Internalization involves internal changing of individual's thought processes in order to adjust to a new environment. Members are advised to carry out soul searching and adopt a new behaviour.

3. **Refreezing:** It is related to integrate the new behaviours into a person's personality and attitude. It is referred to as stabilization. The changed behaviour must necessarily fit into the social surroundings. Refreezing takes place when a new behaviour takes a form of a normal way of life. New behaviour must replace the old on a permanent basis. New behaviours must be re-enforced continuously so that it does not diminish. Change process is not a one-time process but it is continuous phenomenon, hence unfreezing, change and refreezing must also be continues.

SEVEN STAGE MODEL

Another 'change model' was proposed by Ronald Lippitt, Jeanne Watson and Bruce Westley. They expanded the original Lewin's (3 stage) model into seven stage model.

Phase 1: The development of need for change.

Phase 2: The establishment of change relationship (establishment of 'Client' and 'Change agent' relationship).

Phase 3: Diagnosis of client of client system's problems.

Phase 4: The examination of alternative routes and goals; establishing goals and action.

Phase 5: The transformation of moving intentions into actual change efforts.

Phase 6: The generalization and refreezing stabilization of change.

Phase 7: Achieving a terminal relationship with client and change agent.

LEVELS OF CHANGE

Hersey and Blanchard[5] identified four levels of change. These are ***knowledge change, attitudinal change, individual behaviour change and group or organizational performance level change.*** The objective of change is to bring about change in the organization. It is possible through knowledge change, which in turn changes attitude of the individual. Knowledge change is simple as one can improve the level of knowledge by reading or listening. Bringing attitudinal change is difficult, because it is difficult to change the individual and his perception. Change in individual is related to personality traits. A manager may believe that empowering subordinates is essential for organizational growth yet he may not empower them because of his upbringing. Changes in-group and organization is even more complicated than implementing individual level change as it involves change in group norms, customs, and traditions. Change in-group level involves change in organizational culture. This is a long-term process, which must be continuous with active involvement of top management.

1. **Knowledge change:** Change in knowledge can bring change in individual and group behaviour. It is related to the leadership style Hersey and Blanchard refer to it as (1) *participative or democratic change cycle* and (2) *autocratic or directive change cycle.* It is explained below:

   (*a*) Participative leadership style in bringing change in-group or organization is largely based on the style of leadership. Change in knowledge of workforce coupled with participative leadership style can transform an individual in his outlook. It can bring change in his attitude and an individual can be more committed towards the organization. He can be more responsible towards his duties and obligations. New methods and techniques can be implemented to bring change in the group in desired direction. Assistance from like minded leaders having democratic outlook can help mangers to implement desired change. Once this is achieved, getting other people to begin to pattern their behaviour on the lines of successful leaders may effect organizational change. Thus the change cycle works through change in knowledge, attitude, individual behaviour, group behaviour and organizational change.

(*b*) There are autocratic leaders in the organization. This type of leadership announces the desired change all of a sudden. This type of process of change may result in whole hearted acceptance of change or the group may resist the change totally. What is expected in the autocratic change cycle is organizational change, group change, knowledge change and through this cycle to implement individual behaviour change. Since this approach is opposite of participative cycle change as explained above, it is difficult to implement and individuals are not ready to accept change in first place. Secondly, the change may not be of a permanent nature. Participative change is ideal when the employees are achievement oriented having task relevance and willingness to accept responsibilities. It has deeper and longer lasting impact. Autocratic change cycle has fast speed and is revolutionary in nature. It is sustainable where people are not willing and certain amount of is force is required. This change cycles are complimentary to each other and therefore may be used according to the situations.

2. **Attitudinal level change:** It is difficult to bring attitudinal change. Attitudes are formed and conditioned by feelings. The way one feels about change will determine how one is likely to behave. Attitude is formed in early childhood based on social surroundings. When you are part of a group, an attitude is greatly influenced by group norms, expectations of the group members and behavioural code a group adopts. Further the work environment influences the attitudes. Due to complex nature of situations, there is positive or negative impact on individual behaviour. Often actions or reactions of individual are effects of groupthink. It often happens that workers join the strike to show oneness of the group or organization. Individual may not be able to justify a particular behaviour but he does it merely because all others were engaged in a particular behaviour. We are not able to explain our emotions largely that make us behave in a particular manner. These feelings as Davis[6] explains are not a matter of logic. They are neither logical nor illogical; rather they are non-logical hence, logic alone is not enough to modify feelings in modern times, it is however necessary to effect change individual attitude. It is possible by way of delegation of authority, empowering employees in their work. Making work more pleasant and interesting by way of providing the workers wherewithall necessary for its accomplishment, creating autonomy in work and introducing Management By Objective concept in the organization. Cultural change is important MBO for organizational culture must conform to majority of workers' culture and they must feel at home while working. Attitude of leaders also play a vital role in attitude change of subordinates. Participative leadership culture goes a long way in obtaining willing obedience of employees. It must be borne in mind that it is a continuous process and all members must sub-conscientiously attempt to improve work culture in the organization for attitudinal change.

3. **The group level change:** Group plays variety of roles in bringing about change in the organization: The group as medium of change, the group as the target of change and the group as an agent of change. Cartwright[7] has developed the following principles in this regard.

(*a*) The group as a medium of change

(*i*) If group is to be used effectively as a medium of change, those people who are to be changed and those who are to exert influence for change must have a strong sense of belonging to the same group.

(*ii*) The more attractive the group is to its members, the greater is the influence that the group can exert on its members.

(*iii*) In attempts to change attitudes, values, or behaviour the more relevant they are to the basis of attraction to the group, the greater will be the influence that the group can exert upon them.

(*iv*) The greater the prestige of a group member in the eyes of the other members, the greater the influence he can exert.

(*v*) Efforts to change individuals or sub-parts of a group that, if successful, would have the result of making them deviate from; the norms of the group will encounter strong resistance.

(*b*) The group as a target of change

(*i*) Strong pressure for change in the group can be established by creating a shared perception by members of the need for change, thus making the source of pressure for change lie within the group.

(*ii*) Information relating to the need for change plans for change, and all relevant people in the group must share consequences of change.

(*iii*) Changes in one part of a group produce strain in other related parts, which can be reduced only by eliminating the change or by bringing about readjustments in the related parts.

4. **Organizational wide change:** Organizational change is of a mega nature. It starts at the bottom level and acquires a very huge dimension. In defence services if a person is promoted at the top level, there is a chain reaction upward for promotion and resultant placement, transfers etc. If an organization is attempting to change the job of an individual, his role-set is also likely to change that may distrusts the self-concept of the individual. Thus any action for change may also have chain reaction. It is therefore necessary to plan for change carefully Allen has suggested following steps:

(*a*) Development of well defined objectives.

(*b*) Analysis of existing organizations.

(*c*) Preparation of an ideal plan.

(*d*) Trying out the plan.

(*e*) Establishment of uniform nomenclature.

(*f*) Overcoming resistance to change.

In the fast developing world today, there are pressures on the human resources. Due care must be taken to ensure that employees are not disturbed physiologically and psychologically. Careful review of situation to identify the gaps must be carried out. Change costs money and therefore, it is advisable to undertake a pilot project before a universal change is implemented. Status system, titles and appellations attached to it must be protected by introducing uniform nomenclature, designation etc. People must be educated about the impending change so that they are not taken by surprise. Benefits of change must be highlighted. Automation of systems in organization has proved fruitful and cost effective for which it had initial resistance.

'Change Management' has already emerged as a discipline. It requires proper planning, programming, and evolving appropriate procedures and systems. An organization must modify polices, procedures, rules and regulations based on changed objectives. Behavioural science plays an important role by way of ensuring that rewind system is in tune with the time.

TYPES OF CHANGE

1. **Strategic change:** Strategic change requires when mission is changed. A single mission of defence forces participating under UNO banner may require changes in use of weapon system, cooperation at international level, serving under a person not of an Indian origin and the very thought of employing various strategic and tactical doctrines. The multinational companies have to adapt to the culture of the nation where they are providing product and services. Various cultural factors have to be considered in this regard. This is generally carried out as 'planned strategic change'.
2. **Structural change:** Decentralization of authority and introducing flatter organizational structure enable employees to experience a sense of autonomy in work environment. Decentralization leads to empowerment of lower level employees to take appropriate decisions pertaining to their job parameters. It has major impact on the social climate of the organization on one hand and development of team spirit on the other. Structural changes promote acquisition of new skills and improve ability of subordinates to take on the spot decisions even in critical situation.
3. **Process oriented change:** Process changes are necessary to keep pace with the development in technology, automation, information technology, free market environment and availability of trained manpower. The organization must take advantages of these processes. This however needs heavy investment and entails operational changes but cuts down time and energy. This would bring about change in work environment, organizational culture and modify behaviour pattern of employees.

4. **Cultural change:** Due to electrifying changes in communication, an individual is exposed to social changes. This has necessitated introducing a right culture in the organization. It is the responsibility of the top management to ensure proper organizational philosophy, instill culture value system among employees and practice ethical approach in business. These are important inputs for improved performance, group cohesion, and devotion to duty and for development of 'we' feeling in the organization. This can be achieved by close interaction, training in behavioural sciences and building a sense of belonging to the organization. These changes are people oriented and therefore have to be continuous for achievement of organizational mission.

STEPS IN MANAGING CHANGE

Organization must plan to implement change in a systematic manner. It must identify the field in which the change is required whether it is strategic, structural, process oriented or cultural change. Changes can also be affected in all the areas concurrently, but it must be managed appropriately so that there is no bottleneck effect. Once the need for change is identified and the area in which it is to be implemented, the following steps have been suggested by Greiner.

(*a*) **Develop new goals and objectives:** Objectives and goals are derived out of mission statements, objective may need revision due to change in external or internal forces.

(*b*) **Select an agent for change:** It is the responsibility of the management to entrust execution of change to appropriate authority. A manager may be given this responsibility. Outside change agent can also be employed for the purpose. A specialist or a consultant can be brought in to suggest change and monitor implementation.

(*c*) **Diagnose the problem:** Diagnose is the first step to implement change. If an organization has a large number of employee turnover then the data must be collected and made available to the consultant so that the reasons for turnover can be identified and appropriate corrective measures. The process of identification of problem is not simple as it appears. This itself may need a research.

(*d*) **Select methodology:** It is easy to implement material change as a part of change of a system. What is important is to protect the emotions of the employees and they must be made party to select methods so that it is easier to implement at a later stage.

(*e*) **Develop plan:** If the organization wants to reduce employee turnover, it may like to carry out comparative study of other organizations in respect of job content, reward system, employee performance appraisal system, promotion criteria, training and development and the strategy adopted by the organization for its growth. Based on examination of these factors, consultant would be able to develop a plan for change. It may require introducing a new training and development policy that may reduce employee turnover. While developing a plan various other factors must also be reviewed. Plan should not be finalized in isolation. All department heads must be coopted in the exercise.

(*f*) **Strategy for implementation:** Timings of implementation of change is very crucial. A deliberate decision must be taken in this regard like hike in price of a product; the decision to implement change is critical. If the change is related to internal employees, it must be communicated at an appropriate time so that there is no resistance to planned change.

(*g*) **Implementation of plan:** Once the decision to implement the plan and communication through which the plan is to be implemented is decided, it is the responsibility of the various departments to implement the same. This may need notification, briefing sessions or in-house seminars so as to ensure acceptance of all members of the organizations specially those who are likely to get affected. Implementation may be for a short duration as one time change of system or process but its aftermath is of great value. Employee reactions to change of attitudes, aspirations, emotions and behaviour must be canalized in positive directions.

(*h*) **Evaluation and feedback:** The result of the change must be evaluated and suitable feed back given. If modification to training and development causes decrease in employee turnover, the objective of change would deem to have been achieved. If the results are contrary to the expectation, then a new change may be required to diagnosed cause.

CHANGE AGENTS

Change agent are factors that are responsible for the change in individual behaviour. Other changes like change in organization structure, organizational strategy, process, policy and the like can always be introduced in the organization with proper consultations of the employees so that they are accepted by them. Change in human behaviour is a complex phenomenon that may require a number of strategies to make desirable change. These are called change agents. They may either be initiator of change or serve as catalysts for such change. Four types of change agents have been identified (Tichy, N.)

(*a*) **Outside pressures:** External environment like fiscal policy, government policy, technology and social change bring change into the organization. Change is generally executed by the organizations itself. Government may also indulge and help organizations to adapt to new policy like controlling strike in the organizations.

(*b*) **Changes from top management:** The organizational change may come from the top management. It may be in the form of structural, strategic or institutional changes that may be beneficial to the organization with particular reference to employees.

(*c*) **Internal organizational development:** Organizational objectives must be reviewed from time-to-time. This is necessitated because of the environmental changes. Areas where organizational development can be carried out are, work design, delegation of authority, team building, empowerment, autonomy, job enrichment, job rotation etc.

(*d*) **Individual level change:** Individual change refers to change in attitude, skills and behaviour. Management By Objective (MBO) encompasses self-decision-making, setting objective for self-evaluating whether those have been met and resultant modification to work. If such development processes are introduced, individuals are likely to be more responsible and accountable for the work they are assigned. It is therefore necessary to introduce development processes/models in the organization.

(*e*) The change agent may also be in the form of a person who helps the client system to solve organizational problems and bring change. It could be in the form of trainer who trains the client to achieve higher skills that could be used to achieve higher organizational effectiveness. A separate chapter has been devoted to the topic.

RESISTANCE TO CHANGE

Change is a constant phenomenon. Dynamic forces are always at play and therefore individuals must adjust to it and carryout change. If the change in not implemented society will be stagnant and become hopeless. Individuals accept change in the technical field but resist the same as it has far reaching consequences for the social change. Change no matter how beneficial, is generally resented and is always difficult to implement. It must be emphasised that change bring with it new challenges, new experiences, spirit and associated rewards and therefore it should be welcomed and implemented with positive attitude and full support. However, there are certain factors, which resist change these are as follows:

Reasons for resistance	Management of change
– Job security	– Participation and involvement
– Lack of communication	– Communication and education
– Rapidity and extent of change	– Leadership
– Group resistance	– Negotiations and agreement
– Emotional turmoil	– Willingness for sake of group
– Loss of power and control	– Timing of change
– Technology	– Adaptation
– New practices (*a*) Acquisitions and mergers and (*b*) Woman power	– Participation

1. **Job security:** One of the major reasons for change is job security. In recent times there has been the trend in down sizing the organization as a measure of cost cutting. Introduction of modern technology and systems should lead to the growth in productivity of the organization and should not lead to employee turnover.
2. **Lack of communication:** Different people will see different meanings in the proposed change. Management must communicate in advance the need for change, process to adopt for implementation of change. Employees should be coopted right from the beginning in the process of change so that they are party to change and resistance is reduced to a great extent.

3. **Rapidity and extent of change:** Autocratic leader has a tendency to introduce change abruptly with speed. Resistance therefore may be expected to the degree that the persons influenced by the change have pressure put upon them to make it. If the change is of a minor nature and involves routine operations, the resistance would be minimal. If on the contrary the change is major and involves large number of employees, there would be tremendous resistance to it. For example, when Balco was privatised all employees resisted it.
4. **Group phenomenon:** Individual on occasions resists change because group wants it that way. Importance of group cohesion, group norms, code of conduct and the security group provides to individuals, play a dominant role in individual behaviour that makes them to resist change.
5. **Emotions:** Resistance can be expected when those influenced are caught in a jam between forces of change and forces of resistance. Resistance may be expected if the change is made on personal ground and past history of change of identical emotions. If the experience has been pleasant, then the resistance would be negligible. Workers willingly accept technical change if it does not have adverse effect on social fiber of the group. Resistance can be expected if the nature of the people who are going to be influenced by the change. Resistance may also be expected if the change ignores already established institutions in the group with particular reference to customs and group norms. It is therefore necessary that due care must be taken to project the emotions of people.
6. **Loss of power:** Downsizing of department or posting of an executive to different department where there is a reduction of power base will be resisted by the affected individuals though it may be of overall interest to the organization. For example, superintendent of police of a district will resist posting as an instructor to the police training academy.
7. **Technology:** Technology changes are required for the growth of organization. People have now realized that to be competitive, latest technology, which improves the human skills, must be introduced in the organization. It is important to consider that no human resources should be replaced by these changes and certain amount of displacement should be taken in stride. Introduction of technology that causes economic loss and disturb social relationship are generally resisted.
8. **New practices:** Due to advent of technology and education more and more female employees are joining organizations. Some of them are serving in the position of top decision-making. Women domination is not liked by the people and is therefore resisted. For survival, organizations have to adopt the strategy of acquisitions and mergers, which is also resisted by the employees.

MANAGING RESISTANCE TO CHANGE

Change ultimately affects people in the organization. It is always better to explain to them why change is necessary, what benefits are likely to accrue as a result of change and how these benefits are to be shared by employees and the organization. Free flow of information and two-way communication is necessary. If proper communication is not maintained negative attitudes are likely to be formed while change is being implemented. There is a general impression that benefits from change accrue to the organization and management at the cost of workers. This is a false impression and must be corrected by appropriate authority. It must be remembered that without full cooperation of workers, no change can be planned, implemented and the benefits, enjoyed. No growth of the organization can take place unless workers bring it about. Management must understand that workers are the key element of any organization and that they must be involved from planning stage of change. This will result in increased productivity of the organization. Participation should not be simply a mechanical act of calling upon employees to "Participate". It should be clearly understood that there is no one simple panacea to be used in all situations. Participation is not being universally followed. The different combinations of different methods, techniques and procedures may have to be tried. There may be need for the counseling and training of people. If the situation so warrants, the plan even may have to be dropped. Conscious efforts must be made by the leader to remove the fears of employees. Participation should be a part of total treatment of change. Such participation of workers would ensure commitment to implementation of change. Individual involvement right from the planning stage of the change is essential to ensure total involvement. It must ultimately appear that the employees require the change and management is implementing it at the behest of the employees. It has been observed that management is regarded as the instigator of change and unions are considered as forestaller of change. It is therefore for management to take labour leaders in confidence so that they are able to convince the members of the need and utility of change. It is important to make the workers feel that they can discuss the modalities of change and understand the nature of the fears they may have, know for themselves that there is no danger or a trap in the change being planned and that the change is for the benefit of workers and organization. Coch and French's[10] study showed that the group which was not only informed of change and why it was to occur, but also participated in helping to design and plan the new jobs as well as retraining programmes, demonstrated more successful adaptation to change than the other two groups. The other two groups included one group, which had no orientation to change other than a short announcement by management that the change would be made. The another group which was informed by management of the need for change and its implications and the workers were asked to select representative to help devise the necessary retaining programmes. The results were much better in the group involving all, than the group involving only the representative or the group in which only an announcement regarding change was made.

SUMMARY

Change is a permanent phenomenon. It is necessary due to external forces like technology, systems, and social changes interacting with the internal variables of the organization. To implement change Kurt Lewin's model of unfreezing the situation, implementing a change and refreezing must be implemented. Individual, group and organizational changes takes place continuously. Individual change refers to change in attitude, perception and also acquiring new skills to cope with external environment. Group is the important unit of organization. In the present scenario group undertakes work. It is successfully completed because of group norms and groupthink. Organizational level changes can be implemented by clearly defining objectives and plan for change. Driving forces and restraining forces must be evaluated while implementing change. Change is structured when planned and unstructured when change is implemented as a reaction to some situation. There is great resistance to change because of the fear of unknown. Workers in the organization therefore must be educated, trained, made party to change and benefit of change must be divided between the employees and the organization. It is handling of employee emotions and making them psychologically ready to implement change that will ultimately work. The fear must be removed from the minds of people. Dynamic forces are always at play and therefore individuals must adjust to it and carry out change. It must be emphasised that change bringswith it new challenges, new experiences, spirit and associated rewards and therefore it should be welcomed and implemented with positive attitude and full support.

It is difficult to predict which strategy will succeed in implementing the change. Efficient communication, educating the people about impending change, participation, active involvement and last but not the least sharing benefits of change with people is the essential requirement for overcoming resistance to change. The change agent may also be in the form of a person who helps the client system to solve organizational problems and bring change. It could be in the form of trainer who trains the client to achieve higher skills that could be used to achieve higher organizational effectiveness.

TEXT QUESTIONS

1. Explain the meaning of change indicate whether all changes are beneficial.
2. Explain external and internal forces that induce change in the organization.
3. Describe the process of organizational change.
4. Discuss Lewin's model of change.
5. Discuss the functions of change in organizational viability. Why does an organization so often fail to make the necessary changes?
6. Explain the levels of change. How will you bring changes in individual behaviour?
7. Under what conditions does resistance to change develop? Does it show lack of awareness in those who resist?
8. Why individuals and groups resist organization change? Suggest strategies to prevent such resistance.
9. How will you use group as a medium of change if change is to be affected?
10. Write a note on change agent.

BIBLIOGRAPHY

1. Barney, J.B. and Ricky, W. Griffin, *"The Management of Organizations: Structure, Strategy and Behaviour."* Haughton Miffling Publishing, 1992.
2. Lewin, Kurt, *"Field Theory in Social Science."* Harper and Row, 1951.
3. Edgar, H. Schein, *"Organisational Psychology."* Prentice Hall, 1970, p. 120.
4. Kellman, H.C., *"Compliance, Identification and Three Processes of Attitude Change."* Conflict Resolution, 1958.
5. Hersy, P. and Blanchard, *"Management of Organisational Behaviour". Utilising Human Resources*, Prentice Hall of India, New Delhi, 1977.
6. Davis, K. *"Human Behaviour at Work"*, Tata McGraw Hill Publishing Co. Ltd., New Delhi, 1977.
7. Cartwright Dorwin, *"Achieving Changes in People: Some Applications of Group Dynamics Theory"*, Human Relations, Vol. 4, No. 4, 1951.
8. Greiner, Larry E., *"Patterns of Organisational Change"*. Harvard Business Review, 1967.
9. Tichy, N. and H. Hoer Stein, *"Stand when your Number is Called: An Empirical Attempt to Classify Types of Social Change Agents."* Human Relations, Vol. 29, No. 10.
10. Coch, L. and J.R.P. French, Jr., *Overcoming Resistance to Change",* "in:G.E. Swanson *et al.* (Eds), Reading in Social Psychology, Holt, Rinehart and Winston, Inc., New York, 1952.

OD IN PRACTICE
ADJUSTING TO CHANGE IN LIFE

1. Many of us have heard the 'Serenity Prayer' written about 700 years ago—"God grant me the strength to change that, which I need to change, the patience to accept that which I need to change, the patience to accept that which I cannot change, and, above all, the wisdom to know the difference." Even in modern times it captures the essence of the skills required to accept change in life.
2. Changes, both big and small, affect our life from the moment we are born. Although we may cope with small everyday changes pretty well, the major life events can be stressful, because they cause emotional up-heaval and demand major readjustments in life. Some changes, like a change in job can be planned and to some extent controlled. However, other major events like the break-up of a long-term relationship cannot usually be predicted and is beyond our control.

How do you view change?

3. Think about one area of change in your life at the moment, and then answer the following questions to find out how you view change:

- Do you see this change as a challenge or something to avoid?
- What are the advantages?
- What are the disadvantages?
- What aspects of change make you feel threatened?
- What can be the worst possible outcome?
- Are there any long-term effects of this change?
- How does the change affect the people around you?
- What can you do now to make the change better?

4. As you adjust to change, you can expect to experience feelings of loss, anger, and grief at what you are letting go, as well as uncertainty and self-doubt, about the unknown future. If you are to cope well with a major change in your life, you must be prepared to replace old habits and learn new appropriate behaviours. You also need to expect to experience emotional ups and downs, which occur as periods of excitement are followed by periods of calm and returning to routine.
5. Not being able to accept change can lead to emotional problems of depression, anger, resentment, or the inability to forgive. You may find yourself looking back to 'life as it was', rather than accepting 'life as it is'. It takes time to adjust to change, and usually the process is gradual and slow. However, in the constantly changing world in which we live, being able to accept change is an essential life skill.

Case Study
MAGIC KINGDOM

One of the most popular tourist attractions in America is Disney World at Orlando in the State of Florida. It is a theme park with numerous attractions and a visit to America is not considered complete without the visit to Disney World. Prior to the opening of Disney World at Orlando, there was a similar theme park near Los Angeles in the State of California, known as Disneyland. Disneyland was a creation of Walt Disney, a famous family moviemaker who had produced such movie hits as Fantasia and Snow White. Disneyland is a family entertainment phenomenon and is also known as **magic kingdom.**

Following Walt Disney's death, the magic kingdom hit a downward trend. The management rested on the past laurels of its success and the organization stagnated into its status quo. It shunned innovation and stayed in its ivory tower away from the pulse of the audience. It become fearful to change and by all accounts, it was not fully utilizing its potential or its resources and considering the demand for its products and services, it was undercharging for it's licensing of cartoon characters and admission to its theme parks.

Michael Eisner, the head of the Disney organization felt that he had to become more like Walt Disney, an innovator and a risk taker who encouraged creativity and who had built the Disney Empire. After analysing the situation carefully, he devised a plan that would encourage openness to change, and culture of strong creativity, that was always a hallmark of Disney's success.

Wisner himself came up with a number of new and creative ideas including new health food restaurants and he encouraged an induced creativity among others and creativity became one of his top priorities. His idea of creating a Euro Disneyland in Paris came into high focus. He met with 12 of the Worlds most respected architects in a widely creative session to bring out as best design for the theme park as possible. He encouraged and rewarded new ideas, opened the channels of communication and took the members into confidence by sharing with them his strategic plans and ambitious growth strategies.

One change that came into being was the renovation and expansion of its hotel chains. He ordered an ambitious $ 1.0 Billion hotel expansion plan that doubled its room capacity to 20,000 and came at par with the well-known Ritz Carlton chain of hotels.

The movie business that had practically come to a stand still and was hardly reaching break-even point got a boost of creativity. By tightening budget without sacrificing quality and working with adventurous scripts and unknown but talented actors, it became a dominant force in the American movie industry and produced such hit films as Beauty and the Beast, Pretty Woman, Ruthless People and so on.

Michael Wisner's creativity, openness, innovation and team sprit has not been without its rewards. From 1984 to 1990, Disney's sales increased from $ 1.7 billion to almost $ 6.00 billion. Dianey has expanded his family entertainment business to include book publishing and records and has opened a theme park in Japan.

Michael Wisner made a dramatic turnaround of Disney fortune in 1980s. He is even more ambitious during the 1990s and calls it *The Disney Decade.* He has surrounded himself with ambitious, energetic and creative staff and he expects a period of extensive growth for Disney operations around the Globe. With the fall of close societies and advent of instant communications and emphasis on internationalization, he is very optimistic that Disney will become a household name around the World, as it did in America.

Questions

1. Why do you think that the Disney organization, once a highly successful and growing organization become stagnant after the death of its founder Walt Disney? Describe as many reasons as possible.
2. How important is Michael Wisner's role in the process of turn around of the Co's fortunes? Does it mean that the success of the entire organization depends upon the philosophy of its CEOs? Give reasons.
3. List and explain the internal and external forces that necessitated the change in the outlook of Disney operations.
4. Can you identify the change agents that were at work in changing the behaviour of the organizational members?
5. If you were hired as a consultant to the organization, what changes would you suggest, if any, to bring Disney organization into the global limelight?

(Case adapted from Courtland L. Bovey *et al.*, Management, McGraw Hill, 1993, pp. 361-62.)

CHAPTER 16

Power, Politics and Ethics in Organization Development

CHAPTER PLAN

- *Introduction*
- *Definitions*
- *Bases/Sources of Power*
- *Organization Based Power*
- *Politics*
- *Techniques of Political Plays*
- *Machiavellianism (1469–1527)*
- *Strategies Used by Executives Ethics in OD*
- *Ethics in OD*
- *Summary*
- *Text Questions*

INTRODUCTION

Study of power is important in the corporate environment. Power depends from person to person and its use depends upon the attitude of an individual. Power in public life is different than in the corporate world. While former is situational the later is object oriented. In public life, its promises may or may not work as desired. Proper use of power in organization is necessary so that the sources of power is not misused and directed towards attainment of organizational goal. It is important to understand for the manager (who uses power) to understand employee behaviour, because methods of using power are different for different managers in the organization. It is therefore, essential to allow minimum power that may be necessary to maintain peaceful environment. Politics play a decisive role in decision making in the organizations. Politics is considered undesirable. We shall examine the reasons why people play politics and suggest remedial measures. A study to understand how power is acquired and used for attainment of organizational development will be studied in this chapter.

DEFINITIONS

1. Rosabeth Kanter says, ***"Power is the ability to get things done."***
2. According to Wolfe, ***"Power is potential ability of a person to induce forces on another person towards movement or change in a given direction within a given behaviour region, at a given time."***
3. Cavanaugh states *that* ***"Power is a multifaceted concept, which has been analyzed from interpersonal influence process, as a commodity to be traded, as a type of causation and as an issue in the study of values and ethics."***

Understanding Power

Power is derived from the official position held by an individual in an organization; those in power are able to marshal their resources in a way that helps them achieve their goals. They are able to be effective in their jobs and earn the respect of others. Having power as resource can help you gain support, information and supplies—everything and anything that is needed to be productive in your job. Power is a tool and resource, a means as an end while politics represents tactics used by employees to use to manipulate power in organizational setting. Leaders use power as a means of attaining group goals. Leader use power to ensure compliance of job assigned to them. Power is also used to control various activities of individuals and groups. A production manager may be given power to procure raw material worth only Rs. 10,000 in one transaction. This is to control his activities. A leader may use punitive power to prevent individual from restraining undisciplined activities. Power is an ability of a person to possess what he feels as valuable and deprive another person of the same.

Manager having power to promote his subordinates uses it to attain organizational goals. Power should be used for attainment of growth of the organization and should be reward oriented in nature. Threat of power is not desirable as it has negative re-enforcement character inbuilt in it. When we discuss power, authority is associated with it. Authority is acquired from the organizational hierarchy. When we say that HR manager has an authority to employ an individual. This authority is associated with the appointment of an individual as HR manager. It is therefore legitimate. Authority relationship of various individual is contained in organizational pyramid chart, higher one goes, higher the authority. Authority and power go hand in hand. To be effective, power and authority should be equalized. Authority and power are synonymous. But in the present environment, it is observed that while authority remains constant, there is a tendency to exercise more power. This is because of the politics played by an individual to maintain higher influence over resources. On the contrary, there may be situation when an individual does not use full potential of his authority for one reason or the other. Interpersonal and group conflicts are indicative of more influence one wants to exercise in the organizational setting. These happening are common to every layers of organizational hierarchy. Power is therefore personal and acquired.

Politics is a process whereby power is acquired and used to influence behaviour of others. It is endemic to every organization. People form groups, camps or cliques when they play politics. People playing politics for power where ethics, moral values, organizational goals are of little concern. Dalton identified following six areas where politics was being played actively.

Areas where politics is generally played

- Pressure for economy.
- Cooperation of officially powerless experts with their administrative superior line and staff-relationship.
- The conflict between labour and management for interpreting agreements.
- Uncertainly about standards and strategies of promotion.
- Difficulty in linking reward with productivity.
- Practicality of policies.

BASES/SOURCES OF POWER

French and Raven (1959) and Raven (1965) has put forward following six bases of power:

Reward Power

This power source derives from the person's control over resources, for example, power to control human resources and pay and promotion. Grater the perceived values of each rewards the greater the power. These rewards can be extrinsic in nature with tangible values as well as intrinsic such as praise or recognition. This strategy is desirable to implement OD strategies.

Coercive Power

The power to punish or reward, the power to threaten and to use one's position to force others to take action. It reflects the extent to which a manager can deny desired rewards or administer punishment to control other people. If you believed in power coercive strategy of changing, your task would be easy; you would pass the law stating that all person must get vaccinated, and you would achieve compliance.

Legitimate Power

The power, which is exercised in accordance with organizational rules. This power, which is exercised with the authority of the organization. Power derives from our cultural system of rights, obligations and duties, whereby position is accepted by people, *i.e.,* right of private property. The military power relies upon the notion of legitimacy. If it is challenged the whole system will collapse. Person having legitimate power can effectively implement change.

Referent Power

This depends on charisma or personal attraction of the individual. Interpersonal skills and emotional support from others are the source of power for this person. Stronger the association, stronger the power. For example, Amitab Bachan coming on TV screen and requesting parents to take their children for polio vaccination. The famous *'Do boondh campaign'*.

Expert Power

Power that derives from knowledge sometimes called sapient authority is power based on others expertise *e.g.*, Physician. Such people are able to implement OD without any resistance. Power exists within two parties *i.e.*, those exercising it and those responding to power.

Power is the capacity to mobilize resources for effective use. Capacity to exercise power depends upon the situation, which provides opportunities or restrictions on the use of power and the personality of those wishing to exercise the same. Asymetry of power refers to the perceived differences between the power of involved parties and its relationship. Personality refers to physical and psychological advantage an individual has over other persons. For example, Sachin Tendulkar enjoys Charisma and power related to it due to his personality.

ORGANIZATION BASED POWER

Knowledge as Power

Information technology has taken a big leap in the last two decades. Information is necessary for top management to take decisions. Information is vital to carry out various operations in the business environment. Thus a person or a group holding information becomes more powerful than their counter part. Flow of information is necessary for continuous production or service operations. Knowledge is the basic source for implementing change in the organization.

Resource as Power

Resources are necessary for any organization. While material or tangible resources can be procured easily, it is the availability of these resources, at right time, at right place in a required quality and at a competitive price. Any person having monopoly over scares resources wield power. When project is required to be started, it is government agencies, which delay the project for want of various resources, like power, water, etc. Human resources are critical. Any person having direct or indirect control over making skilled persons available holds power. Organization cannot servive without adequate availability of various resources.

Decision-making as Power

Decision-making rests with the head of the organization. Decision-making is delegated to departmental heads depending upon the nature of the work, ability of the departmental heads and the trust enjoyed by them. Decision-making is one of the most important processes of management. Decisions are influenced, may be by subordinates, peers, friend or even family members who are psychologically close to decision-maker. Therefore, both a person having decision-making authority and a person who can influence decision-making have power in the organization.

Power Centers

There exist people in the organization who desire to be stronger. They also want people dependent on them. Specialists, people with special powers deliberately delay decisions or hold resources so that they become more demanding. Power centers exist in various departments. It may in form of reservoir of power.

Dependency

Strength of power depends upon degree of dependency. Greater the dependency on the power holder greater influence will the power holder exercise over his subordinates. Dependency is directly related between power holder and those do not have it. Power holder holds power of retention to be able to increase dependency. All managers have two dimensional power bases. One is the power generated by the organizational authority and the second, the personal power by virtue of personality.

Centrality

Centrality refers to activities, which are central to organizations. Finance is central activity in the organization hence the finance manager holds power in excess of his authority. Finance manager further allocates funds to various departments. Department heads therefore also become powerful not because they can further allocate funds to their subordinates but because centrality of activity. Managers of various departments have power based on their position by virtue of their departmental position. In addition they enhance their power position by virtue of opportunities they get to control activities that are central to the organization. This gives managers authority to control various units and subunits.

Scarcity

When resources are in abundance there is no problem, as everybody would get them based on their requirement. When resources become scares, a person obtaining it will appear to be more powerful. Finance is a scares resource. If a Director of an Institute manages to obtain additional funds from AICTE or by way of consultancy obviously he becomes more powerful in the eyes of the management. It is true of a faculty that may not be judged by efficiency of imparting knowledge but by obtaining finance for the Institute from external sources.

Uncertainty

Management is related to planning for organization. It is basically related to identification of organizational objectives, evaluation of various alternatives and selection of best course of action and planning resources to put in action the course selected. Uncertainty of availability of required manpower with specific skills, raw material, finance can play havoc with the plans. There are situations when government policies change with the change of government that further makes situation more critical. A manager who has a vision and can appreciate what is likely to happen in future and takes corrective actions in advance, obviously garner additional power. According to Kanter most power goes to those people in those functions that provide greater control over what the organization finds currently problematic. Sales and marketing people when markets are competitive, production experts when materials are scares and demand is high; personnel or labour relations specialists when government regulations impinge; finance and accounting types when business is bad and money tight. There is a turning to those elements of the system that seem to have the power to create more certainty in the face of dependency, and to generate a more advantageous position for the organization.

Allocation of Power

Organization allocates power in two ways:

Structural power: Organization structure has hierarchy of authority. Higher the position higher the legitimate authority. Mere granting of authority does not make a person powerful unless he uses it effectively. Invoking sanctions, awarding promotions or even punishments makes a manager powerful. If a leader does not use power, displays lack of interest, does not keep pace with development, delays decisions and lacks effective communication makes a manager ineffective and powerless.

Functional power: Functional power is related to a job a person does. By virtue of division of labour, people in organization do a very specific element of a job. Interdependence of employees develops rather smoothly, which culminates in completion of a job. Any specialization in isolation does not lead to power generation; rather it diminishes its effect. Scarce skills, longer duration of a person in organization, extent of access to vital information are some of the factors that make a person more powerful. Power comes from functional exclusiveness that can be achieved as under:

(*a*) Devote more effort; time energy on unbeaten, unattended fields.

(*b*) Develop friendly work relations.

(*c*) Share information with your subordinates and make them part of decision-making. By seemingly sharing, one attains more power.

(*d*) Communicate judgments rather than justifying it.

(*e*) Handle expertise carefully and yet let there be exclusiveness of skill.

(*f*) Be available when required. Gather relevant information before decision is made.

POLITICS

Politics is about access to power. How organization structures promotes opportunities or enhance access to power is therefore of considerable importance. Pffeffer defines, ***"Politics as those activities taken within organizations to acquire, develop and use power and other resources to obtain one's preferred outcome in a situation in which there is uncertainty or dispenses about choices."*** He further states that power is a force, a store of potential influence through which events can be affected. Politics involves those activities or behaviours through which power is developed and used in organizational settings. *Power is a property of system at rest; politics* *is the study of power in action.* An individual, sub-unit or department may have power within organizational context at some period of time. Politics involves the exercise of power to get something accomplished as well as those activities that are undertaken to expand the power already possessed or the scope over which it can be exercised. Departments in organizations are dependant on each other in varying degree. It is the degree of dependency between departments, the power relationship is expressed. Such relationship can be collaborative or conflicting depending upon the variables. Chief among the variables is mutual task dependence. This is an incentive for collaboration, but also an occasion for conflict and the means for bargaining over inter-departmental issues. Walton and Dutton have stated that role problems cause interdepartmental friction. Blocked promotions, role ambiguity and faulty performance appraisal leads to scapegoat. An interpersonal skill plays a vital role in management of political influence. Sub-units control contingencies for one another's activities and draw power from the dependencies thereby created. A sub-unit power is related to its coping with uncertainty (which includes preventing uncertainty) to substitutability (whether there are alternative means of performing the operations) and centrality (the degree to which sub-unit is linked into the organizations systems).

Organizational Politics

Political behaviour is designed and initiated to overcome opposition. These are illustrated as under:

Resolution of non-programmed decision is a complicated matter as there are no set solutions. This unique problem involves consideration of various factors and variables. They remain ambiguous in nature and subject to political maneuvering by those who have knowledge and techniques to solve them. Politics plays a vital role in organizations to create decisions in favour pertaining to sensitive areas like strategic planning, mergers and acquisitions, policy change and so on.

Organizational Change

Organizational change is continuous process. People who are in position to take decision can very effectively influence the decisions. These change may include vital areas like restructuring, creating new departments, launching a new product line, appointment of key personnel at top levels and thus creating a *lobby* within the organization. This may prove to be counter productive and harmful for maintaining peaceful atmosphere.

External Environment

External environment is highly mobile and generally unpredictable. It is the ability of the organization to meet the challenges effectively by appropriately maneuvering internal environmental factors, technology and processes. Thus political behaviour is heightened when interested people manage these. Rechard (1988) states that "resources are continuously becoming scares and competitive and the ever changing technology makes the environment more complex to handle, requiring organizations to continuously evaluate their goals and strategies. This would make most organizations political in nature so that managers in responsible positions must become sensitive to political processes and games in order to play their role in acquiring and maintaining political power."

TECHNIQUES OF POLITICAL PLAYS

Mintzberg (1983) has suggested the following strategies to wield political power in the organizations.

Cultivate Right Allies

One must have alliance with right people who are rising in the corporate ladder. It is necessary to develop friendship with upper level management. It may also be advisable to form alliance with boss's secretary or someone who is close to powerful person.

Be Positive Towards Others

Human being wants to be appreciated and complemented for any work done. When you appreciate other people they will develop a positive outlook towards you and may be helped when situation demands.

Reciprocity

It is good to help others. Accordingly, recognize those members of the organization who will be more powerful in future. Help them so that they reciprocate the same when you need their support.

Be Persuasive

It is necessary to develop a persuasive technique to get the job done. Forceful agreements when stated eloquently are often highly influencing. It improves your image and substantial pay offs in a future time.

Image Building

One must build a positive image and create good impression in the organization. One must therefore be honest, sincere, attentive, and sociable and display organizational citizenship behaviour.

Control Information

More the critical information and fewer the people who have axis to it, stronger the power base. It is therefore necessary to control and disseminate critical information when it is likely to have impact and serve self-interest.

MACHIAVELLIANISM (1469–1527)

Niccolo Machiavelli, an Italian philosopher has formulated a set of behaviour for maintaining political power. Christie and Geis have formulated an attitude scale in conformity with some basic tenets of Machiavelli. The aim of the scale is to measure the extent to which an individual follows Machiavelli views. This attitude is known as "Mach Scale". The characteristics of people who measure high on mach scale are as follows:

- They have high esteem and self-confidence and behave in their own self-interest even at the expense of others.
- Others consider them, as cool and calculating and they would not hesitate to take advantage of others.
- They tend to form alliances with people in power for the sole purpose of benefiting themselves.
- They believe that end justify means even if it involves lies, deceit and moral compromise.
- They manipulate others by false flatter and exaggerated praise and they will make friends only for the purpose of using them.
- They have very unfavourable views of human nature. They believe that "anyone who completely trusts anyone else is asking for trouble."
- They will say that others want to hear but they will not set others stand in the way of their personal gain.
- They are on the look out and select situations where their tactics would work most effectively such as face-to-face emotional, unstructured and ambiguous condition.
- They are able to exert control over such unclear situations.

The above attitude indicates selfish and unproductive in organizational setting. Management must identify such individuals in the organization who muster political power by adopting Machiavellian tendencies and be prepared to take measures to counter their designs. This will ensure healthy work environment.

Pettigrew (1974) has identified some behavioural patterns that executives generally use to follow to enhance the political power in organization. The catalog shown below refers to influence process between specialists and executives. Pettigrew describes the way specialists credibility is undermined by the executives in Table 16.1 below:

STRATEGIES USED BY EXECUTIVES ETHICS IN OD

Table 16.1 A Catalog of Ploys adopted by Managers

S.No.	Strategies	Actions
1.	Strategic rejection	If executive is self-assured and powerful, rejects the report.
2.	"Bottom drawer it"	Executive sends a memo praising the specialist's the technicality, and then puts it away and forgets it.
3.	Mobilising political support	Executives call it the credits from colleagues.
4.	Nitty-gritty tactics	Minor details are questioned, and mistakes in details are raised to try to discredit the whole report.

Contd...

5.	Emotional tactics	Relies on appeals to emotional states.
6.	But in the future	Argument that data may be historically accurate but does not consider future changes.
7.	Invisible man	Avoidance, often with the support of a secretary, so no discussion can take place.
8.	Further investigation is required	Specialist is sent away to collect more information, either because terms of references are changed, or to follow up the more interesting issues raise in the support.
9.	Scapegoat	A suitable scapegoat, who is raised as a threat to any change proposed.
10.	Deflection	Discussion is deflected away from the main areas by concentrating the attention on less crucial matters.

Political behaviour is of two types first an ethical behaviour that is acceptable and an unethical behaviour. Baddeley and James (1990) seek to distinguish between *'politicking' and 'maneuvering'*. The former refers to acting in self-defence, self-oriented where people defend their ego by employing tactics that is called 'game playing'. The latter approach is distinguished by the sense of personal inequity where conscious decisions (choices) are made in different situations. The other dimension in the organization is political awareness, generally referred to the extent a person is able to understand and interpret the political behaviour in the organization. In simple word, how one is able to 'read' a political situation. Baddeley and James have suggested the behaviour model of various managers as indicated in Figure 16.1 below:

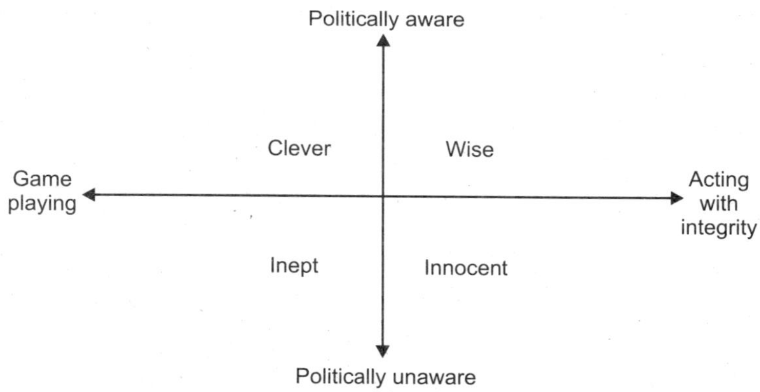

Figure 16.1 Behavioural Model—reading political situations

Reading Political Situation

Each of the four boxes above presents behaviour i.e., **clever, inept, wise** and **innocent,** depending upon the person's capacity to read situations and their propensity to play games or to act with integrity.

ETHICS IN OD

Ethics is related to value, assumptions and beliefs in the organization. It is essential that all organizations have ethical systems inbuilt in all their organizational practices. (1) Belief is proposition about how the world works that the individual accepts as true; it is a cognitive fact for the person. (2) Values are also beliefs, and are defined as; beliefs about what is desirable or 'good' (freedom) and what is undesirable and 'bad' (dishonesty). (3) Assumptions are beliefs that are regarded as so valuable and obviously correct that they are taken for granted and rarely examined or questioned. Thus values, assumptions and beliefs are all cognitive facts or proposition with values being belief about good and bad and assumptions being strongly held. Values are of three types:

(*a*) **Humanistic value:** It proclaims the very importance of the individual in the organization. Humanistic values treats people with respect and dignity and assume that every individual has intrinsic worth. It views all people having potential for growth and development.

(*b*) **Optimistic value:** It emphasizes that the people are basically good, progress is possible and desirable in all human dealings in the organization. Rationality, reason and goodwill are the tools for making progress.

(*c*) **Democratic value:** Asserts the sanctity of the individual, the right of people to be free from arbitrary misuse of power, fair, equitable treatment for all. It emphasizes justice through the rule of law and due process.

Events that Lead to Promotion of Ethics in the Organization

Taylor, in his work gave a scientific connotation to the work. His major contribution has been Time and motion theory, introduction of piece rate of payment, breaking jobs into small parts and thus promoting specialization, standardization that led to organized work culture. Mayo made the ethical treatment to the individual in his research during the beginning of the 20th century. He emphasized the concept of group phenomenon. Identified that it is the group norms and cohesiveness that improves productivity. He emphasized that individuals be treated with utmost dignity and they will accept change voluntarily. Hawthorne studies done by Mayo led to the following ethical practices in the organization between 1940–60s:

- Participative management.
- Greater attention to workers needs.
- Social revolution in the work environment.
- Greater stress on training and development.
- Promotion and development of individual skills.
- Humanizing work place.
- Promotion of group tasks.

Later social scientist laid more stress on the organizational philosophy based on the human value system. Maslow evolved need hierarchy theory of motivating workers and emphasized that organizational policies follow a set pattern of administration that would lead to need fulfillment of employees. Likert in 1960s has very emphatically promoted leadership theories. He recommended democratic way of leadership as against the autocratic leadership. His work promoted among other things group orientation in work setting, group decision-making, and promoted social psychology in the work environment.

Early statements of OD practitioners laid stress on the following democratic and humanistic values:

(*a*) Development of increased understanding between and within working groups in order to reduce tension.

(*b*) Development of better methods of conflict resolution.

(*c*) They identified improvement in interpersonal competence, a shift of value so that human factors and feelings come to be considered to be legitimate.

(*d*) Development of organic rather than mechanical way of various systems that support ethical values in the organizations.

OD practitioners held several assumptions about the *nature and functioning* of the organizations:

1. A basic building block of the organization is groups/teams. Basic change is therefore required in the teams/groups and not in the individual.
2. Relevant change goal is the reduction of inappropriate competition between parts of the organization. For change to be effective, development of collaborative conditions are necessary.
3. Decision-making should be promoted at the grass route levels of the individuals and freedom of action should be ensured.
4. Organizations, units, sub-units and individuals continuously manage their affairs against goals. Controls are interim measurements and not final/basic managerial strategy.
5. A goal of a healthy organization is to develop trust and open communication, mutual trust and confidence between and across levels.
6. People support what they create. Permit them to participate in decision-making. It is called ownership value.

It is therefore necessary to understand that though the individuals have drive for attaining their personal goals, most people desire to attain higher levels goals. They try and make greater contribution to attain organizational goals. Management therefore should adopt the following approach towards the groups/teams and even the individuals:

- Ask — Risk taking
- Listen — Permit failures
- Support — Remove obstacles and barriers
- Challenge — Give autonomy
- Encourage — Give responsibility

Value Study

A study was carried out to answer the following three questions and the answer are given along with:

Question 1: What are the various reasons that attracted an OD practitioner to OD?

Answers:
(*a*) To create change.
(*b*) To positively impact people and the organizations.
(*c*) To enhance effectiveness and profitability of the organizations.
(*d*) Learn and grow.
(*e*) Exercise power and influence.

Question 2: Which value do you believe are associated with OD work?

Answers:
(*a*) Increasing efficiency and effectiveness of the organization.
(*b*) Creating openness in communication.
(*c*) Empowering employees to act.
(*d*) Enhancing productivity.
(*e*) Promoting organizational participation.

Question 3: Which value do you think should be associated with the OD work?

Answers:
(*a*) Empowerment of employees.
(*b*) Creating openness in the organization.
(*c*) Facilitating ownership of processes.
(*d*) Promoting a culture of collaboration and its outcome.
(*e*) Continuous learning.

SUMMARY

Power is derived from the official position one holds. Those in power are able to marshal resources to their advantage. Power, authority and responsibility are inter-related. French and Raven have identified six bases of power. These are reward, coercive, legitimate, referent, expert and information power. Effectiveness of power depends upon the situation, perceived differences between the power of involved parties and its acceptance of legitimacy. The people having charismatic personality can also enjoy power. In organizational setting power base can be enhanced by using knowledge and other resources. Managers can improve their importance by delaying decision-making and creating power centers. Creation of dependency, resorting to centrality of resources, creating scarcity of resources and uncertainty leads to a feeling of an enhanced authority. For efficient working, it is necessary to delegate power to subordinates, resort to division of work to the maximum extent, modify organization structure if required and give functional powers to all the individuals so that they feel empowered and develops a sense of responsibility. Politics is about access to power. Power is the property of systems at rest while politics is the study of power in action. It is the dependency between departments, the power relationship is expressed. Managers can play power game to their advantage by creating scarcity of resources, resorting to non-programmed decisions, and setting ambiguous goals, introducing organizational changes in vital areas and managing external environment. There are various techniques of political play. These included to cultivate right allies, being positive in dealing with others, being reciprocal and persuasive thus building a right image.

Machiavelli suggests that end justifies the means and that the job must be accomplished at any cost. He has suggested various techniques of manipulating power. Pettigrew has identified some behavioural patters that executive generally follow to influence management process. Among other things it includes rejection, mobilizing political support, questioning of minor details with an aim to discredit the individual, avoidance, deflecting the main issue and making a person scapegoat if situation demands. Baddeley and James have suggested a model of reading political situations. They have classified individuals as clever, wise, inept and innocent depending upon the political awareness a person has and his ability to read situations and their propensity.

Ethics in organizations have been studied in greater details. It is related to achieve organization effectiveness. OD strategies lay stress on development of the group/teams and empowering them so that they function effectively. Organizations must lay greater attention on team building, open communication, problem-solving, group dynamics, and managing the systems effectively. It will promote self-indulgence in the organization and achievement of organizational goals.

TEXT QUESTIONS

1. Define organization development.
2. Explain the concept of power.
3. What are the various areas where politics is played?
4. What are various bases of power?
5. Explain politics that is generally played in the organization.
6. What are various techniques of political play?
7. What theory has been propagated by Machiavelli?
8. Explain various ethical concepts that are necessary to implement OD.
9. What are various events that lead to organizational development?

Exercise

Visit an organization in your neighbourhood. Study the following aspects:

- The culture the organization is propagating?
- Where is the power base in the organization?
- What are various ethical practices, the organization is good in?
- Politics in the organization is a common phenomenon, what politics did you notice during your visit?

CHAPTER 17

Quality of Work Life (QWL)

CHAPTER PLAN

- *Introduction*
- *Definitions*
- *Features of Quality of Work Life*
- *Model of QWL*
- *Mental Health*
- *Burnout*
- *Quality Circle (QC)*
- *Summary*
- *Text Questions*
- *Bibliography*
- *Case Study: QWL in Bhilai Steel Plant*

INTRODUCTION

Information technology, knowledge management, adoption of new technology and introduction of various processes has had tremendous impact on human behaviour. Individuals are aware as to what is happening around the world. Standards of living have increased. Material demands of the people have enhanced and people are no more interested in what is required? They are interested as to what is desirable, seeing the world around. The social changes has made it necessary to evaluate the desired quality of work forces taking into consideration the globalised environment prevailing now in India. An attempt is therefore being made in this chapter to study the concept of Quality of Work Life (QWL).

DEFINITIONS

1. Nadler and Lawler[1] define QWL as ***"A way of thinking about people, work and organizations. Its distinctive elements are, (1) A concern about the impact of work on people as well as on organizational effectiveness and, (2) The idea of participation in organizational problem-solving and decision-making."***
2. According to Luthans[2], ***"The overriding purpose of QWL is to change the climate at work so that the human-technological-organizational interface leads to a better quality of work life."***
3. Sangeeta Jain[3] viewed QWL as consisting of a ***"Whole parcel of terms and notions all of which really belong under the quality of working life umbrella. They include industrial effectiveness, human resource development, organizational effectiveness, work restructure, job enrichment, socio-technical systems, working humanization, group-work concepts, labour management, cooperation, working together, workers participation, workers involvement, labour management and work structures."***
4. (Hunt et al.), ***QWL is the overall quality of human experience in the work place. Today many concepts and theories are discussed and adopted for organizational development that reflects QWL and Theory Y themes.***

   The hallmark of excellence in management of organization includes the following:

   (*a*) **Empowerment:** Involving people from all levels of responsibility in decision-making.

   (*b*) **Trust:** Redesigning jobs, systems, and structures to give people more personal discretion in their work.

   (*c*) **Rewards:** Building reward systems that are fair, relevant and consistent, while contingent on work performance.

   (*d*) **Responsiveness:** Making the work setting more pleasant and supportive of individual needs and family responsibilities.

   (*e*) **Work life balance:** Organizations should ensure that the demands of the job are a reasonable fit with one's personal life and non-work responsibilities.

FEATURES OF QUALITY OF WORK LIFE

Quality of work life is a concept evolved to solve problems and achieve organizational development. Some of the features of QWL are as under:

1. Team building and voluntary participation of employees in organizational developmental programme.
2. Training of employees in team problem-solving.
3. An understanding of no loss of job in the event of loss caused due to implementation of QWL programmes.

4. Training and development of employees.
5. Use of quality circles and organization for periodic meetings to review the progress of quality of products and to study the problems affecting employee performance at the plant level and general work environment.
6. Organization of meetings, brainstorming sessions to discuss on the matters of customer welfare, quality, safety, customer care and production schedules.
7. Job designing.
8. Skill training.
9. Autonomy of planning.
10. Evolving various methods to promote responsiveness of workers.
11. Any other issue, which promotes employee autonomy, problem-solving and improvement of work culture within the overall umbrella of development of organization.

MODEL OF QWL@

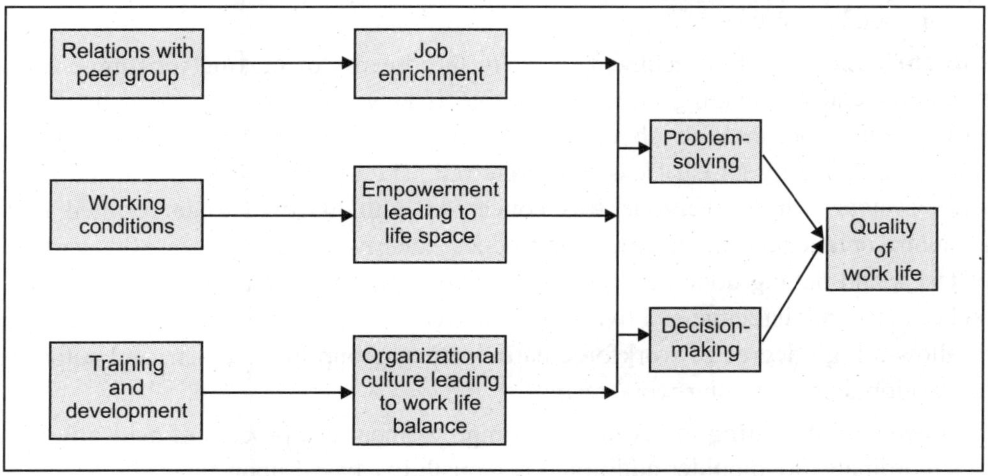

Figure 17.1 Model of QWL (Kondalkar)@

1. **Relations with the peer group:** Workers should enjoy freedom of action and they should undertake their work without any psychological burden. Relationship with the peer group and with superiors must be cordial. Each one should be able to express ones views without any fear and that expressed views should be considered by all and accepted if there is any merit in it. Interpersonal communication should be of a very high order.
2. **Working conditions:** Physical working conditions and layout of the plant should be scientific. It should render physical comfort to the employees when undertaking any physical movement. Tools and literature should be available and that they should not have to run

around for the same. Advice of the superior must always be at hand. Factors like reasonable hours of work, zero risk conditions and devoid of age restrictions create good work environment. Provisions of Factories Act, 1948 should be followed and any compromise on implementation is likely to have hazardous consequences in the work environment.

3. **Training and development:** Nothing gives greater pleasure to the employees than when they are considered fit for the next promotions. It is possible when all employees are imparted training on a regular basis. While workers can be trained on the job, it is executives training that matters most. Following points should be considered:
   (*a*) Organize regular seminars, group discussions and workshops.
   (*b*) Tie-up with professional institutes for training of your employees for upgradation of skills.
   (*c*) Initiate research projects.
   (*d*) Collaborate with sister concern for training and development of employees.
   (*e*) Have knowledge management concept prevailing in your organization.
   (*f*) Obtain regular feedback from your employees about their perception on training and development. Money spent on this aspect is an investment. It is bound to pay rich dividends in future.
4. **Job enrichment:** Job enrichment refers to the process of making jobs more interesting, satisfying and challenging. This is possible if new contents are added to the job. Job enrichment is done through job redesign. Among the job redesign studies conducted in India, study conducted by Nitish De is often referred. The study diagnosed that the fragmented work system, where everyone was concerned with his own trade resulted in lack of emotional or rational commitment to the product, extensive idle time because of interdependence of tasks, and having done the same job for years, workers felt bored with the task. They lacked sense of challenge and overall productivity was 26.8 per cent. They are encouraged to allow a high degree of workforce participation, group involvement and autonomy, and to develop self-managing work teams.
5. **Empowerment leading to life space:** "Empowerment is a process of delegating authority to subordinates to shoulder additional responsibility based upon their ability, knowledge, experience and power to achieve autonomy, independence and quality of work life for organizational effectiveness." It is unleashing of power within the work domain of employees that they already possess. Those organizations are likely to survive that has excellent, skilled, experienced and dedicated manpower. To achieve this end, organizations should empower their employees in the turbulent times. Empowerment is an effective management tool to achieve maximum potential of employee. The old order of bureaucracy proposed by Max Weber is no more valid in the present times. To achieve greater degree of involvement and responsibility a process of empowerment is necessary. Empowerment is the process of passing authority and responsibility to individuals at lower levels in the organizational hierarchy to enhance feeling of self-efficacy and a sense of owing a job (Kondalkar, 2007).[4] Manager's

management styles are to empower employees and thereby to increase workplace environment, in turn, are intended to result in empowerments in work performance and good citizenship behaviours as well as quality of work life. QWL should be so enriching that the employees carry home the pleasant memories of the work place. It should not impinge upon the personal life of the individuals. Frequent transfers, late hour working, frequent tours are not recommended as it saps the energy of the employees. It disturbs the life style and is counter productive for smooth organizational functioning. It causes stress amongst the employees and imbalances work environment.

6. **Organizational culture:** It is defined, as ***"the shared attitude and perceptions in an organization that are based on a set of fundamental norms and values and help members understand the organization."*** Organizational culture is not inborn. It has to be invented and later developed over a period of time. It enables employees to perform within the framework of the organization's culture. Environment both internal and external plays a dominant role in developing the culture and so does demographic factors organizational culture ***"consists of norms, values and unwritten rules of conduct of an organization as well as management styles, priorities, belief and interpersonal behaviours that prevail. Together they create climate that influences how well people communicate, plan and make decisions."***[5] It originates from the founders of the organization based on value system held by them. It is further passed on, down the line. Organizational culture is also a function of the nature of work and goals of the organization. While decentralized work culture will promote autonomy that will lead to greater job satisfaction. Peters and Waterman state, "Without exception, the dominance and coherence of culture proved to be an essential quality of the excellent companies. Moreover, the stronger the culture and more it was directed towards the market place, the less need was there for policy manuals, organization charts and detailed procedures and rules. In these companies, people, way down the line know what they are supposed to do in most situations because the handful of guiding values is crystal clear.[6] Organizations should ensure that job demands are not excessive on the employee that it clashes with one's personal life. If an appropriate organizational culture is introduced in the organization, the quality of work life of the employees will improve. It will bring growth and higher productivity leading to achievement of competitive edge.

7. **Problem-solving:** Group decisions are better than the decisions taken by the individual. In the same way group problem solving is recommended in the organization. It is a general practice that the departmental heads/representatives meet periodically (generally once a week) to take a stock of the situations and resolve any problem that may be faced by a particular group/department/section. It is recommended that all individuals be trained in such a fashion that corrective measures are taken in the process and that the problem creation is avoided. The psychological bent is important in this regard. If the employees are satisfied, happy, and have developed a sense of belonging to the organization, the problems are generally reduced. Quality circles play a decisive role in problem-solving in the organization.

8. **Decision-making:** No business can survive without effective decision-making. Decision-making is an essential part of very function of management. In the words of Peter F. Drucker, "Whatever a manager does, he does it through decision-making." Decision lies deeply embedded in the process of management. Decision-making involves thinking and deciding before doing and so is inherent in every managerial functions. A decision-maker should ask these questions: (1) What is my objective? (2) What does it involve? (3) How far can I plan now? This is why; decision-making is often called the *essence of managing.* Rational decision-making involves following stages:
   (*a*) Diagnosing and defining the problem.
   (*b*) Analyzing the problem.
   (*c*) Collection of data.
   (*d*) Developing alternatives.
   (*e*) Review of key factors.
   (*f*) Selecting the best alternatives.
   (*g*) Putting the decision into practice.
   (*h*) Follow up.
9. **Effective decision-making must be rational.** *Rationality is the ability to follow a systematic, logical, thorough approach in decision-making.* Thus, if a decision is taken after a thorough analysis and reasoning and weighing the consequences of various alternatives, such a decision will be called an objective or rational decision. In the present scenario decisions are highly supported by decision support systems and quantitative techniques are available for the manager to take decisions. He must make extensive use of the same. Large volume of data is also available through electronic media. Knowledge management has added an extra function to already available functions the manager has. It is the responsibility of the management to promote creativity and innovative ideas among the working class. These must be rewarded. All individuals must make an effort to contribute to the over all efficiency of the organization. It is only possible if the employees develop the sense of belonging to the organization.
10. **Quality of work life:** If the above factors are attended to on a long-term basis the human-technological-organizational interface will be achieved. Organizations will get willing workers who are progressive and dedicate themselves to the growth of the organization. Objective of quality of work life (QWL) is to improve the general working environment of the organization so that the employees enjoy working because they feel pleasant experience interacting with each other. Lawler (1975) suggest that one of the ways of measuring QWL is to focus on the behavioural outcomes such as rate of turnover, absenteeism, drug abuse, alcoholism, and mental and physical illness resulting from psychologically harmful jobs. Dubin (1975) point out that job involvement or the self-investment of individuals at work is a good index of QWL experienced at work. Uma Sekaran has explained QWL encompassing the

extent of job involvement or self-investment at work, their sense of competence (*i.e.,* the extent of their confidence in their own competence at work), the job satisfaction or the satisfaction they derive from the various facets of their work such as from the nature of the job itself, the supervision, co-workers, pay, promotion opportunities, growth and development on the job, and other aspects of work environment. Mental health of the employees is also an important factor to measure QWL.

11. While deliberating on QWL, International Labour Office (ILO)[7] enumerates the following areas as determinants of QWL:

(*a*) Hours of work and arrangements of working time.

(*b*) Work organization and job content.

(*c*) Impact of new technologies on working conditions.

(*d*) Working conditions of women, young workers, older workers and other special categories.

(*e*) Work-related welfare services and facilities.

(*f*) Shop floor participation in the improvement of working conditions.

MENTAL HEALTH

Uma Sekaran[8] has carried out research and developed a model of mental health. He has considered individual, job, organisation and other network factors as independent variables. Job involvement, sense of competence and job satisfaction as intervening variables and mental health as dependant variable, which is an ultimate indicator of QWL. The model is explained in Figure 17.2 below:

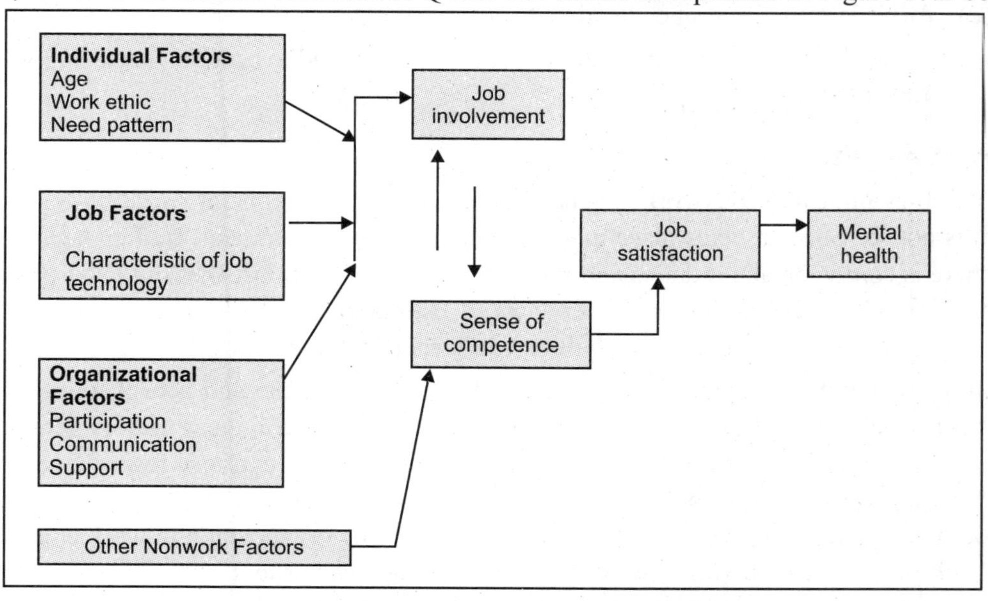

Figure 17.2 Paths to the mental health of employees

QWL, apart from employee point of view is also considered from organizational point of view that includes factors that measures organizational growth and effectiveness. These include profits, market share, customer satisfaction, product quality, product innovativeness, services after sales and the image they carry. Social aspect of the QWL measures factors like ecology maintenance, pollution control generating additional employment, social responsiveness etc. QWL is therefore measured by combined impact of individuals delight, organizational growth and societal gains.

BURNOUT

Burnout is a type of existential crisis in which work is no longer a meaningful function. Workers who experience burnout may no longer view their job as meaningful. They feel work as tedious, redundant and insignificant. They experience total fatigue that may show itself in the form of boredom, depression and a powerful sense of alienation. Work related behaviour of executives indicates very little concern for quality, creativity, enthusiasm and contribution to organizational goals.

Morely and Katherine (1982)[9] in their work on the subject have identified the pattern of behaviour of burned out executives. They concluded that predictable behaviour is as under:

(*a*) Tendency to balance others in the organization for their burnout.

(*b*) To complain bitterly about aspects of work which in the past were not areas of concern.

(*c*) To miss work because of non-specific and increasingly prevalent illness.

(*d*) To daydream and sleep on the job.

(*e*) To be last to come and the first to leave.

(*f*) To bicker with co-workers or appear uncooperative and to become increasingly isolated from others.

Causes of Burnout

1. **Work estimation:** Overwork is generally considered to be a major cause for burnout. But it is not so. Burnout takes place in a chaotic, unstable environment. It often happens when there is confusion about duties and future managerial directions. Burnout takes place when there is management by crises. Low work estimation may also cause burnout. When executive feel that there is no challenge and innovativeness in the work.
2. **Job mismatch:** It has been observed that executive choose and accept jobs which has higher extrinsic reward like high salaries and power. These hygiene factors generally fail to motivate executives for a longer time. Decision to choose extrinsic reward over intrinsic rewards results in unhappiness. Job mismatch may be observed in personal value and organizational value system and autonomy provided by organization in work environment. Lack of gratification from the work generally leads to burnout.
3. **Organizational productivity:** When executive are not able to meet organizational objective due to external environmental factors like shortage of raw material, governmental rules,

market demand etc., they experience a burnout. They feel a sense of helplessness. Burnout may also be noticed where there is a strict bureaucratic way of doing things and very little scope for exploitation of personal skills, innovation and creativity.

4. **Personal problems:** Personal problems like unhappy married life, financial instability children education/job security may cause stress leading to burnout. Persons with a predisposition to burnout may be badly affected by problems unrelated to work.

Prevention of Burnout

As seen in the preceding reading, burnout emanate from the organizational policy, structure, practices, nature of the work and personal characteristics of the individual. Probability of burnout increases if there is a mismatch between individual and job fit. Preventive measures include diagnosis, prevention and treatment.

1. *Diagnosis*

It is the responsibility of all individuals to ensure that his subordinate is not subjected to burnout. This can be identified from the early warning by observing clinical sings that include the following:

(*a*) Feeling of lethargy.

(*b*) Lack of productivity.

(*c*) Lack of interest in the present job and feeling that change of job and place may change the present situation without even considering upward mobility.

(*d*) Feeling of loneliness, forced isolation and acute discomfort.

(*e*) Feeling of lack direction less.

(*f*) Traumatic personal problems like death in the family or major accident.

2. *Prevention*

Morley and Katherine have suggested the following preventive and treatment strategies:

(*a*) Seeking a fit between characteristics of the individual, complexity of the job and type organizational structure.

(*b*) Developing programmes that help individuals cope with the causes of stress that lead to burnout.

(*c*) Teaching and supporting self-diagnosis and individual adaptation strategies for addressing burnout symptoms.

3. *Treatment*

(*a*) Evaluate and understand the causes of burnout.

(*b*) Determine change both personal and organizational to return to normal work related functioning.

(*c*) Develop sensitivity to the sings of burnout to cope with likelyhood of the same in future.

(*d*) Develop skills to deal with feelings and emotions to avoid burnout to fellow employees.

QUALITY CIRCLE (QC)

1. The Japanese Union of Scientists and Engineers originated the concept of QC in Japan in the year 1949 as vehicle for statistical quality control. Ohamae[10] explained the concept of QC. According to him, "Quality circle is a group of about 10 relatively autonomous workers from same division of a company who volunteer to meet for an hour or so, once or twice a month. After work, they discuss ways to improve the quality of their products, the production process in their part of plant and the working environment. The long-term objective is to build a sense of responsibility for improving quality but the immediate goal is to exchange ideas in a place uninhibited by barriers of age, sex, or company ranks."
2. ***Objectives***
   (*a*) To develop an organization.
   (*b*) To develop respect for human-relations and induce job satisfaction.
   (*c*) To deploy human capabilities to the fullest extent and draw out their infinite potential.
3. ***Characteristics***
   (*a*) It is a group effort.
   (*b*) It is voluntary in nature.
   (*c*) Efforts of employees are directed towards quality control in their respective place of work.
   (*d*) Members of quality control meet frequently at company cost. (They are paid extra by the company for the work of quality control they put in).
   (*e*) The quality control group is a team of volunteers without any bias of rank, sex, or the age.
   (*f*) Their main aim is to find out ways and means to improve quality of product and services without incurring additional cost.

Quality Control in India

Bharat Heavy Electricals Limited (BHEL) is the pioneer organization in India to have started the QC functions way back in 1981. The objectives of BHEL for QC are as under.[11]

(*a*) Reduce human error and enhance quality.
(*b*) Inspire more effective teamwork.
(*c*) Promote job involvement.
(*d*) Increase employee motivation.
(*e*) Build an attitude of problem prevention.
(*f*) Improve company communication.
(*g*) Develop harmonious manager/worker relationship.
(*h*) Promote personal and leadership development.

Suggestions for improvement of quality control in India [12]:

1. The employer should:
   (*a*) Provide physical amenities at the work place, health and safety, and welfare provisions.
   (*b*) Involve workers in decision-making on all matters.
   (*c*) Initiate suitable forms of work design.
   (*d*) Formalise QWL experience for future use.
   (*e*) Re-examine policies of work.
   (*f*) Develop an appreciation of changing environment.
2. The unions and workers should:
   (*a*) Educate and make workers aware of QWL.
   (*b*) Identify areas of collaboration with management.
   (*c*) Identify ways and means to satisfy workers needs through non-monetary alternatives.
   (*d*) Encourage workers to participate in QWL activities.
   (*e*) Organize labour in unorganized sector and specially make them aware of QWL.
3. The professional organizations should:
   (*a*) Organize workshops and seminars to bring about greater awareness of QWL.
   (*b*) Initiate specific research projects in this field.
   (*c*) Provide professional assistance to organizations to help generate internal competence.
   (*d*) Develop state-of-art profiles on QWL.
   (*e*) Develop a network for collection, storage and dissemination of information on QWL.
4. The government should:
   (*a*) Legislate standards and norms in newer areas.
   (*b*) Change in policy to provide greater autonomy to experiments with QWL.
   (*c*) Execute actions to ensure implementation of legislated facilities.
   (*d*) Encourage and adopt appropriate technology.
   (*e*) Find projects on QWL.
   (*f*) Modify the structure and scope of education in the country.

SUMMARY

QWL is a way of thinking about people, work and organizations. The overriding purpose of QWL is to change the climate at work so that the human-technological-organizational interface leads to a better quality of work life. Some of the important elements are; team building and voluntary participation of employees, training of employees in problem-solving. An understanding of no loss of job in the event of loss caused due to implementation of QWL programmes. Training and development of employees. Use of quality circles, organization of meetings, brainstorming sessions to discuss on the matters of customer welfare, quality, safety, and customer care and production schedules. Job redesigning and skill training.

The author has suggested a model of QWL. It involves attention on various factors like relations with peer group, working conditions, training and development. Employees should be empowered leading to life space. Suitable organizational culture is pre-requirement of any QWL project to be successful. QC groups should solve problem and the team involved in the jobs should resort to group decision-making. QWL is successful where workers are progressive and dedicate themselves to the growth of the organization. Objective of Quality of Work Life (QWL) is to improve the general working environment of the organization so that the employees enjoy working because they feel pleasant experience interacting with each other. International Labour Office (ILO) has enumerated determinants of QWL: It is the responsibility of the organization to promote mental health of the workers. Quality Circle (QC) should be introduced in the organization that can take care of the quality of product and services.

Burnout is a type of existential crisis in which work is no longer a meaningful function. Workers who experience burnout may no longer view their job as meaningful. They feel work as tedious, redundant and insignificant. They experience total fatigue that may show itself in the form of boredom, depression and a powerful sense of alienation. Work related behaviour of executives indicates very little concern for quality, creativity, enthusiasm and contribution to organizational goals.

Causes of burnout are work estimation, job mismatch, organizational productivity, and personal problems. It is the responsibility of the team members to diagnose, prevention and treat the burnout. Following steps are recommended:

(*a*) Evaluate and understand the causes of burnout.

(*b*) Determine change both personal and organizational to return to normal work related functioning.

(*c*) Develop sensitivity to the sings of burnout to cope with likelyhood of the same in future.

(*d*) Develop skills to deal with feelings and emotions to avoid burnout to fellow employees.

The objectives of QC is to develop an organization and to develop respect for human-relations and induce job satisfaction. Bharat Heavy Electricals Limited is the pioneer organization in India to have started the QC functions way back in 1981. The objectives have been laid down by BHEL for QC. The Government should lay down policy document in this regard and promote employee living standards.

TEXT QUESTIONS

1. Explain the concept of QWL. Why is QWL required?
2. With the help of diagram, explain the model of QWL.
3. What is the basic philosophy behind quality circles? What are its objectives?

4. Take an example of your university and describe the constituents of its QWL. Suggest how can the QWL be improved in your university?
5. Explain QWL model.
6. Explain burnout. How will you as a manager of an organization dignoe, prevent and treat the cases of burnout?

BIBLIOGRAPHY

1. David, A. Nadler and Edward, E. Lawler, Quality of Work Life, Perspectives and Directions, *Organisational Dynamics,* Winter, 1983, pp. 20-30.
2. Fred Luthans, *op. cit.* 1991, p. 17.
3. Sangeeta Jain, *op. cit.*1991, p. 17.
4. Kondalkar, V.G., *Organizational Behaviour*, New Age International (P) Ltd, Publisher, New Delhi, First Edition, 2007.
5. Sinn, larry, *"Corporate Culture"* in Readings in management and organizations, edited by Moniqe A. Pelletier Kendall, Hund Publishing, 1991, p. 378.
6 Peters Thomas, J. and Robert, H. Waterman, *"In Search of Excellence",* Harper and Row, 1982.
7. ILO: Recommendations from the National Seminar on *Improving Quality of Working Life, Productivity,* Vol. 22, No. 4, 1982, pp. 79–83.
8. Uma Sekaran, *Organisation Behaviour, Text and Cases,* Tata McGraw Hills, Fourth reprint 2006.
9. Morely, D. Glickon and Katherine Janka *Executive Under Fire : The Burnout Syndrome,* California Management Review, Vol. 24, No. 3, 1982.
10. K. Ohamae, Quality Control Circles, What Makes Them Work? *The Asian Wall Street Journal,* March 31, 1982.
11. M.G. Kargaonkar, *Quality Circles at BHEL-Case*, Indian Institute of Management, Ahmedabad, 1986.
12. *Ibid*.

OD IN PRACTICE
QWL—THE BALANCING ACT

By
Sonali Majumdar

Jim Bird, the President of worklifebalance.com, a leader in work life balance solutions, has a simple philosophy: "I just want to achieve something today and enjoy something too. And if I do both of these things everyday, for the rest of my life, I'm going to have a pretty good life," he says.

A simple, yet profound concept, and is probably the best advice anyone can offer you for incorporating balance into your work life. Balance is necessary, for it gives you a measure of control over your life. As work schedules become hectic and the customer expects 24 × 7 service from a company, the employee is under constant pressure to perform. "Today, most employees are reeling under long working hours and pressure," says Sanjay Salooja, Founder and CEO, Empower, a work life value company. And if the pressure gets to you, then the balance could tip. The effect is, of course disastrous, with the employer and the employee suffering in the long run. A survey conducted on how personal problems could impact you work life, pointed out that 30 per cent of absenteeism is related to an employee's inability to cope with personal problems. And that nearly two out of every five employees are dissatisfied with the balance between their work and personal lives.

The symptoms of living in imbalance are quite obvious—mental duress and lack of concentration. "The employee is usually in a tearing hurry to shift from one task to the other and is unable to do justice to any," says Ajay Oberoi, Senior Vice-President, Aptech Limited. As a result, he feels tired constantly and eventually burnout sets in. "One can quote the example of Amitabh Bachchan who used to pump 17 hours into his workday. And this is, no doubt, one plausible reason for his illness," says Dr. R.L. Bhatia, CEO, Fun and Joy At Work.

So how does one go about achieving a work life balance? There are five stages that one must go through to achieve this, the first one being the phase where you struggle, to understand what is wrong and what you are missing in life. Says Bhatia, "You just feel out of control." In the second stage, you juggle various responsibilities and develop tricks and techniques that allow you to create a sense of control. "This is a precarious stage and the skills that allow you to juggle two balls may fail as soon as a third ball is added to juggle," he says. Now comes the third stage work life balance where you actually begin to fulfill your multiple responsibilities and enjoy a sense of equilibrium. The trick is to focus on all your energies and get through the day. The fourth is work life integration where you are not only able to fulfill all your work responsibilities but also have enough energy to put towards career planning, career development and personal growth. You have a personal growth. You have a sense of where you are going, says Bhatia. In the final stage of work life harmony, you are completely in control of all aspects of your work-life.

Even organizations have started realizing the importance of work-life balance and are taking some concrete steps to help employees snap out of the imbroglio. A company, for instance, has come up with a Wednesday Blackout policy, which essentially means that lights are switched off at 6 pm every Wednesday—a signal for employees to wrap up and push off. Then there are companies that have formulated flexi-hour policies for their employees. This allows people to adjust their workday while maintaining full-time hours-an ideal arrangement for someone who might want to start work early and leave early. "I know of a manager in a company who worked flexi-hours from December to May to meet with a family responsibility," says Bhatia.

A compressed workweek is another option, "Companies even allow employees to work the entire week and club the holidays together to meet family," says an Editor of publishing house.

For that to happen, you'll obviously have to look for an opportunity to talk to your employer. "It's better to be prepared in advance and not spring it onto a manager on a Friday afternoon in a fit of tears after an exhausting week," says Salooja. Let them know exactly what you are looking for and explain why. Do this not from the perspective of "I need to spend more time with my kids" but in terms of "In order for me to be the most effective employee possible, this is the work arrangement that I need in order to fulfill my commitment."

And if you are wondering whether flexi-arrangements would hamper your career, then let me tell you a flexible schedule does not always limit your career. "It can slow down your career path slightly because it may take you longer to get the necessary experience for promotion, but it shouldn't limit growth in the long run," says Bhatia. After all, it's good to remember that the more out of balance or out of control your life is, the more you pay in terms of physical and emotional health. "You probably won't eat properly or consume more caffeine, more alcohol, more sugar, and you are less likely to exercise on a regular basis. Your relationships, too, could become unstable quite a heavy price to pay for an unbalance life," says Salooja. A stressed employee may spell trouble for companies too. (Source: *Hindustan Times*, dated: 30 May, 2006)

CASE STUDY
QWL IN BHILAI STEEL PLANT

Non-statutory welfare programmes in the Bhilai Steel Plant (BSP) initially emerged because of its geographic location. Housing was the main problem. Though BSP undertook extensive construction programmes, it also provided loans to its employees to construct their own houses.

Medical and educational facilities followed, BSP now has a 520 bed hospital with the most modern facilities. Persons suffering from cancer or requiring artificial limbs are sent to other hospital with an escort and the expenses are reimbursed. BSP spends Rs. 3 crores annually on this operation. There are 40,000 children receiving free education with 1800 teachers on the roll. Car, scooter, and cycle loans are easily available with long-term interest free payment plan. BSP also supports the Bhilai Mahila Samaj, a voluntary all-women organization that stitches uniform and manufactures soap—all of which bought by the 110 Bhilai Cooperatives. It has also initiated a village adoption scheme.

BSP's most significant programme was the establishment of the Steel Employees Welfare Association (SEWA) in 1973 to promote social and welfare activities, to foster fellow feelings among employees, to create a social security fund, and to render financial assistance to nominees in the event of the death of a member, irrespective of the cause or place of death (SEWA, 1975). These activities are over and above those provided by statutory welfare. Contributions come from over 50,000 employees (Rs. 125 per month per member). By the end of April 1976, SEWA had settled 151 cases and paid out Rs. 8,48,750. A members contribution is refunded to him consequent upon his retirement/resignation/termination transfer to another establishment; and in the termination on medical grounds, his contribution is doubled irrespective of the period of membership.

Analyse the above case and also suggest how to use SEWA to improve QWL in BSP.

(Source: Organizational Behaviour, S.S.Khanka, S.Chand and Co. Ltd., 2005)

CHAPTER 18

Emotional Intelligence and Employee Productivity

CHAPTER PLAN

- *Emotions*
- *Terminology*
- *Emotional Dimensions*
- *Emotional Intelligence at Work*
- *Framework of Emotional Competence*
- *Affective Events Theory*
- *Summary*
- *Text Questions*
- *Bibliography*
- *Case Study: Emotions*

EMOTIONS

1. For many years wisdom of a person and his ability to perform was measured by Intelligence Quotient (IQ). IQ was a measure for admission to schools, measurement of performance in studies, for seeking jobs and performance evaluation while on the job. However studies indicate that Emotional Intelligence (EI) is now considered as greater predictor of success than IQ.
2. Wechsler and Robert Thornadike carried out work on non-cognitive aspects of intelligence like social intelligence. In 1990 Salovey and Mayer coined the term 'Emotional intelligence'. They described emotional intelligence as ***"A form of social intelligence that involves the ability to monitor one's own and others' feelings and emotions, to discriminate among them, and to use this information to guide one's thinking and action."*** Cognitive abilities are related to IQ of an individual and non-cognitive with emotions. It has been found that emotional and social skills actually help to improve cognitive functioning also.

TERMINOLOGY

1. **Affect:** A broad range of feelings that people experience.
2. **Emotions:** Intense feelings that are directed at someone or something.
3. **Moods:** Feeling that tend to be less intense than emotions and that lack a contextual stimulus.
4. **Emotional labour:** A situation in which an employee expresses organizationally desired emotions during interpersonal transactions.
5. **Emotional dissonance:** Inconsistencies between the emotions, we feel and emotions we project.
6. **Felt emotions:** An individuals actual emotions.
7. **Displayed emotions:** Emotions that are organizationally required and considered appropriate in a given job.

EMOTIONAL DIMENSIONS

There are literally dozens of emotions. These include anger, contempt, enthusiasm, envy, fear, frustration, disappointment, disgust, happiness, hate, hope, jealousy, joy, love, pride, surprise, and sadness. These are either positive or negative. Positive emotions express a favourable evaluation or feelings. Negative emotions seem to have greater impact on individual. Negative emotions are as strong as five times of positive emotions. That is why negative feelings or fear is remembered over a long period of time. There are essentially six universal emotions and the emotions mention above fall in one of the five emotions. The six emotions are anger, fear, sadness, happiness, disgust and surprise (Woodworth)[1]. These are reflected on one continuum as under:

Emotional Continuum

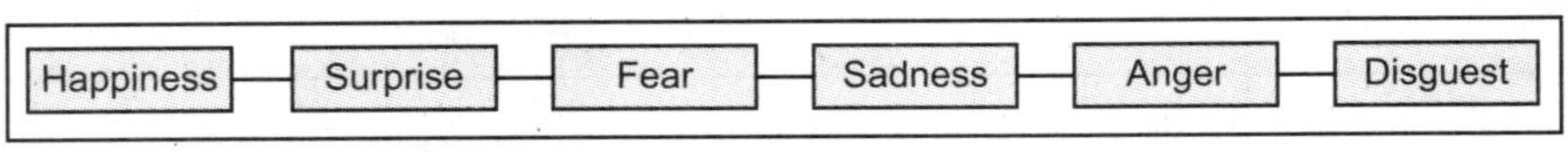

(Source: Based on Woodworth, Experimental Psychology, New York, 1938)

These six emotions have been depicted on one continuum in the above diagram. The closer any two emotions are to each other on this continuum, the more people are likely to confuse them. For instance, happiness and surprise are frequently mistaken for each other, while happiness and disgust are rarely confused.

1. **Intensity:** Different people express emotions differently. You undoubtedly know individuals who almost never show their feelings. They rarely get angry. They never show rage. In contrast, you would have noticed people on an emotional roller coaster. When they are happy. When they are happy they are ecstatic. When they are sad they are deeply

depressed. Jobs make different intensity demands in terms of emotional labour. Aircrew is expected to be cool in extreme situation. Nurses and doctors are required to be calm when patient is in critical situation.

2. **Gender and emotions:** It is widely assumed that women are more "in touch" with their feelings than men–that they react more emotionally and are better able to read emotions in others. Evidence does confirm differences between men and women when it comes to emotional reactions and ability to read others. In contrasting the genders, women show greater emotional expression than men; they experience emotions more intensely; and they display more frequent expressions of both positive and negative emotions, except anger. In contrast to men, women also report comfort in expressing emotions. Finally, women are better at reading non-verbal and paralinguistic cues than are men.[2] This may due to following reasons:
   (*a*) Different ways men and women are socialized.
   (*b*) Men are taught to be tough and brave.
   (*c*) Women are socialized to be nurturing, they are generally warmer and friendlier than men.
   (*d*) Women have more innate ability to read others and prevent their emotion than do men.
   (*e*) Women may have a greater need for social approval and a higher propensity to show positive emotions, such as happiness.

EMOTIONAL INTELLIGENCE AT WORK

Optimism: Martin Seligman developed a construct that he calls "learned optimism". It refers to the causal attributions people make when confronted with failure or setbacks. Optimists tend to make specific, temporary, external causal attributions while pessimist make global, permanent, internal attributions. In research at Met Life, Seligman and his colleagues found that new salesman who was optimists sold 37 per cent more insurance in their first two years than did pessimist. When the company hired a special group of individuals who scored high on optimism but failed the normal screening, they outsold the pessimist by 21 per cent in their first year and 57 per cent in the second. They even outsold the average agent by 27 per cent. Optimism was a better predictor of students' actual grades during the freshman year than high school grades. The ability to manage feelings and handle stress is another aspect of emotional intelligence that has been found to be important for success. A study of store managers in a retail chain found that the ability to handle stress predicted net profits, sales per squire foot, sales per employee and per dollar of inventory investment. A study carried out at Yale University by Sigdal and Barsade indicated that emotional intelligence has as much to do with knowing when and how to express emotions. Good feelings led to improved cooperation, fairness, and overall group performance. It has been established that most effective leaders in the US Navy were warmer, more outgoing, emotionally expressive, dramatic and sociable. Empathy is a particularly important aspect of emotional intelligence, and researchers have known for years that it contributes to occupational success. People who are best at identifying others' emotions are move successful in their work as well as in their social life.

Emotional intelligence is important for success in work and in life. Goleman and Mayer, Salovey and Caruso have argued that by itself emotional intelligence probably is not a strong predictor of job performance. Rather it provides the bedrock for competencies that are. Goleman has tried to represent this idea by making a distinction between emotional intelligence and emotional competence. **"Emotional competence refers to the personal and social skills that lead to superior performance in the world of work. The emotional competencies are linked to and based on emotional intelligence. A certain level of emotional intelligence is necessary to learn the emotional competencies"**, for instance, the ability to recognize accurately what another person is feeling, enables one to develop a specific competency such as 'influence'. Similarly, people who are better able to regulate their emotions will find it easier to develop a competency such as initiative or achievement drive. Ultimately it is these social and emotional competencies that we need to identify and measure, if we want to be able to predict performance.

FRAMEWORK OF EMOTIONAL COMPETENCE

A model of emotional competencies is given below in Figure 18.1 below:

	Self Personal competence	**Other** Social competence
	Self-awareness	**Social awareness**
Recognition	Emotional self-awareness Accurate self-assessment Self-confidence	Empathy Service orientation Organizational awareness
	Self-management	**Relationship management**
Management	Self-control Trustworthiness Consciousness Adaptability Achievement drive Initiative	Developing others Influence Communication Conflict management Leadership Change Catalyst Building bonds Teamwork and Collaboration

Figure 18.1 Framework of emotional competencies

The model reflects recent statistical analysis by Richard Boyatzis that supported four domains as seen in the diagram. These are self-awareness, self-management, social-awareness, and relationship management (Boyatzis, Goleman and Rhee, 2000). They administered the emotional competence inventory, a questionnaire designed to assess the twenty EI competencies to nearly six hundred corporate managers and professionals and engineering, management, and social work graduate students. Respondents were then asked to indicate the degree to which statements about EI related behaviours for instance, the ability to remain calm under pressure were characteristic of themselves. Their ratings were then compared to ratings of those who worked with them. Three key clusters into which the twenty EI competencies were grouped emerged: self-awareness, self-management and social awareness (which subsumes empathy), along with relationship management, which, in the statistical analysis, subsumed the social awareness cluster. While the analysis verifies that the competencies rest within each EI domain, it also suggests that the distinction between the social awareness cluster and the relationship management cluster may be more theoretical than empirical.

AFFECTIVE EVENTS THEORY

Weiss and Cropanzano has suggested a model called Affective Events Theory (AET)[5] has significantly helped study of emotions at work. AET demonstrates that employees react emotionally to things that happen to them at work and that this influences their job performance and satisfaction. This is explained in Figure 18.2 below:

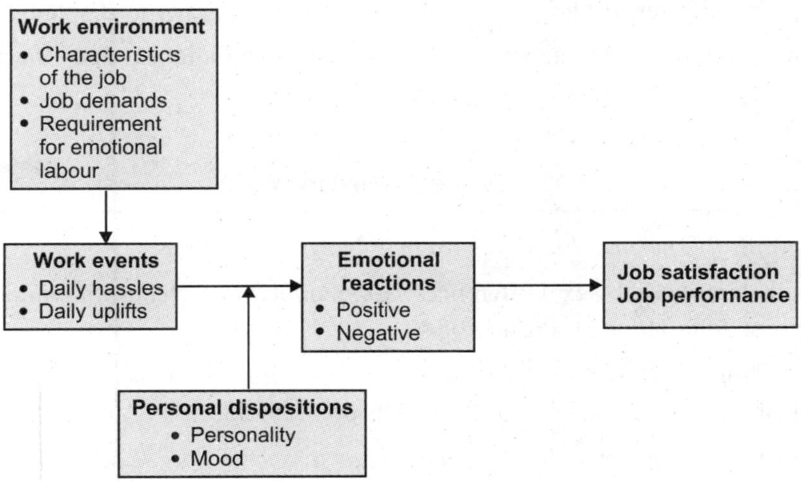

Figure 18.2 Affective events theory

(Source: Emotions in the Work place: New Challenges for Managers—By N.M.Ashkanasy and C.S. Daus, Academy of Management Executives February, 2002).

SUMMARY

In 1990, Salovey and Mayer coined the term 'emotional intelligence'. They described emotional intelligence as "a form of social intelligence that involves the ability to monitor one's own and others' feelings and emotions, to discriminate among them, and to use this information to guide one's thinking and action."

Optimism. Martin Seligman developed a construct that he calls "learned optimism". It refers to the causal attributions people make when confronted with failure or setbacks. Optimists tend to make specific, temporary, external causal attributions while pessimist make global, permanent, internal attributions. The ability to manage feelings and handle stress is another aspect of emotional intelligence that has been found to be important for success. Barsade indicated that emotional intelligence has as much to do with knowing when and how to express emotions. Good feelings led to improved cooperation, fairness, and overall group performance. Studies indicate that Emotional Intelligence (EI) is now considered as greater predictor of success than IQ. AET demonstrates that employees react emotionally to things that happen to them at work and that this influences their job performance and satisfaction.

TEXT QUESTIONS

1. Define emotions. What is the difference between felt emotions and displayed emotions?
2. Explain emotional dimensions with the help of emotional continuum.
3. What is the difference between men and women as regard to display of emotions?
4. Explain Emotional Competencies Model of Boyatzis, Goleman and Rhee.
5. Write in details the Affective Events Theory (AET).

BIBLIOGRAPHY

1. Woodworth, "*Experimental Psychology*", New York, 1938.
2. J.A. Hall, Non-verbal Sex Differences: *Communication, Accuracy and Expressive Style* (Baltimore: John Hopkins Press, 1984).
3. L.W. Hoffman, *"Early Childhood Experiences and Women's Achievement Motives."* Journal of Social Issues 28, No. 2 (1972), pp. 129–52.
4. Cherniss Cary, *Emotional Intelligence: What it is and Why it Matters,* Graduate School of Applied and Professional Psychology Rutgers University Piscataway, NJ 08854.
5. Weiss and Cropanzano, *"Affective Events Theory"*.

OD IN PRACTICE
INTELLIGENCE TESTS FOR INDIAN ARMY

THE DEFENCE Research and Development Organization has developed a new method to assess the intelligence of the officers of the Armed Forces.

In future warfare, abilities like higher order mental function involving concept formation, attention ability and decision-making would be more crucial than simple intellectual abilities.

While earlier tests were confined to testing of reasoning capabilities, the prototype of the new method called Comprehensive Battery of Cognitive Assessment (CBCA) measures a wider spectrum of cognition including attention, memory, problem-solving, decision-making, reasoning and concept formation. The assessment test comprise of a set of sub-tests, which measure registration of a stimulus, processing of information and planning strategies and higher order functioning for application of that information.

A comprehensive cognitive profile can be generated through the CBCA within and hour and 15 minutes. (Source HT-17, August, 2007)

CASE STUDY
EMOTIONS

For 11 years Kumara Mangal worked as a network administrator at Rajdhani Engineering. Kumar builds measurement and instrumentation devices for the defence forces. In the last couple of years of his tenure, Kumar's performance reviews had turned negative. He could see the inevitable coming and he was angry. So he concocted a revenge plot to sabotage the network he helped create. Just before the company fired him, Kumar put a software time bomb in the computer and stole the only back-up tape. A week after he was fired, the timebomb went off. The company's server crashed and destroyed all of the critical tooling and manufacturing programmes. Kumar's anger and resulting sabotage caused Rs.100 million in damage, dislodged Rajdhani Engineering's footing in its industry, and eventually led to the layoff of 80 employees.

Computer sabotage is an extreme example but it does dramatically illustrate the theme – Emotions are critical factor in employee behaviour.

(Source: Stephen P. Robbins and Seema Sanghi, Organization Behaviour, Eleventh Edition, 2007)

CHAPTER 19

Organization Culture and Climate

CHAPTER PLAN

- *Introduction*
- *Definitions*
- *Understanding Organization Culture*
- *Functions of Organization Culture*
- *Levels of Culture*
- *Organizational Climate*
- *Summary*
- *Text Questions*
- *Bibliography*

INTRODUCTION

Organizational culture is one constant factor that propelles organization development.

Study of organization culture and climate has become necessary to achieve change. Management has realized this and there are laying stress on good governance that includes organization culture.

Achieving and maintaining quality of product and customer satisfaction are two most important factors of successful organization. To achieve these twin objectives, an organization has to marshal various resources, plan its use over a period of time and produce products or services, which meets the consumer needs, desire and aspirations. For an entrepreneur, the most important and difficult task is to manage human resource. The task becomes more pronounced if the employees are from different geographical areas having different culture. In such situations, manager should evolve a technique where a strong organizational culture is established. Culture is invisible power of any organization. When thinking and actions of employees are institutionalized, an organizational culture is deemed to have taken birth. It guides the employees.

DEFINITIONS

Edgar Schein defined culture as **"A pattern of basic assumptions invented, discovered or developed by given group as it learns to cope with its problems of external adoption and internal integration worked well-enough to be considered valuable and therefore, to be taught to new members as a correct way to perceive, think and feel, in relation to those problems."** Wagner III and Hollenbeck have defined organizational culture as **"The shared attitude and perceptions in an organization that are based on a set of fundamental norms and values and help members understand the organization."**

UNDERSTANDING ORGANIZATION CULTURE

Organizational culture is not inborn. It has to be invented and later developed over a period of time. It enables employees to perform within the framework of the organization's culture. Environment both internal and external plays a dominant role in developing the culture and so does demographic factors. That is why we generally refer to Japanese culture or Indian culture. It is therefore environment specific in nature. On examination it reveals that the organization's culture is informal in nature and relates to shared way of living. It is a common binding factor in the organization. Organization culture help develop professionalism among its employees. Value system is the corner stone of the organization culture. It promotes standardization in various systems and sub-systems, which reduce role conflict to a great extent. Once the culture is developed, it virtually becomes a people's organization from a functional point of view that promotes risk-taking among managerial cadre and generates novel ideas. It promotes formal communication that improves productivity and job satisfaction. India is a multi-religious, multi-lingual and multi-cultural society. Organization culture promotes equality and work culture. The corporate culture ***"consists of norms, values and unwritten rules of conduct of an organization as well as management styles, priorities, belief and interpersonal behaviours that prevail. Together they create climate that influences how well people communicate, plan and make decisions."***[1]

Organizational culture originates from the founders of the organization based on value system held by them. It is further passed on, down the line. Organizational culture is also a function of the nature of work and goals of the organization. It is visible from the organizational structure. Centralized command and control, strict hierarchy and fixed communication are indicative of formal culture with little freedom of action and with scant attention to innovation and creativity. While decentralized work culture will promote autonomy that will lead to greater job satisfaction. Peters and Waterman state, "Without exception, the dominance and coherence of culture proved to be an essential quality of the excellent companies. Moreover, the stronger the culture and more it was directed towards the market place, the less need was there for policy manuals, organization charts and detailed procedures and rules. In these companies, people, way down the line know what they are supposed to do in most situations because the handful of guiding values is crystal clear.

FUNCTIONS OF ORGANIZATION CULTURE

(*a*) **It gives members an organizational identity:** Sharing norms, values and perceptions gives people a sense of togetherness that helps promote a feeling of common purpose. Culture provides shared pattern of cognitive perceptions or understanding about the values or beliefs held by the organization. This enables the organizational members how to think and behave as expected of them.

(*b*) **It facilitates collective commitment:** The common purpose that grows out of shared culture tends to elicit strong commitment from all those who accept the culture as their own. It provides shared pattern of feelings to the organizational members to make them know what they are expected to value and feel.

(*c*) **It promotes systems stability:** By encouraging a shared sense of identity and commitment, culture encourages lasting integration and cooperation among the members of an organization. It enhances social stability by holding the organizational members together by providing them appropriate standards for which the members should stand for.

(*d*) **IT shapes behaviour by helping members make sense of their surroundings:** An organization culture serves as a source of shared meaning that explains why things occur the way they do. Organizational culture is not fully visible but felt. At less visible level culture reflects the value shared by organizational members.

(*e*) **It provides a boundary:** Culture creates distinction between one organization and the other. Such boundary defining helps identify members and non-members of the organization. Culture facilitates the generation of commitment to something larger them one's individual self-interest. It serves as a control mechanism that guides and shapes the attitude and behaviour of organizational members.

(*f*) It helps organizational members stick to conformity and expected mode of behaviour. Culture ensures that everyone thinks and behaves in a prescribed manner.

Managing Organizational Culture

Once the culture is formed, it is the duty of the organization to enrich it. Management of organizational culture is explained below in Figure 19.1 below:

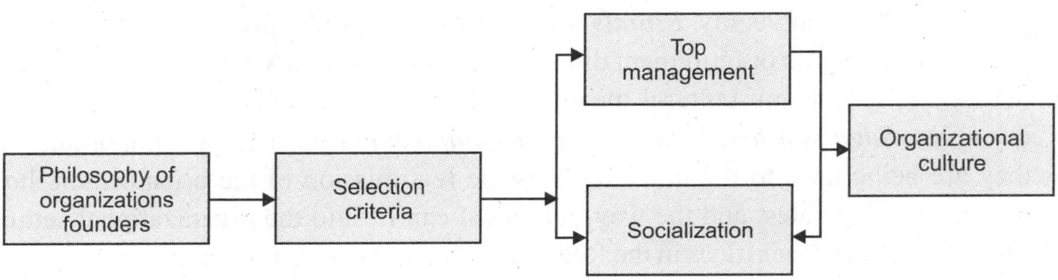

Figure 19.1 Management of organizational culture

Philosophy of organization's founders: Culture is valuable for the organization because it enhances organizational commitment. It guides employees towards right direction. Culture is also marked by dysfunctional aspect as well when shared values conflict with the aspects of organizational effectiveness. Such situations take place in dynamic organizational environment where organization do not change with changed environmental factors. Early traditions are the basis of culture in the organization. The vision of founders and various functions of the organization create culture. The ideology and customs are bedrock of any organizational culture. The mission and vision of founder members, hard work, competitive spirit and the way of life is important as it establishes cultural value of any organization. The vision of Ratanji Tata has created a Tata culture. Luthans has suggested following two steps in creation of culture:

1. A single person (founder) has an idea for a new enterprise.
2. The founder brings in one or more other key people and creates a core group that shares a common vision with the founder. That is, all in the core group believe that the idea is good one, is workable, is worth running some risk for.

LEVELS OF CULTURE

According to Edgar Schein, there are three levels of culture, these are discussed in the succeeding paragraphs.

(*a*) **Observable artifacts of culture:** These are the symbols of culture in the physical and social work environment. These are visible and most accessible. They include ***organizational heroes***. As mentioned earlier, organizational culture emanates from the top management and their leadership styles. These leaders become the role model. Employees would like to copy their behaviour, work ethics and represent what an organization stands for. ***Modelled behaviour*** is a powerful tool and organization should continuously learn. They should re-inforce organizational value system**.** ***Rites and rituals*** are recurring activities that are used at special times to influence the behaviour and for understanding of organizational members. For example, taking out **Colors** when oath ceremony is underway in the Defence Services. Colors remind soldiers of the excellent work done by their predecessors and the sacrifices they have made. Presentations of certificates at convocation ceremony in the university. ***Rituals are systems of rites*** like departmental song, colours, and company picnic or retirement dinners. "***Cultural symbols*** are an object, act, or event that serves to transmit cultural meaning." Corporate uniform, tie, buttons etc., are the examples. ***Saga is a heroic account of accomplishments.*** Sagas are important because they are being used to tell new members the real mission of the organization, how the organization operates, and the way individual can fit into the organizational settings. A saga of valour and sacrifices in the Regimental history is a good example of organizational culture. It communicates organizational culture. Certain dress **logo** can reflect its value and orientation. Many people wear buttons on the uniform suggesting that they are members of golf club or rotary club thus reflecting a sense of value. Some of the material artifacts are reserve parking, air conditioned office, luxury automobiles given to senior members of the organization. These carry with it the value system prevailing in an organization.

(*b*) **Shared values**: We have studied two types of values, *i.e.,* ***terminal values*** that reflects end state of existence and instrumental values. ***Instrumental values*** are means to achieve terminal values being hard working (instrumental value) may lead to achieve solace (terminal value). Shared value lie at the very heart of the organizational culture. It helps turn routine activities into valuable, important actions, tie the corporation to important value of society, which may provide a very distinctive source of competitive advantage. Employees should be taken into confidence and good work done by them should be recognized so that other workers are motivated to work for the organization. Values should be linked with work. A person should feel that he is producing an umbrella that keeps health of the society. He is not merely working for material gain but for the good of society. Organizations should therefore develop a "dominant and coherent set of shared values", so that individual behaves in a graduated manner in line with the organizational philosophy.

(*c*) **Common assumptions:** Common assumptions are fallout of shared value system and observable artifacts of culture. Employees, over a period of time form within themselves a common culture. In Bajaj Automobiles, everybody comes in time to the plant. Punctuality is therefore a common assumption that is embedded in their organizational culture. In Maruti Udhog, safety is accorded a high priority. Workers health and safety in plant therefore is assumed a common assumption. The cultural artifacts develop cohesiveness that leads to operational productivity. Indians believes in truth and non- violence. Therefore, it is a common assumption of our national culture.

Management Philosophy

Every organization exists for fulfillment of social objectives whatever it may be. Automobile industry is there to fulfill the social need of transportation (movement). Organization therefore should spell out their mission and objectives. This will reflect the management philosophy of the organization. It is necessary because (1) it establishes boundaries of operations for each member. (2) It provides the way that situations can be effectively handled and (3) it provides unity of thoughts and known path towards success. Management philosophy should be documented. To promote management philosophy/corporate culture, following actions are recommended:

1. Slogan should be prominently displayed indicating organizational mission.
2. Policies, rules, procedures, regulations should be made known to all employees.
3. Recognition of heroes.

4. Belief that rituals and ceremonies would be observed for unity of employees.
5. Informal set of behaviours.
6. Sharing of information and free flow of communication.
7. Adherence to all social, religious norms.
8. Reaching beyond organizational boundaries to dependants of employees and other connected organizations, which can directly/indirectly assist parent organization.
9. Belief in value system and adherence to business ethics.
10. Faith that workers hand would be held in difficult situation.

Myths

Unproven and often unstated beliefs that are accepted by employees. For example, 'safe plant is an efficient plant'. 'Safety over rides every other process in nuclear power plant.' In spite of that there are plants where accidents have taken place. Therefore 'safety is a myth'.

Sub-culture

There is typical and unique dominant culture within each organization. There is usually a sub-culture within a particular group or department with its own pattern of values and philosophy that is not inconsistent with the values of the larger culture of the organization itself.[3] In an organization, finance department may have its own sub-culture that may be part of larger culture of the organization. It is typical of R and D departments to have its own sub-culture in which every individual enjoys a comparatively greater freedom of action. These sub-cultures coexist with and enhance the overall organizational culture. This is especially true in functionally structured organizations.

Counterculture

Countercultures have a pattern of values and beliefs that sharply contracts the dominant social norms, values and behaviour patterns. This counterculture tends to emerge when individuals or group strongly feel that the existing organizational culture is too rigid and does not support their creativity or the style of operation. Countercultures are distinctly visible in the organizations that have been merged or acquisitioned. In Balco, there is an original culture when it was a government undertaking. Counterculture has probably emerged after it has been privatized. Both type of culture are coexisting in the organization. In relation to dominant organizational culture, the counterculture groups usually engage in three types of dissent: (1) direct opposition to organization's dominant values; (2) opposition to the dominant culture's power base and (3) oppositions to the methods of interaction with dominate culture (Yinger, J.M.).

Top Management

Organizational culture is an important aspect of organization success. Once the organizational culture is established, it is the duty of managers to ensure that all workers respect the organizational culture and run the organization as per its philosophy. It is the duty of the management to lay down organizational mission, which is achievable. Too much of ambitious mission is likely to fail resulting in low morale of the employees. It is therefore important that managers play a significant role in keeping values, behaviours and opinions of the organizational members under control and guide them appropriately. Leaders should pay continuous attention to maintaining the established standard and send clear signals to all the members as to what is expected of them. Some of the important points are as under:

(*a*) **Selection:** Standardized procedure should be used to hire right people for right job. Experts should interview the candidates and try to screen out those whose value system does not conflict with that of the organization. Additionally, the selection process provide to the applicants, information about the organizational culture. Should they do not match; the applicants should be given freedom to join other organization. It is important that organizations lay down detailed process selection criteria and selects a team who can employ right people for right jobs. Personality-job fit must be carefully worked out without any bias. People who are qualified and experienced must be appointed ignoring those with pull and push. The vision, mission, and policy of a sound organization must not be bypassed while selecting the people for work performance. People who do not have core values of an organization must not be appointed because one-day they might destroy the very foundation of value system in an organization. Once this happens the whole organization is likely to collapse and suffer losses. In India some of the public sector undertakings have survived because of correct selection process not heeding to political pulls and pushes. While others have discredited because they have fallen pray to whims and fancies of people who have destroyed cultural and value system.

(*b*) **Socialization:** Employees should be properly inducted in the organization. Organization policy should lay down procedure in this respect. Individual employee should be briefed on the organization structure, his department and the immediate superior to whom he is to report. On the job training would go a long way for the growth of an employee. Induction also involves lying down career path for managerial cadre. Training and development programmes, promotional cadres should be planned on a regular basis so that an appropriate message is passed on to the employees. As stated earlier it is the duty of the senior managers to ensure that organizational culture is enriched by their way of handling things under stress and strain where emotions have to be controlled and canalized in the desired direction. It is here that the employees receive a positive signal of the level of organizational culture. Less productive workers should be encouraged and not treated as second class citizens of the organization. Good managers are able to support and reinforce existing organizational culture by being strong role models and by handling situation that may result deviation with skill and diplomacy.

Newly recruited employees are put through adaptation process called socialization. Socialization starts once an individual is selected. A proper brief of the organization is sent to him at his home. Individual or group of individuals are received at railway, bus stations or at air terminus. They are taken around to various departments and introduced to key appointments. They are later put through the culture of an organization through intensive training programme. Special attention is paid to each of the individuals who are put through all the activities of the organization. The aim being to make him aware of the problems and difficulties envisaged. The importance of doing a minor job and its contribution towards a 'whole' job is also an important consideration. The training programme is scheduled in such a fashion that 'on the job training' is given to an individual along with making him aware of organizational culture. The organizational culture is maintained not only in work functions but also in dining, dressing and other developmental activities. Employees on their part prove their commitment with the organization. In case employees fail to adapt to the organization's culture are called ***'non conformist'*** and are further put through an intensive training programmed as under.

- **Pre-arrival stage:** The values, attitudes, personality and learning aptitude is assessed towards driving the individual towards organizational culture. It is diagnosis stage, which identifies, in an individual the possibilities of socialization (adaptation) of the organization's culture. Psychologists and behavioural scientists are invited to smoothen individual values to suit the organizational requirement.
- **Encounter stage:** It is an induction stage where a recruit joins an organization and is put through the job. He compares his expectations and image that he has formed with the organizational set up. If the expectations are far from reality, they are expected to learn and follow organizational value system. Those who modify and learn are taken into the mainstream of the organization. Those who resist have to quit the organization being misfit.
- **Metamorphosis stage:** It is a consolidation stage where individual learn the values, norms, culture of the organization. They are made to familiarize with various individuals, and adapt to various prevailing organizational systems and processes. It is voluntary process where an individual is put under a facilitator for learning process. Individual master skills required for job performance, he adopts new role and adjust himself to changed life style. This becomes a stepping-stone to be an effective member of the team. It is **"refreeze stage"** of change process.

  In the defense services socialization has a great importance where leaders are born and made. Socialization is called 'regimentation'. An individual officer is required to follow daily routine that soldiers follow. In initial stages he has to go through the duties and responsibilities of a soldier by physically doing it. An officer even has to eat the food prepared for troops, share the same barracks to sleep. The aim of the exercise is to make him aware of the criticality and knowing each function from grass route level. This also enables his troops to understand him and his commitment towards them in exercise of command. This type of induction has paid rich dividends. An officer is taken into the fold of the regiment who sacrifices for cause when time comes and obtains willing obedience and ultimate sacrifice of his subordinates. They live like a family for whole life (duration of service). This exercise continues for about six month to a year. During this period an officers masters skills of handling solders, he knows regimental customs and traditions. He commits himself to the regiment, he serves and becomes part of the organization that cannot be detached. Organizational commitment, and commitment to troops you command is total. In Chetwood hall at Indian Military Academy Dehradun from where the commission is sought, there exist and advice to officer cadets **"Welfare and dignity of my country comes first always and everytime, welfare and dignity of troops comes second always and everytime. Welfare of self comes last always and every time."** That is the socialization (regimentation) all about.

(*c*) Following additional points contribute to enrich the organizational culture:

(*i*) Carry out job analysis periodically.

(*ii*) Encourage an individual in public for good work done.

(*iii*) Define clearly the job requirements.

(*iv*) Celebrate festivals that employees greatly value.

(*v*) Publicize stories, encourage hero worship.

(*vi*) Organize social functions.

(*vii*) Ensure quality decisions.

(*viii*) Show concern to all employees.

(*ix*) Encourage innovative ideas and reward them.

(*x*) Lay down promotion policy; create a healthy and competitive work environment.

(*xi*) Ensure quality of work life.

ORGANIZATIONAL CLIMATE

According to Bowditch and Buono[4] "Organizational culture is with the nature of belief and expectations about organizational life, while climate is an indicator of whether those beliefs and expectations are being fulfilled." Employees in the organization keep studying the management philosophy and various actions they take to deal with organizational factors that are of a routine nature. These include the following:

(*a*) Selection process of the employees.

(*b*) Leadership style and approach to solve-problems of the employees.

(*c*) Wage administration.

(*d*) Attitude to implement change and incorporate latest technology.

(*e*) Job description.

(*f*) Organizational structure and frequency to modify the same based on need.

(*g*) Performance evaluation.

(*h*) Promotion policy and its implementation.

(*i*) Efforts involved in promoting creativity and innovations.

(*j*) Availability of resources for research and development.

(*k*) Organizational values and promotion of culture.

Richard, M. Hodgetts [5] has classified organizational climate into two factors as under:

(*a*) Overt Factors

- Hierarchy
- Goals of the organization
- Financial resources
- Skills and abilities of employees
- Technological state of the organization
- Performance standards adopted
- Efficiency measurement.

(*b*) Covert Factors

- Values
- Attitude
- Norms
- Feelings
- Interaction
- Supportiveness
- Satisfaction.

Overt factors can be measured and fair assessment can therefore be made about the intentions of the management and efforts they are putting in to build an appropriate organizational climate. While on the other hand, covert factors can not quantified being of subjective nature. To measure the level of organizational climate a questionnaire is prepared and feedback is obtained from the employees on the five points scale

(*a*) Strongly agree — 5 points

(*b*) Moderately disagree — 4 points

(*c*) Neutral — 3 points

(*d*) Moderately agree — 2 points

(*e*) Strongly disagree — 1 points

Likert[6] has carried out studies an organizational climate by isolating six different variables namely decision-making, leadership style, motivation, goal setting communication and control. Each variable was then evaluated on four dimensions. Each of the dimensions can then be studied on the five-point scale enumerated above. Based on the inputs so received on the specific study of a particular variable an appropriate conclusion of the prevailing organizational climate can be drawn. Suitable remedial measures then can be initiated to modify the climate to desired level.

SUMMARY

Achieving required quality of product and managing customer satisfaction are important factors in running a growth oriented organization. While all the resources can be managed, it is difficult to manage human resource especially when globalization is the order of the day in all facet of our life. Therefore, culture plays a decisive role in running of an organization smoothly. Culture is an invisible power of any organization. When the thinking and actions of employees are institutionalized, an organizational culture deemed to have been formed. Organizational culture is a pattern of basic assumption discovered or invented by the people of the organization. Organization culture deemed to have been born when people have learned to cope up with problems of external adoption of various systems, processes and technology and achieved internal integration. Organizational culture is required to be passed on to new members as correct way of thinking, perceiving and behaving. Organizational culture is not inborn, it has to be invented over a period of time and nurtured by all members of the organization. The corporate culture consists of values, norms, and unwritten rules of conduct and the style of governance. Following are functions of organizational culture: (*a*) It gives members an organizational identity; (*b*) it facilitates collective commitment; (*c*) it promotes systems stability; and (*d*) it shapes behaviour by helping members make sense of their surrounding.

Organization culture help develop professionalism among its employees. Edgar Schein who has carried out in depth study on the subject has identified three levels of culture. They are observable artifacts of culture and include organizational heroes, rites and rituals, dress and logo. These are organizational symbols of culture in the physical and social work environment. They are visible and most accessible. Second is shared values and the third level of culture is common assumptions that actually fall out of shared value system. Myth may also be considered as one of the cultural aspects as the Indians are having faith in these types of happenings. Every organization has a dominant culture and each of the group of workers or department may have its sub-culture. It is the responsibility of the management to evolve, initiate and promote its own philosophy. It is necessary because (1) it establishes boundaries of operations for each member, (2) it provides the way that situations can be effectively handled, and (3) it provides unity of thoughts and known path towards success. Management must pay proper attention to selection and socialization of employees. While carrying out social adaptation activity a newly recruited individual passes through pre-arrival stage, encounter stage and metamorphosis stage.

"Organizational culture is with the nature of belief and expectations about organizational life, while climate is an indicator of whether those beliefs and expectations are being fulfilled." Richard M. Hodgetts has classified organizational climate into two factors. (1) Overt factors, which can be analyzed and (2) Covert factors that cannot be analyzed being subjective in nature. Likert has carried out studies on organizational climate by isolating six different variables namely decision-making, leadership style, motivation, goal setting communication and control. Each variable was then evaluated on four dimensions. Each of the dimensions can then be studied on the five-point scale as explained in text of the chapter above.

TEXT QUESTIONS

1. Define organizational culture. How does it differ from social culture?
2. Organizational cultures generally reflect the belief and ideologies of the founder. Do you agree with the above statement? Give reasons.
3. As a manager of an organization having 400 employees, how will you promote organizational culture?
4. What are various levels of culture? Explain in details.
5. What are various functions of organizational culture? Give examples.
6. How do sub-culture and counter cultures within the dominant organizational culture exist? Should the management tolerate the counterculture? If so, give your views.

BIBLIOGRAPHY

1. Sinn, larry, *"Corporate Culture"* in readings in management and organizations, edited by Moniqe A. Pelletier Kendall, Hund Publishing, 1991, p. 378.
2. Peters Thomas J. and Robert, H. Waterman, *"In Search of Excellence"*, Harper and Row, 1982.
3. Martin, J. and C. Siehl, *"Organisational Culture and Counterculture: An Uneasy Symbiosis"*, Organizational Dynamics, Vol. 12, No. 2, 1983, pp. 52–64.
4. Bowdwitch, J.L. and A.F. Buono, *"A Primer on Organizational Behaviour,"* John Wiley & Sons, 1990, p. 247.
5. Godgetts, Richards M. *Organizational Behaviour: Theory and Practice,* Macmillan Publishing, 1991.
6. Likert, Rensis, *"The Human Organization,"* McGraw Hill, 1967.

CHAPTER 20

Future of Organization Development

CHAPTER PLAN

- *Introduction*
- *Strength of OD*
- *Challenges for the Organization*
- *Summary*
- *Text Questions*
- *Bibliography*
- *Case Study:*
  1. *Esprit De Corporate*
  2. *Rebuilding Nalanda*

INTRODUCTION

External environment is totally turbulent. Old paradigm is no more valid. There is a global competition for product and services. Competitiveness is the order of the day. Organizations are adopting acquisitions and mergers to remain valid in the present environment. Interdependencies are increasing day-to-day. Information technology and managing knowledge has become necessary for organizations to achieve growth. Human being is subjected to greater stress and strain while performing his job. Downsizing and restructuring of organizations have become rampant. Business strategies therefore need change as the environment changes. The old pattern of managing people is no more valid today. Bureaucratic model where rules, regulations and standing orders were absolute is giving away to something new. The present paradigm proclaims that organizations would have flatter structures; high performing teams will carry out work; empowerment will be the way of working; minimum central staff for controlling; more delegation and autonomy in the work environment; customer oriented products; and high quality of services with an obligation of protecting social values and maintaining/promoting environmental balance. Work will be carried out faster with minimum cycle time. Training and development of employees would be necessary for high skills. Globalized work environment that leads to working with transnational culture will be more prevalent and play an effective role in the future. Continuous quality improvement; achieving total customer satisfaction and putting very high value on the human resources would be futuristic scenario. OD will have to play an active role in the situations mentioned above. The future of OD is bright provided it is able to evolve new paradigms as the situation demands. An attempt is made to discuss present strengths of OD and sketching down certain contingencies that may be evolved as the growth of the organization take place. There are greater demands on the human beings. We are sure that the human resources would meet the demands of society and the organizations would be able to serve humanity with greater challenge.

STRENGTH OF OD

1. Organization development is ***about people and organizations***. How they function and steps that may be required to improve its effectiveness. It is a long-term planned effort. It pertains to solving problems that concerns human side of the organization. The target of OD is to make organization function by improving human behaviour and organizational processes. Basic strength of OD is the people; their skills, their zeal and strong desires to change to cater for the environmental requirements. This is implemented by identifying strengths and weaknesses of the organization (diagnosis) deciding on the intervention to be applied (intervention); selecting a change agent for application (change Agent/Facilitator); implementing the intervention (process); and evaluation its effectiveness (feedback). Desired results are achieved by focusing on the teams and other independent configuration, redesigning organizational structure and jobs; adopting to participative leadership and developing an open people oriented climate where decision-making is decentralized and teams are empowered.
2. Second fundamental strength of OD is its ***democratic nature***. We have in earlier chapters explained that joint decision-making; participative nature of implementing jobs; team building strategies; training and upgrading skills of the people; all leads to democratic nature of the OD efforts. It is therefore highly practical approach of implementing organization development intervention to nations where democratic governments exist. Indeed OD efforts promote such norms based on value system and democratic way of life.
3. ***OD is a blend of people oriented processes*** with human, technical systems and socio-technical systems. To illustrate, this blend can be seen in increasing use of parallel or collateral organizations in large-scale change projects. People in organizations are adapting to new technological change that render organizations to facilitate growth. We have already studied socio-technical systems of organizational development. Extensive use of Change agent/OD Practioner/Facilitator in training and development and implementing OD interventions is indicative of the nature of human resources that are able to mould itself to the current requirements of the organization. The elasticity displayed by human behaviour is the very core of the organization development intervention application.

4. All large organizations have a HR department. It not only deals with HR maintenance factors, but also deals with ***development of human resources by applying various OD*** strategies. Organizations are now filtering their employees through psychometric tests at entry level only. The objective being right people (psychologically) for the job to avoid intraorganizationl conflict at a later stage. Organizations have a cell that is dedicated to form policies on organizational and transorganizational matters and developing latest processes to make thing better in the organizations. OD has a vital role to play in the present scenario. The role of OD is increasing day-by-day. Time is not far that the OD will be re-invented under a new label of **organizational transformation.**

CHALLENGES FOR THE ORGANIZATION

Change is coming upon us like an avalanche, and people are utterly unprepared to cope with it. Tomorrow's world will be different from todays, calling for new organizational approaches. Organizations will need to adapt to changing market conditions and at the same time cope up with the need for renewing rather than reactive work force. Reengineering, restructuring, transformation, flattening, downsizing, rightsizing, and a quest for global competitiveness—is real, it is radical and it has already arrived. The successful twenty-first century managers must deal with a chaotic world of new competitors and constant innovations. In the future, the only winning companies will be the ones that respond quickly to change. Many companies are facing global as well as domestic competition. Changing customer life style and technological breakthroughs all act on the organization to cause change. The degree of change may vary from one organization to another, but all face the need to adapt to external forces. Many of these changes are forced upon the organization, whereas others are generated internally. Because change is coming rapidly, it is important for management gurus, social scientists, psychologists, and entrepreneurs to evolve and apply new OD strategies to manage change. Factors that affect OD are as under:

(*a*) **Organizational values and leadership:** In defence services it is common saying that it is not the gun that matters but a man behind it. It is universally true of business organizations too. Management must place high value on the employees, groups and their performance. As O' Toole[1] says, "Management can choose to try to create organizations that have both profitability and humanistic/developmental objectives whether or not the two are necessarily correlated." OD consultant can play a very decisive role in advising the management. There may be two situations in the organization for it to be effective. (1) "*Slash and burn*" and (2) *"democratic and humanistic approach"*. Does the consultant remain silent and assist management in carrying out a large downsizing or does he question the proposed course of action? Warner Burke opines, "For the good of the organization and its individual members, consultative help may mean confrontation, questioning, and challenging—when an OD practitioners client contemplating downsizing, the intervention of choice is to test the wisdom of such a decision.[2] All the organizations should understand their social responsibility. They must design each job appropriately and it should be fitted to the people (do not fit people to the job). Employees must be given autonomy so that they are accountable to their job. Organizations should be viewed as a place people learn and achieve personal growth. When individual grows, organization automatically achieves growth. Organization policies should promote employee satisfaction that lead to high morale and motivation. This aspect has gain added importance due to technological and engineering considerations that are required for the decision-making. Organization should take value-based decisions and possess strong leadership skills that can be applied based on various situations. We should be able to align people, establish purpose direction and transform them to undertake challenging jobs.

(*b*) **Awareness about OD programme:** OD is generally considered as a long-term continuous process. It aims at modifying individual behaviour, group dynamics thus classifying OD as a behavioural science. OD approaches seem to over emphasize changing the behaviour pattern of members, with a consequent lack of recognition of other significant factors such as structural and technological elements. Many consultants call for a broadening of OD practices to a more systematic, comprehensive integrated approach to change. There is therefore a need to develop total awareness about OD that also emphasizes *social responsibility, self-control, and democratic ideals.* Time factor is irrelevant. We may have to evolve strategies to answer questions like: what does it offer organizations in crisis that may be fighting for survival? Is there a need for short-term crisis OD interventions that can help introduce change under conditions where urgency and survival may be the immediate concern? There is need for more detailed, published cases of OD efforts and the use of OD processes in conjunction with other improvement strategies.

(*c*) **Second generation OD:** More and more, practitioners and scholars are talking and writing about *"organizational transformation."* Amir Levy and Uri Merry define it as ***"Second order change (Organizational transformation) is a multi-dimensional; multi-level; qualitative; discontinuous; radical organizational change involving a paradigmatic shift."*** Increasingly, OD professionals distinguish between the more modest, or evolutionary, efforts towards organization improvement and those that are massive in a sense, revolutionary. Goodstein and Burke contrast ***"fine tuning" and fundamental, large-scale change in organization's strategy and culture".*** Beckhard and Prichard contrast ***"incremental"*** change strategies and ***"fundamental"*** change strategies. Organizational transformation is seen as requiring more demands on top leadership, more visioning, more experimenting, more time, and the simultaneous management of many additional variables.

(*d*) **Certification of OD practitioners:** OD, as an independent field of study has emerged. Many organizations conduct various developmental programmes like seminars, conferences, workshops, and role-play, on various organizational issues round the year. They cover subjects ranging from individual development, group dynamics organizational communications and review various systems and processes to meet the current requirement of the time. There are number of organization with full OD orientation in India but there is no organization that accredits the skill agents or OD practitioners. There is therefore a need for certification at the apex level or even organizations of repute in the field of OD should undertake the responsibility of certification. This will prevent unqualified persons undertaking the job of OD practitioners that would be detrimental to organization development in times to come.

(*e*) **Canvass of OD:** OD has been highly interdisciplinary in nature. It has been built on theory, research and practice. Various fields that have been benefited from OD are Social Psychology, Anthropology, Philosophy, Management, and Human Resources Management. Apart from the above, OD has made inroads in-group dynamics, systems theory, community development, counseling and psychiatry. Due to technological advancement and knowledge explosion, there is a need for evolve new OD strategies/interventions and find out newer fields/areas where such practices can be applied. We may examine as to what we can learn from say Yoga or religion and how new OD interventions can be evolved. There is a great challenge that lay ahead for OD scientists, academician, researchers, social workers, and management experts.

(*f*) **Mergers, acquisitions and alliances:** Organizations have to adopt strategies of mergers, acquisitions or/and alliances to be able to face the competition in the world. This is more important today due to technological advances, knowledge explosion, and speed with which the information can be transferred from one location to the other. Computers have practically changed the face of the world. The recent mergers of Tata-Corus (steel), Mittal-Ancelor (steel), Tata-Tetley (tea), Sahara-Kingfisher (aviation), and Tata's acquisitions of Dewoo Motors of Korea are the landmark examples of such strategies. This has led to dealing with people of transnational culture, values and handling different types of processes and systems. It is a great challenge to the OD practitioner to instill in the organization the semblance of uniformity in its day-to-day functioning. OD practitioners need to be knowledgeable as possible about structural interventions integrations. At the same time, experts in the technological aspects of these fields also need to knowledgeable about OD interventions and its application to the real situations. As an extension of these ideas, additional conceptualization about large-scale systems change is necessary. As Warner Burke says[3], " We are on the threshold of a paradigm of the effective management of large-scale organization change. We are beginning to understand much more clearly what the primary levers are for initiating and implementing organization change, levers such as culture, values, key leadership acts (providing a vision and clear sense of direction), the reward system, and management/executive programmes."

(*g*) **Sense of community feeling:** We, at times surprise to find out that the western countries do not have a sense of community feeling as it is evidenced in India. In fact, the whole nation is a community. In India it is easy to find cohesive groups functioning by itself and producing fantastic results, may it be in government organizations, hospitals, defence services, or in the functioning of the people in municipality across the country. OD heavily depends on the behaviour of the people in the organization. What is required is that the people have a common objective and try to canalize their energies, skills for the achievement of the same. The main objectives of any organization can be spelt out as under:

1. Production of high quality of products and services.
2. Staying viable and competitive in the market.
3. Protect the interests of the stakeholders.
4. Achieve ultimate satisfaction of the customers/consumers of the product and services.
5. Ensure that the organization has total peace, achieving employees' growth, improving their skills and creating such organizational practices that are beneficial to the employees, thereby achieving higher levels of job satisfaction.
6. Social transformation.

To achieve the above objectives, it is but natural that the employees work in groups and complete their task in time. In doing so, establish the *"sense of community"* within the organization. *"Organizational citizenship"* is also an important way of achieving togetherness in the organization. OD practitioners are likely to face an uphill task of transformation, where the diversity in culture, value system, and behaviour exists. It is the responsibility of the society to see that the human resources that come from the social stream are able to mould themselves in the organization's mould and that they are able to function effectively. It is the responsibility of the schools, colleges, technical organizations and management institutes that they understand the requirements of the organizations and prepare young people accordingly. They have a great responsibility in shaping the individuals in the right form. High organizational performance can be congruent with and supportive of a sense of community, and vice versa. Obviously it requires vision, time, empathy, skills, commitment, and hard work to achieve either or both.

OD is about people helping each other to unleash the human spirit, energy, wisdom and capabilities to achieve the objectives mentioned above for the social upliftment of the society. It is our responsibility and we have to shoulder it with great wisdom and intellect. Enormous opportunities and potential exist for the OD movement in future. OD practitioners must be well qualified to undertake the OD work and implement intervention strategies with full dedication. OD future is very bright, having great challenges for the OD practitioners.

SUMMARY

OD is a continuous process. External environment is turbulent and therefore old paradigm is no more valid today. Downsizing and restructuring of organizations is the order of the day. Organizations are trying hard for acquisitions, mergers and alliances to remain competitive and growth oriented, as otherwise the existence may be difficult. Employees are subjected to more stress and strain. The present paradigm proclaims that the organizations would have flatter organization structures; high performance teams; empowerment; minimum staff for controlling; more delegation; and autonomy in the work environment.

We must study the strength of the present system for us to understand the future of OD. Basic strengths of OD are the people, zeal, their skills and strong desire to work. The second strength of OD is its democratic nature. Blend of people with full orientation to various processes and systems makes OD field very interesting and pose challenge to the OD practitioners. The basic challenges are competition, implementation of OD interventions with particular reference to protection of value system by the client system. OD programmes have to keep pace with the changing situations. Awareness of broad OD competencies is necessary. OD has probably lived its life in the present form. A new face of OD is "Organizational transformation". OD practitioners must achieve certification from a competent organization. Organization development is applicable to all the organizations that have to grow with time. It therefore has a broad canvass to work for. Mergers, acquisitions, and alliances pose a great challenge for change agent to implement change, for it has to deal with multiple-cultural workforces. It should be understood that we are at threshold of the paradigm where large-scale organizational change is anticipated. This can be achieved by developing a sense of community that will promote implementation of OD interventions to enable organizations to achieve their objectives. OD has a bright future that is full of challenges for the OD practitioners and client organizations.

TEXT QUESTIONS

1. What is various strength of OD?
2. What are various challenges that is posed by the external environment?
3. Explain organizational transformation.
4. Write shorts notes on the following:
   (*a*) Sense of community feeling.
   (*b*) Additional responsibility that OD practitioners have to bear due to policies of acquisitions, mergers and alliances.

BIBLIOGRAPHY

1. James, O' Toole *"Do Good, Do Well: The Business Enterprise Awards"*, California Management Review, 33 (September, 1991), p. 21.
2. W. Warner Burke, *"The New Agenda for Organisation Development"*, Organisational Dynamics, 26 (summer 1997), p. 11.
3. W. Warner Burke, *"Organisation Development"* (Reading, M.A.: Addition-Winsley Publishing Company (1994), p. 200.

Case Study 1
ESPRIT DE CORPORATE
(ECONOMIC TIMES, DATED 14 MARCH, 2006)

The Indian army can teach corporations things or two about managing their most important resource: human beings. Nikhil Menon finds out what makes the Indian Army probably the best—run organization in the country.

If you thought that the size of your company presented a mammoth HR management challenge, you might want to think again. In comparison, the Indian army, consisting of over a million men, equipment and infrastructure should be an operational and logistic nightmare. But it isn't, in fact, the army is known for being an institution in a class of its own. Compare it with an organization—any organization and admittedly the similarities are many. There are hierarchies and functions, leaders and followers, teams, meetings and strategy sessions, very high emphasis on 'delivering the goods' and above all, a sense of organizational social responsibility that makes it our most reliable asset during times of crisis. Perhaps the only differentiator between the armed forces and corporations, then, is the ***raison d'etre***. The objective of the armed forces is task orientation instead of profit-orientation. The attitude is to do 'whatever-it-takes'. "The army's rules and procedures are rigid," admits (retd.) Maj Gen. Satur. Adding, "But the rules in the corporate world are bent at the drop of a hat."

However, it's neither possible to run an organization in the same way as the army nor can companies put employees through the same grueling degree of training and spit-and-polish regimentation. However, here are a few things to be learnt by every corporation that wants to create a battle-ready organization that runs smoothly on the back of a loyal and motivated workforce.

Finesse Under Fire

Soldiers learn to maintain their mental calm and respond instinctively to extreme provocation. "It is a very high pressure job," says Col. Mathew Abraham, HR head, Oberoi Flight and Airport Services, adding, "We ask from them the supreme sacrifice: their lives. But their training and the institutional culture of the army ensures that their physical standards, mentally robustness and professional competence see them through even the biggest crises." Abraham, who has seen the best of both worlds, says that the army's high standards ensure that only the fittest get in at the entry level. The filtering that is subsequently done ensures that it is only the best that make it into the forces and are eligible for higher office.

Lesson to be Learnt

Recruiting a candidate is extremely crucial. You have to be sure he/she can handle duress, and actually relish it to an extent.

Take Charge

"I sometimes see people grumbling and saying, 'why should I do it? It's not my job," says Abraham. The military's way to get things done is to put your back into the task until it gets done. Sometimes people are not keen to take risks, lest their plans backfire. The support of one's superiors and the knowledge that mistakes are all right as long as they lead to further learning can do wonders for anybody. When in the armed forces, split-second decisions have to be taken and risks are inevitable. "Remember that those under your command are constantly watching you," says Col. CPS Waraich, GM-Personnel, Admin and HR, Supermax. "You have to take your role seriously and keep your own conduct above reproach. You cannot afford to wash your hands off a problem," he adds.

Lesson to be Learnt

Responsibilities shouldn't prevent you from going out of your way to do something that needs to be done. Also, put your people in the job that best suit them. If you have an energetic young executive on your hands, give him a position that best utilizes his energy. Don't forbid mistakes, it only encourages quick fixes and shoddy work.

Learning Lasts a Lifetime

The army is a staunch believer in continuous training and learning. It begins with the military training administered at the beginning of a candidate's entry into the armed forces, then regimental training and then examinations and further regimental training and then examinations and further training at the time of entry into higher levels of authority. Officers are routinely sent for refresher courses and higher studies to improve their skills and knowledge. The Indian army today, some of its people go to the IIMs and other institutes for six-month management courses. Says Col. S. Khare, a consultant with an Indian MNC, "There is need based skill enrichment. Training is not a one-time affair. Like you see in organizations or even the civil services. Soldiers receive training even for retirement."

Specialization and continuous practice is the key. People wonder what the army does during peacetime. The answer is, train harder, and improve learning to ensure that people and equipment don't fail when the hour of reckoning comes.

Take Pride in Your Regiment

"The feeling of ownership comes naturally in the army," says Col.Waraish, "You have to create a situation where a person is proud of his Company and his Battalion." The awe-inspiring image that the army has built up over decades creates a feeling of belonging that is intensely powerful. Sports and other competitive events build pride in one's own Regiment. Officers and their men also intermingle freely at parties, during celebrations, and in the camp. The communication between a CO (Commanding Officer) and a soldier takes place on a very personal level too. Adds Col. Waraich, "For the first year or so, officers are told to be seen and not heard. This ensures that they observe and understand their environment and comrades closely before they become mature enough to form opinions about them."

Maj. Gen. Satur says, "Any jawan has the right to approach the General and get his grievances dealt with. It doesn't work like that in the corporate world. If I don't like your face, I just might remove you and bring someone else in!"

Lesson to be Learnt

Reinforce pride in the organization through fair and equal treatment. It is important for the administration to reach every person, instead of the other way round. Only then would he or she want to work with you.

Organizations have always borrowed heavily from the military's strategies and management models. But somehow they haven't been able to attain the same level of discipline that is so essential for the military to function and deliver beyond all expectations. "Perhaps the difference is that the army corporatises the individual, while civilian organization individualise the corporation," theorises Col. Khare. Add to that a scenario where different strata and echelons of employees rarely interact with each other and watertight responsibilities that confine individuals to a series of tasks instead of aligning them with the eventual all-important objective, and you begin to see why companies are still entrenched in their old ways, while the army marches on towards dizzying heights of organizational excellence.

Questions

1. Draw a sketch of organizational culture of the Army.
2. How will you design and implement training and development in your organization?
3. In Army interpersonal communication has been key for developing awareness. How will you promote the same in your organization?
4. Visit one of the Army units in your neighbourhood and write an essay on regimentation.

CASE STUDY 2
REBUILDING NALANDA

By: *V.G. Kondalkar*

1. Introduction

Grand plans are on to rebuild greatest residential university of the 5th century. Like the mythical phoenix, Nalanda University is all set to rise from the ruins, thanks to the national and international efforts that are on to rebuild it as a "Centre of intellectual excellence". A period which is witnessing the re-emergence of Asia as an economic hub, Nalanda has the potential of becoming a beacon of global understanding and world peace."

2. Vision

(*a*) Visualize Nalanda as a unique institution considering the present ambiance of the world.

(*b*) Draw inspiration from the rich historical traditions of Nalanda and Buddhism, where Lord Buddha got enlightenment.

(*c*) Importance of meeting of minds from the national and international arena to do research on the unity of minds linking human welfare, science, technology, economics and spirituality.

3. Mission

(*a*) Recapturing of holistic traditions of knowledge creation, acquisition, and dissemination as practiced in ancient Nalanda.

(*b*) Working towards building an inclusive society in a world free of violence. Terror, war, and fear.

(*c*) Making Nalanda a meeting place for equitable societal welfare, scientific, spiritual, philosophical and religious thoughts.

(*d*) Creating one of the largest libraries in the world including a digital library.

(*e*) Providing leadership for world peace.

4. Rebuilding Plans

The proposed university will be situated 16 km from the ruins of Nalanda. It will be spread over 600 acres of land. The site will be close to six-lane expressway and the Budhist tourist circuit corridor and the proposed new airport.

5. Rebuilding Organization

The Nalanda Mentor Group (NMG) headed by Nobel laureate Amaritya Sen is overseeing the revival project. Other members of the NMG includes Singapore Foreign Minister George Yeo, Government officials from China and Japan, Lord Meghnad Desai, Sugata Bose, a grand nephew of Subhash Chandra Bose who is teaching at Harvard University and some experts on Budhisim. It will be fully residential, like the ancient Nalanda seat of learning and will not be a monastic centre. Even the old Nalanda had educational arrangements in many secular subjects, such as medicine, philosophy, public health care, mathematics, languages, and literature. It will have the international character and also have involvement in global intellectual interaction. It will be unique university in which there will be joint arrangements and international partnership between a number of Asian countries including China, Japan, Singapore and others who would interest.

6. Courses to be Taught

Following courses are likely to be taught:

(*a*) Philosophy and Buddhist study.

(*b*) Regional history focussing on comparison and connections among Asian countries fostered through cultural and trade.

(*c*) Business and management studies.

(*d*) International and peace studies.

(*e*) Study of languages.

(*f*) Neuron-sciences at the cutting edge of scientific studies.

Questions

1. Analyze the above case, how do you visualize the organization to come up?
2. What contribution, it is likely to make for the world peace?
3. What are various restructing factors that have been considered in this case?

Index

A

Accommodating 113
Adaptive learning 59
Affective events theory 233
Appraisal and recognition 143
Attitudinal level change 186
Autocratic/feudal culture 7
Autonomy/independence 154
Avoidance 112

B

Bases/sources of power 201
Belief 16
Benchmarking 61, 128, 147
Biofeedback 118
Blind self 109
Bureaucratic culture 7
Burnout 220

C

Canvass of OD 253
Career Anchors 154
Career-life planning 118, 169
Centrality 203
Challenges for the organization 251
Change agents 190
Changes in awareness 110
Changing through cognitive restructuring 184
Classification of OD strategies 38
Coaching and mentoring 153
Coercive power 201
Collaborating 113
Collaboration and conflict 106
Committees 85
Competencies 10
Competing 112
Compromising 114
Conflict resolution model 112
Confrontation 120
Counterculture 242
Creativity 58
Culture 139

D

Decision-making 147, 163
Decision-making as power 202
Deming's pioneering work 140
Dependency 203
Development of self-managed teams 40
Diagnosis 26
Dynamics of OD 4

E

Emotional continuum 230
Emotional dimensions 230
Emotions 192, 229
Empirical rational strategies 173
Empowerment leading to life space 216
Entrepreneurial creativity 154
Entrepreneurial culture 8
Ethical standards 73
Ethics in OD 209
Expert power 202
External environment 205

F

Factors contributing to empowerment 164
Features of quality of work life 214
Feedback 131
Force field analysis 95, 183
Forces of change 182
Framework of emotional competence 232
Functional power 204
Functions of organization culture 239

G

Generative learning 59
Goal setting 166

H

Hidden self 110
High performance teams 87

I

Impartiality 58
Individual counseling 42
Instrumented training 154
Inter group team building interventions 119

J

Job burnout 116
Job enrichment 216
Job evaluation 45
Job evaluation and role analysis techniques 46
Job redesign 128
Job redesign strategies 45
Job security 191
Job sharing 46
Juran's framework of TQM 141

K

Knowledge as power 202
Knowledge change 185

L

Lack of communication 191
Latest trends in OD 3
Leadership 143, 166
Learning organizations 47, 60
Legitimate power 201
Levels of culture 240
Life style 157

M

Machiavellianism (1469–1527) 206
Managing change 29
Mechanistic view of empowerment 167
Meditation 118
Mental health 219
Mergers, acquisitions and alliances 253
Model of QWL 215
Myths 242

N

Nature of OD Interventions 28

O

Objectives of organizational development programme 10
OD characteristics 10
OD values and assumptions 18
Open self 109
Optimism 231

Organic view of empowerment 167
Organization transformation 31
Organizational change 205
Organizational climate 245
Organizational culture 5, 163, 217
Organizational mirroring 121
Organizational politics 205
Organizational transformation 9
Organizational wide change 187

P

Performance appraisal 166
Personal efficacy 58
Personality conflict 109
Phases of learning 62
Phases of OD programme management 29
Philip B Crosby's approach 142
Politics 204
Power centers 203
Power coercive strategies 173
Power sub-system 147
Problem-solving 217
Problem-solving teams 85
Process consultation 41
Process of confrontation meeting 102
Process of empowerment 164
Process of MBO 134

Q

Quality circles 87, 131, 222
Quality circles and self-managed teams 40
Quality of work-life 63, 131, 218

R

Re-engineering 144
Redesigning organizational structure 165
Referent power 201
Refreezing 184
Relations with the peer group 215
Resistance to change 191
Resource as power 202
Responsibilities of the client system 74
Reward power 201
Role ambiguity 108
Role analysis technique 93
Role conflict 108
Role negotiation 94
Roleplaying 44

S

Scarcity 203
Second generation OD 252
Self-managed work teams 85
Six sigma 138
Social sub-system 146
Social support 117
Socialization 243
Socio-technical interventions 45
Sources of stress 115
Strategic change 188
Strategies for reducing inter group conflict 114
Strategies normative re-educative 173
Strength of OD 250
Stress management 114
Stress management intervention strategies 116
Structural change 188
Structural interventions 46
Structural power 204
Study of awareness—Johari window 109
Sub-culture 242
Sub-optimization 107
Systems approach to management 145
Systems thinking 58

T

T-group 152
Task force 85
Task significance 130
Team based work environment 167
Team building 90
Team building interventions 39, 88
Team roles 88

Teams and work-groups 39
Technical sub-system 146
Techniques of political plays 206
Techniques of team building 93
Technocratic culture 8
Technology 192
The change agents 75
The client-consultant system 69
Third party peace-making interventions 42, 120
Total quality in human resources management 140
Training and development 166, 216
Transactional analysis 41, 109
Types of change 188
Types of empowerment 167
Types of teams 85

U

Uncertainty 203
Understanding action research 52
Unfreezing 183
Unknown self 110

V

Values 16
Virtual teams 87
Vision 165
Visioning 9

W

Workflow 44
Working conditions 215